THE AMNESTY OF GRACE

"*The Amnesty of Grace* liberates the doctrine of justification from its individualistic, subjective, and middle-class captivity and provides fresh understanding of God's grace expressed in solidarity with the poor and excluded. The author's sound scholarship, accessible literary style, and engaging faith converge in an exceptional book that exposes the popular 'logic oriented toward death' which permeates much North American thinking."

Bishop Kenneth L. Carder
Nashville Area, The United Methodist Church

"Most turning points in the history of Christian thought have been marked by a return to Paul, and in particular to Romans. *The Amnesty of Grace* is a landmark book which shows that Latin American Liberation Theology has reached its maturity. It will be a necessary reference, not only for those interested in liberation theology, but also for any further interpretation of Romans and of Paul himself."

Justo L. González
Columbia Theological Seminary

"The thesis that justification by grace through faith is the way God creates justice in the world by making the poor agents of transformation stands over against traditional views that make the theme of justification an alibi for the perpetuation of patterns of injustice. The readable and intriguing book by one of Latin America's finest biblical theologians demonstrates that Pauline and liberation theology actually enrich and strengthen one another."

Theodore W. Jennings, Jr.
Chicago Theological Seminary

"In this excellent volume Elsa Tamez offers a sharp rereading and reappropriation of the Pauline teaching of justification by faith from a Latin American perspective, from the perspective of the poor and marginalized of the continent. The result is not only a highly innovative and challenging interpretation of this teaching—with justice and solidarity at its very core—but also an excellent example of theological dialogue with the Scriptures—thoroughly immersed in the sociopolitical realities of both the Roman Empire and present-day Latin America."

Fernando F. Segovia
Vanderbilt Divinity School

THE
AMNESTY
OF GRACE

*Justification by Faith
from a Latin American Perspective*

ELSA TAMEZ

TRANSLATED BY
Sharon H. Ringe

Wipf and Stock Publishers
150 West Broadway • Eugene OR 97401

THE AMNESTY OF GRACE

JUSTIFICATION BY FAITH FROM A LATIN AMERICAN PERSPECTIVE

Wipf and Stock Publishers
150 West Broadway
Eugene, Oregon 97401

The Amnesty of Grace
By Tamez, Elsa
©1991 Tamez, Elsa
ISBN: 1-57910-865-2
Publication Date: January, 2002
Previously published by Abingdon Press, 1991.

CONTENTS

CONTENTS

INTRODUCTION

In recent years the theme of justification has begun to appear on the Latin American theological agenda, especially among Protestants. With the flourishing of liberation theology, short articles have occasionally appeared that establish the need to reinterpret that doctrine from a liberating perspective more appropriate to the reality of our continent. However, despite several studies of the doctrine of grace, especially by Roman Catholic theologians,[1] we still lack a deeper and more complete study of the doctrine of justification.

It seemed important, therefore, to take on the task of a rereading of justification by faith from the perspective of Latin America. The principal motivation for this study lies in the fact that the present understanding of the doctrine, detached as it is from the concrete details of the Latin American reality, has led to practices that have negative consequences for the present process of liberation. Furthermore, I believe that a biblical-theological rereading of justification in light of our reality can illuminate our understanding of Christian life and faith, independently of any confessional relevance such a rereading might have.[2]

The approach followed in this study is not objective. I began from the reality of poverty, oppression, repression, discrimination, and struggles that large sectors of our peoples are experiencing, and from their experience of God in that situation. For what interested me was to learn whether the doctrine of justification is good news for the poor and for those discriminated against on the basis of color or sex, in what sense it is good news, and how this good news is revealed in our particular context. This study explores the meaning of justification in the framework of Latin American theology of liberation, which is a particular way of doing theology welcomed by both Catholics and Protestants. In this theology, the poor, "oppressed and believing," constitute the privileged locus of theology. That is to say, theology is done from their reality of oppression-liberation and their experience of God. Every great theological theme, every biblical reading, must be reexamined from that angle of vision.[3]

My basic desire was not to return to the usual discussions of the disjuncture between faith and works, or to juxtapose the initiative of God to that of the human being. The current situation demands instead that we search for new theological discussions of justification that respond to a reality marked by the deaths of millions of innocent people caused by structural sin.[4] I choose in this discussion to join with the voice of the Asian theologian Raymond Fung, in his desire to speak the following word to the churches:

> We wish to report to the churches that a person is not only a sinner, a person is also the sinned against. That men and women are not only wilful violators of God's laws, they are also those violated. This is not to be understood in a behaviouristic sense, but in a theological sense. . . . We would like to report to the churches that man is lost, lost not only in the sins in his own heart but also in the sinning grasp of principalities and powers of the world, demonic forces which cast a bondage over human lives and human institutions and infiltrate their very textures.[5]

Condemnation to physical death by hunger and the experience of "insignificance"[6] were two urgent dimensions of the experience of excluded or marginalized people that moved me to examine the doctrine from its very roots. The first entails condemnation to death due to the nature of exclusion in the economic system currently in force, and the second results from not being accorded one's dignity as a human person.

The study of justification by faith from this perspective led me to take on that doctrine as a concrete affirmation of the life of all human beings. The revelation of the justice of God and its realization in justification proclaim and bring about the good news of the right to life for all people.[7] The life granted in justification is recognized as an inalienable gift, because it proceeds from the solidarity of God, in Jesus Christ, with those who are excluded. Such a life of dignity makes human beings subjects of their own history. God "justifies" (makes and declares just) the human being in order to transform the unjust world that excludes, kills, and dehumanizes that same human being.

I decided to leave aside for now the contributions of the theological and confessional tradition, many of which arose in the midst of heated controversies. I believe that the heavy confessional burden borne for historical reasons by the theme of justification will preclude the recovery of additional liberating meanings through the biblical text. Moreover, since the Bible has become a central and renewing document for Latin American Christians through the rereadings of the Bible that have proliferated on all levels,[8] I considered it both appropriate and effective to return to the biblical source for the reexamination of justification.

This book is divided into three parts. The first discusses the need to reformulate the doctrine of justification by faith in contexts of poverty and discrimination: The phrase "justification of the sinner" requires a sketch of the profile of those human beings who receive the message. I offer a critique of the usual meaning of that phrase, and I propose new challenges. In the same section of the book, I analyze the contributions or intuitions that have already emerged in Latin America concerning the theme under investigation.

The second part returns to the biblical text in the search for new light to illuminate liberating meanings of justification by faith. The focus is on Paul, and on relating his theological proposals with his historical moment, without reducing that relationship to abstract theological disputes. The socioeconomic and political situation of the Roman Empire and the particular situation of Paul as a "plural subject" help to delimit the theme of justification within the framework of human history.

The third part of the book attempts a rereading of the doctrine of justification by faith from the perspective of Latin America today. The reading of the biblical text and the challenges of that historical reality, respectively, lay the foundation for that study. The theological discussion is developed under two headings: (1) justification by faith and the threatened life of the poor, and (2) the gift of being subjects of history as an expression of the power of justification by faith. This last section concludes with some elaborations of the meaning of sacrifice, judgment, and forgiveness.

The bibliography used (cited in the notes) is varied and merits an explanation. At the outset of the work, I became aware of a point of inconsistency: I wanted to reread the doctrine of justification from the perspective of Latin America, but the legitimation of that reading came from European and North American research. In view of this inconsistency, and without disdaining the contemporary contributions of the theology of the First World, I have opted to develop the first and third chapters using principally a theological and economic bibliography drawn from our own continent. Needless to say, contributions from representative writers or from those congenial to our context, but who come from other latitudes, are not absent. I have recognized especially those contributions that are basic to or inherent in our own theological formation. But I chose to leave them in the margin—specifically, in the notes—in order to delineate

15

more neatly the theological voices of our continent—voices that in some moments resonate with those other voices, but in other moments are dissonant. Biblical research, though not hermeneutics, is principally supported by a bibliography from the First World. The reasons are obvious: Beyond the acknowledgedly great tradition of exegesis, tools of every type for doing biblical research, as well as recent documentation concerning antiquity, are within reach in those places, and we recognize that Latin American biblical criticism depends in large measure on the fruits of researchers from outside the continent.

Finally, I intend to shape my analysis and discourse having as my principal though not exclusive point of reference a Latin American audience: pastors, lay leaders of Christian communities, and students. For that reason I have tried to combine language accessible to those groups with the academic requirements that all research demands. I want to thank the Faculty of Theology of the University of Lausanne for their kind welcome given to my family and me at all times, for their opening of new avenues of thought, and for the excellent physical surroundings, propitious for research. Most especially I thank Professor Klauspeter Blaser for his genuine, persistent, and timely accompaniment. I thank also the community of the Seminario Bíblico Latinoamericano and the Departamento Ecuménico de Investigaciones in Costa Rica for the confidence and stimulation they offered.

I am grateful for the financial support of the Board of Global Ministries of The United Methodist Church in the United States, the Presbyterian Church (U.S.A.), and the Evangelisches Missionswerk in Germany. Thanks also to the Program for Theological Education of the World Council of Churches, which, through its director Samuel Amirtham and his team (especially the representative for Latin America, Ofelia Ortega), cared without ceasing for our well-being during our stay in Switzerland.

Thanks to José for his love, and to my children for their patience with me. I ask forgiveness from Tairo and Xipatly for not having given them the time necessary to play, talk, and help them with their homework—an attitude inconsistent with the results of this work, which needs to be confessed!

PART I

JUSTIFICATION BY FAITH
IN LATIN AMERICA:
TOWARD A REFORMULATION
OF THE DOCTRINE

CHAPTER ONE

PERSPECTIVES ON JUSTIFICATION BY FAITH FROM LATIN AMERICA

I s the question of justification by faith relevant today in Latin America? The validity or relevance of the theological question of justification is accountable to the life experience and practice of Christians, churches, and poor people in general. From that beginning point, this Christian doctrine must be examined in light of the Word as it is known in Scripture and in history, and as it has been and continues to be appealed to in the life of many Christians of Latin America who seek to be faithful to God. Moreover, often when the presence of the crucified and risen Word is lived intensely (as in acute cases of oppression and repression), those situations themselves carry the voice of God that makes its appeal to all of us, to every theology, and to every doctrine.[1]

A CRITIQUE OF THE MEANING OF JUSTIFICATION IN LATIN AMERICA

The effort to reformulate the doctrine of justification by faith in Latin America is motivated initially by the usual meaning uncritically assigned to it. This meaning is not recorded in any specific book, but it can easily be perceived in the majority of the sermons or other common oral expressions of Christians in our churches.[2]

No one will deny, for example, that in the common theological understanding of our peoples, justification by faith is perceived essentially as (1) forgiveness of the sinner's sins; (2) liberation from guilt by the blood of Christ on the cross; and (3) reconciliation with God or being at peace with God, through the unique and absolute deed of God.[3] From the semantic point of view, these three perspectives arise automatically out of

19

people's awareness that justification by faith functions as a sort of code phrase, in which the disjuncture with our reality is evident: Forgiveness of sin is spoken of in an individual and generic sense, and reconciliation too is seen on an individual and abstract plane. Active human participation in the event of justification is denied, with no examination of the meaning of that denial.[4]

Two difficulties arise with this commonplace conception. One is the transference by our Protestant evangelizers—without examining the consequences of their doing so—of a doctrine that arose in a social and political context different from ours. The other difficulty is that these echoes of the Protestant heritage from Europe and North America arrive on our continent in a garbled form, as when static interferes with a message or signal sent from one place to another. The result is that, by force of repetition or emphasis of some aspect related to the theme of justification, a certain confused assimilation has taken place. In that process, justification is made on the one hand into a synonym of forgiveness of the godless or cruel, and on the other hand into a synonym of reconciliation with God.

But the fundamental problem is not rooted in the formula that is simply repeated like a mantra, with no attention to its specific content. That would indicate simply the irrelevance of the doctrine in our world, and its corresponding demotion to second rank. The problem consists rather in the fact that the usual understanding, disconnected from reality, has generated and generates a practice that has negative consequences for the current process of liberation. The attitudes or doubts of certain Christians concerning the popular movements have as their background the discussion of the fact that God saves us by faith and not by works.[5]

It is clear that such affirmations are not false: God does justify and pardon the ungodly, reconciles all humanity in Jesus Christ, and does so by pure grace, without human collaboration. But the abyss between the doctrine and the reality of our poor people allows the doctrine to remain floating in ambiguity, which in turn is conducive to its facile manipulation.[6] For that reason, each of those affirmations about the meaning of justification must be examined more closely.

Justification as Forgiveness of Sins

How can one affirm the relevance of an interpretation of justification by faith as the forgiveness of the ungodly in a situation where the most obvious sin is structural?[7] It is not that the poor do not feel that they are sinners. On the contrary, they have internalized to a profound degree the fact that they are sinners. To ask forgiveness from God for everything is central to their piety.[8] But in Latin America the sins that kill are very tangible. Following a cold and simplistic logic, we would have to recognize that justification viewed from an abstract, individual, and generic plane is good news more for the oppressors than for the poor. By beginning with the event of justification, the former can feel relieved of guilt—pardoned of their sins—by grace, without confronting the "wrath of God," or judgment, or the justice of God, and without the need for any conversion or change of practice.

This reading, obviously, contradicts the salvific and liberating message of the doctrine of justification in the time of Paul and in the time of the Reformation. Such an interpretation is not "justification by grace through faith" from the biblical point of view. Moreover, such an ahistorical interpretation leads us to fatal consequences: the accommodation of a doctrine removed from its context, which serves to erase the challenges of reality and to allow the doctrine itself to be "conformed to this age" (Rom. 12:2).

This does not imply that anyone is deliberately acting in bad faith. People can have a good heart. The problem is rooted in the fact that in Latin America the usual meaning of justification is confusing or misplaced. The historical dimension, which is capable of challenging both conscience and concrete practice, is absent. What does justification say to the poor indigenous peoples of Peru, Guatemala, Bolivia, or Mexico, who suffer both hunger and permanent discrimination? It is shameful to bring them the message that God has justified the sinner with no contextual specificity, or with nothing to distinguish the faces of the sinners. If we accept that sin has to do with social reality, justification also has to be understood within that same horizon.

Clearly, as the Bible asserts, all human beings are sinners. In practice, however, there is a paradox: The poor, whose sins cannot be compared to those of the powerful, are those who more consistently recognize their faults. Injustice becomes more obvious when it is committed against those who, with greater frequency, remember that they are sinners. We know that sin cannot be reduced to social injustice, but in the present moment in Latin America, it is vital to make people see that any dehumanizing situation is an offense to God, and for that reason it is a manifestation of sin. The spiritualization of sin has often made it difficult to identify in concrete realities—an identification that is the precondition for fighting against sin.

Tomás Hanks has warned of the possible distortions of an irresponsible reading of sin that emphasizes the inferiority of the human being:

> The Reformers worked at the time of the Renaissance, in the midst of a humanism that was not secular but most profoundly religious, often Christian. They were able to proclaim boldly that "all have sinned," and not ask

21

themselves how incoherent, absurd, or irrelevant that might sound to beings who see themselves as being like a pig at a trough or like complex machines that soon will be displaced by the most recent computer. . . . In a context like this, Christian evangelists should not ignore the biblical teaching about creation: the fact that we are created in the image of God and for God's glory provides the necessary complement and the indispensable presupposition for the teaching about sin.[9]

On the other hand, to reflect on forgiveness between human beings in situations of conflict is both serious and difficult, but it is part of being a Christian. How can one say to the Mothers of the Plaza de Mayo in Argentina that they should forgive the soldiers, the torturers and assassins of their children? No one with a minimum of integrity has authority to do so.[10] However, it is necessary to reflect on justification and its relationship to forgiveness in historical situations where the powerful will not emerge victorious again, but where God's justice will shine forth. This is one of the important reasons to take up the theme again in Latin America, namely, to reject every approach that favors the rich to the detriment of the poor.

The Exclusive Role of God

Another problem underlying the understanding of the doctrine is related to the principle of the absolute initiative and participation of God in the salvation of the human being (an aspect that in turn is connected to what is often erroneously called the disjuncture between faith and works). We understand the absolute divine initiative as a biblical truth.[11] The difficulty resides in the fact that this principle is almost always read from the opposite direction, as meaning that human beings have no role in their salvation. This belief leads in a natural way to consequences for the historical reality in which human life is lived. At worst, the conclusion is drawn that what a person does with his or her life counts for nothing, or that human efforts in history are of no worth, since one is justified by grace and not by works.[12] In this way the historical practice of human beings working for their liberation is called into question or deemed irrelevant.

In his rereading of Wesley, José Míguez Bonino mentions the problem of the exclusion out of hand of all synergism or active human participation in the work of God, which, he says, "has been fateful for Protestantism":

It has prevented giving human action an intrinsic place in the work of God in making present God's reign. . . . This monergism at any cost not only relativizes but also trivializes historical action for justice and peace, transforming it into an exercise of derivative value, transitory and not transcendant, merely the creation of a stage setting where the truly important occurs—the salvation of the soul—a setting destined to disappear.[13]

Clearly no one in Protestant circles would deny the fact that participation in the construction of a more human society is part of the mission of the creature obedient to the Creator. Furthermore, especially in ecumenical sectors, there are new languages that overcome the dualism of faith and works with phrases such as Paul's own formulation, "faith working through love" (Gal. 5:6). But frequently this truth is relegated to a secondary place when the question of the historical subject—the agent of transformation and construction of society—comes into focus. It is in this debate about the historical subject who liberates that the polemic emerges about the understanding of justification by faith and not works.

This polemic is due not only to the echoes of the tradition heard incorrectly by our people, but also to the traditional language of the Reformation itself.[14] The problem is not only theoretical. In our present sociopolitically and economically conflictive situation, the participation of our poor people in the struggle for their liberation is affected positively or negatively in the moment when the poor (such as peasants, workers, indigenous peoples, Blacks, women, or the unemployed) have risen up in all sectors of society and are declaring themselves the protagonists of today's history.[15]

Misreadings of the Protestant heritage from Europe and North America (which can be heard endlessly in evangelistic sermons) underline the inferiority of the human being before God. One of the great dangers in human attitudes and actions cited to justify such readings is the human bent toward self-aggrandizement or the desire to be God. To highlight this danger is correct, prophetic, and virtually indispensable in societies where wealth abounds and where people hold the power to control and determine commercial relationships with poor countries.[16] However, in societies where poverty and marginalization abound, and with them, the insignificance that comes from powerlessness, this same reading can be inappropriate and even violent. Míguez Bonino raises the same concern:

> Luther invited those who had power, wisdom, and justice—those who saw themselves as created in "the image of God"—to empty themselves and assimilate themselves to the weak, ill, and "little ones." But should the same sorts of things be said to those whom the world has convinced that they are only servants, not only distant from God, but less than human? What does it mean to invite such people to self-renunciation? Would it not be preferable to call them to affirm with confidence their worth as "children of the

Father"—brothers and sisters of Jesus Christ, "heirs of the inheritance of God"?[17]

In keeping with this reasoning, in our Latin American context it would be better to emphasize the grace that dignifies and humanizes the disfigured face of the oppressed, and to recognize the gift of the vocation to be free subjects of history, as inherent in the act of justification. The historical situation demands overcoming these traditional theological bonds, and rereading the theme from new angles.[18]

Justification as Reconciliation

The interpretation that limits justification to reconciliation with God has principally an individual and abstract meaning. The leap from one to the other is probably promoted by the generalized understanding of "to justify" and "justification" as "to make or to be in good relationship with God." This understanding may eliminate the traditional Catholic-Protestant polemic: "To be in right relationship with God" can include "to make just" and "to declare just" someone who is a sinner. At the same time, however, the connotations of the verb *dikaioō*, "to justify," are reduced to only one—the "vertical" relationship of humankind to God—neglecting implications on the "horizontal" plane concerning relationships between human beings. Such a reduction of meaning is impossible unless one reads in *dikaioō* uniquely and exclusively the forensic aspect removed from human history, a reduction overcome today by many Protestant theologians.[19]

The interpretation of the doctrine of justification based on an ahistorical reconciliation with God falls inevitably into individualism, as can be observed in many of our Protestant churches, and against which their leaders and theologians are struggling.[20] In contexts of urgent praxis, such individualism remains an insuperable obstacle—an attitude that obviously, and often unconsciously, relegates solidarity to a secondary position.

Certainly from the biblical point of view, justification and reconciliation with God are related (2 Cor. 5:19-21; Rom. 5:1).[21] What in our judgment affects negatively the interpretation of the doctrine of justification is that "reconciliation with God" is identified with "right relation with God," with the latter made synonymous with justification. With that identification, both justification and the theology of reconciliation so important today in our midst[22] remain one-dimensional. Both are limited to the divine-human relationship, leaving semantically at a distance relationships between human beings and with the rest of the world. The justice of God and justification cannot be reduced to "being at peace with God," for peace with God is seen when peace is realized. In 2 Corinthians, Paul

24

affirms that God reconciled us through Christ and conferred upon us the ministry (*diakonia*) of reconciliation (2 Cor. 5:18); in Christ's name, adds the apostle, we are ambassadors of that ministry (2 Cor. 5:20).

Of course we are not speaking of a cheap reconciliation between human beings that conceals sin. The *Kairos* document from South Africa, whose radicality responds to a situation of unbearable racial and economic oppression, is clear in this respect:

> In our situation in South Africa today it would be totally unChristian to plead for reconciliation and peace before the present injustices have been removed. Any such plea plays into the hands of the oppressor by trying to persuade those of us who are oppressed to accept our oppression and to become reconciled to the intolerable crimes that are committed against us. This is not Christian reconciliation, it is sin.[23]

Finally, the substitution of "the justice of God" and "justification" with the phrases "right relation with God," "being accepted by God," or "reconciliation with God" drastically reduces the dimension of divine and interhuman justice that the terms *dikaiosynē theou, dikaios, dikaioō, dikaiosynē* and other words based on the same root could include. Furthermore, that reduction could occur independently of the discussion about the freely offered or "gracious" initiative of God.

From this analysis it is clear that the doctrine of justification has been invested with meaning both explicitly and implicitly, with or without people's awareness of doing so. The need to reformulate the doctrine of justification is equally evident now that individualism, subjectivism, universalism, passivity, and general misinterpretation (whether explicit or implicit, conscious or unconscious) have contributed to the confusion of its meaning. This confusion becomes even more obvious when one recognizes that the same word "justification" in Spanish is very far removed from the original meaning of the word in Paul, having lost the connection to "justice" that is so central to Paul's usage. However, this *via negativa* does not exhaust the possibilities for finding the validity or relevance of the doctrine in Latin America today. Rather, that doctrine offers a liberating meaning for our countries and for others of the Third World who are going through similar situations. That meaning must be sought in light of the Bible examined from the perspective of our reality, and in light of our reality examined from the perspective of the Bible.

Contributions from Latin America to the Theme of Justification by Faith

The many examples in Latin America of the rediscovery of relevant dimensions of the Bible and tradition include various articles by authors from different confessional backgrounds. Examining these articles through the lenses of current meanings of the doctrine and current challenges of our reality allows one to see the need to reinterpret the doctrine of justification by faith, and to propose important elements by which to reread it.[24]

For example, from the Lutheran perspective, Walter Altmann proposes the following rereading of the doctrine:

> In Luther's time, the juridical terminology of justification became important: the problem of guilt and condemnation worried not only Luther but a whole people and a whole era. But we would be deceiving ourselves if we thought that the doctrine of justification, as Luther formulated it, could retain the same relevance for all eras and situations. Such a perennial theology does not exist.[25]

In relation to Lutheran conservatism in the sociopolitical sphere, Roberto Hoeferkamp observes:

> If the accusation is well founded that large sectors of Lutheranism have justified their ethical passivity by hiding themselves behind a fear of salvation by works, it is necessary to indicate that such an attitude manifests a gross misunderstanding and an abysmal ignorance of the teaching of Luther about faith, love, and good works.[26]

Lutherans are not alone in their interest in rereading justification from new angles. In fact, all of the Protestant churches assume this as the heritage appropriate to our tradition. For example, Victorio Araya, a Methodist, is concerned to seek a historically specific and concrete reading of justification by faith "through the scandal of the structural injustice that is anti-life." His purpose is to answer the often-asked question concerning justification by faith and theological reflection from the perspective of the poor:

> There are some who have said that an emphasis on reflection on the faith that begins in a liberating praxis of the faith, omits or does not consider seriously the doctrine of justification by faith. On the other hand, the affirmation of justification by faith imprisoned in a concept of abstract, ahistorical, theological orthodoxy has taken captive its prophetic and liberating force appropriate to the justice that comes from God. . . . How can we live justified by faith in such a way that, in response to the saving initiative of God in Jesus Christ, an evangelical dynamism will emerge from within the world that is in conflict and move us in the constructive direction of a just history in which all live as sisters and brothers, and which leads toward the justice of the Reign of God?[27]

A reading of these contributions to the discussion of justification by faith shows us that there is in Latin America an impetus toward contextualizing justification by faith beginning with the reality of poverty and struggle, leading people to recover or rediscover in it dimensions relevant for that reality, and thereby to enrich Latin American theological thought.[28] The concern is not polemical or confessional.[29] One could better say that it is existential, but from the point of view of the experience of suffering of innocent people. With such a motive, the question Luther asked himself is repeatedly posed in a different way: The personal anxiety of how to bring about a merciful God changes to, "How can we bring about a just world?"[30] or "How can we be merciful?"[31]

Three concerns emerge in these discussions. The first and most prominent is the task of relating justification to the justice of God.[32] The second important concern, although it has received less attention, is the affirmation of human dignity by the event of justification.[33] Finally, in some of these articles one can see an interest in underlining the sense of free grace in the practice of justice and in a utilitarian society.[34]

Justification and Justice

In order to examine more fully the meaning of the justice of God in Paul, it is important to examine the meanings of justice in the Hebrew Bible.[35] Such words as ṣĕdāqâ, mišpāt, ḥesed, and others[36] reveal the liberating dimension of God's concern for the poor, or God's appeal to human beings to practice justice. Since doing justice is what it means to know God,[37] idolatry appears intimately related to interhuman injustice, which is equivalent to ignorance of God.[38]

This same dimension is generally recognized to be present in the works of the apostle Paul as well. José Porfirio Miranda, for example, following a detailed study of justice in the Hebrew Bible in which those elements are exegetically grounded, explains (as a key for understanding all of the letter to the Romans) that the sin of which Paul speaks "acquires its permanent meaning for the first time in Rom. 3:9 as a summary of the adikia of Jews and Gentiles."[39] He recognizes that the terms adikia (injustice) and hamartia (sin) are not interchangeable, but "adikia constitutes the qualitative characterization of that which Paul understands by hamartia (sin) in all the rest of the letter."[40] Sin is incarnate in social structures, in the very powerful wisdom of the world, and in human civilization, whose "most characteristic and quintessential expression is the law."[41] And it was that incarnation of sin that condemned Jesus Christ. Therefore, for Porfirio Miranda the most important thing in Paul is his affirmation that justice does not come by the law but by faith.[42] According to Paul and the whole

27

New Testament, to have faith is "to believe that the definitive reign of justice and life has arrived."[43]

Other authors likewise point to the influence of the Hebrew Bible on the Pauline concept of the justice of God. For example, Pablo Leggett writes:

> We find ourselves here in the central part of the argument that Paul develops in Romans and Galatians: God has witnessed the unjust actions of humankind since the fall. What God requires most of humankind are justice and righteousness. To fulfill this requirement is why God called one people in particular, Israel, to be God's own (Gen. 18:19), God revealed Godself to Israel in an act of justice (Exod. 6:1-4). God gave them the law so that they would know and obey God by acting justly (Mic. 6:8). But Israel disobeyed. They forgot the true knowledge of God, in order to worship idols and commit injustices. Both of these actions represent a lack of knowledge of God. For the Hebrew Bible that knowledge and the work of justice are intimately bound together. Paul accepts the message of the Hebrew Bible but introduces a crucial revelation: Paul maintains that the purpose of the law was not to make humankind just. Rather, the law was to serve as a guide to lead people to Christ (Gal. 3:24). However, there is no reason to think that Paul's concept of justice differs from that of the prophets. Paul makes the same identification between idolatry and injustice that they do.[44]

For Néstor Míguez also, the idea of justice found in the Hebrew Bible (which includes the expectation of reciprocity and the necessity to restore the poor, weak, and oppressed to a full human condition) is not lacking in Paul's thought. However, for Paul the law failed, since no structure or individual is capable of producing justice.

> The only alternative to this system of injustice is to enter into a new reality, that of the justice created by Christ and by the Spirit of God. [Therefore] the justice of the God of all justice is not as much the formal decree of a neutral judge, as it is the activity of a God who does justice in order to renew the entire order of the world.[45]

To the extent that, by faith, we are part of this proclamation, we are justified and created in the image of the "new nature." Therefore for Míguez the social dimension of justice can only be conceived through the messianic praxis of Jesus, the messiah who is poor and without power, and who disqualifies the powerful of this world.[46]

We need to turn not only to the Hebrew Bible to explain the social dimension of the justice of God and justification in Paul, but also to the Gospels and other non-Pauline letters. Ricardo Pietrantonio summarizes the concept of justice in the New Testament, analyzing it for Latin Americans and Spaniards:

> For many exegetes justice has a more salvific meaning, be that interpreted as external or be it considered personal—in other words, justice has a salvific meaning for those who receive it as well as for the one who exercises it. On the other hand, justice has an earthly and interhuman meaning. There is no great concern with justice as *coram Deo*. In the face of the great misery, marginality, poverty, and injustice in the distribution of the goods produced by the majority, this theme is approached from the side of social justice. Therefore, the point of departure for the study of the New Testament does not originate in a concern for interiority, or for what is personal. Even the question about how to be saved, made just, or liberated is of no importance. And when the theme is important *coram Deo,* it is always marked by the concern for its implications *coram hominibus.*[47]

Pietrantonio further examines the concept of justice in three passages of the New Testament (Matthew 5–7, 23–25; Romans 3–6; and James 2:13-23) with the intention of noting the various ways of conceiving of justice in those texts. He concludes that in Matthew interhuman justice is fundamental, and entrance into the Reign of God depends on this response to justice. The action of God and fidelity intersect. In James, faith is dead if it does not demonstrate the practice of justice. In Romans, on the other hand, we meet a Paul who "is more concerned with justice *coram Deo,* although he then uses *dikaiosynē* to mean interhuman justice (Romans 6) after justification." That is why, according to Pietrantonio,

> the central concern of Paul is not that justice be sought, but rather that justice by grace through faith be also accessible to the circumcised. The great Pauline polemic has as a background the specific problem of the judaizers, and not an antinomianism or an indifference to justice. The big question is whether or not the people accede to that justice of God.[48]

Irene Foulkes, intending to combat the usual interpretations that separate Paul from the Gospels, compares the Reign of God and the thought of the apostle Paul, in particular justification by faith. She arrives at the conclusion that there is no basis for claiming that there is a contradiction between Paul and Jesus, or between the message of the Reign of God and that of justification by faith. Rather what one observes is the movement of the same message from one environment and historical epoch to another setting.[49] She also compares what can be understood by justification in the parable of Matthew 18:23-34 (where the king condemns and forgives, hoping for the same attitude on the part of the one forgiven) with the corresponding Pauline concept.

> As evangelical Protestants we have insisted that justification is by faith, and we like to cite the declarations of Paul on the subject. Together with this insistence goes the responsibility to investigate what type of faith comes into play here. . . . The faith which leads to justification, to liberation, carries within itself the transformation of the justified one, like the great king-judge. To repeat this indispensable point, the parable ends with the categorical disqualification of the forgiven one who does not forgive, of the unjust "justified one." In the words of James, that type of faith does not save.[50]

In order to analyze justice in Romans, Emilio Castro turns to other Pauline letters, as well as to the roots of that concept in the Hebrew Bible. His purpose is to discern the dynamic character of selected passages of the letter to the Romans. For him, Romans 1:16-17, 3:21-26, and 6:17-23 "summarize the doctrinal thought of the Apostle in relation to the justice of God as divine action and as the summons of human beings to action." He concludes, "The object of the justice of God is not my salvation as an end in itself, but rather my salvation is my incorporation into the project of the Reign of God."[51]

Mortimer Arias, in his study of the Jubilee as a paradigm of the action of the Reign of God in the world, speaks of justification as rectification:

> It is interesting to see, especially for us Protestants, that the word "justification," so dear to us, means literally rectification! God is the Great Rectifier of history. [God] is the Mighty God of Mary: "Who has brought down the mighty from their throne and lifted up the lowly" (Luke 1:52).[52]

The proclamation of liberation by Jesus (Luke 4:16-21) does not result in the forgiveness of sins, but goes far beyond that to liberate also from illness and false relationships. Therefore mission cannot be limited to the ministry of absolution. For Arias, the Christian has been called to proclaim the all-encompassing liberation of God, to liberate the captives from the concrete chains of historical oppression—that is to say, from impoverishment, from the international economic system, from foreign debt, from the laws and practices governing land tenure.

In his study of the paschal mystery in Paul, Severino Croatto does not speak of justification by faith, but rather limits himself to saying that the justice of God is not juridical but salvific.[53] His interest is to show the meaning of the saving event of the death and resurrection of Christ, in categories of liberation. According to Croatto, in Romans 3–8 the event of Christ picks up, extends, and deepens the kerygma of the Exodus.[54] This kerygmatic focus is presented on a continuum of other foci (Exodus-Genesis-Prophets-Gospels). It is deepened by the development of a theology of liberation from structures, in order to speak adequately of liberation from the three forms of alienation experienced by human beings—sin, the law, and death. In contrast to other kerygmatic foci, here the oppressors also can be liberated. Paul definitively speaks of a radical liberation of the human being in his or her being and vocation.

Juan Luis Segundo analyzes Romans 1–8 in the course of developing his Christology.[55] The key for reading Paul, he says, cannot be political, as it is in the Gospels, but anthropological and existential. These two dimensions introduce factors of historical and political causality. Paul deals instead with powers that intervene significantly in every human existence. The human being must be liberated from the mechanism of sin that enslaves him or her. Acting through a person's egotism or injustice, the sin to which one is enslaved obscures one's judgment concerning the truth, using religion to cover up ideologically one's unjust practice. God counters that slavery by faith, declaring one to be just according to the criterion of faith. But faith is not something God requires in order to give something else in return.

> What God gives in Jesus Christ is the possibility of a coherent maturity, that is to say, of a complete human fulfillment, and that assumes the substitution of the mechanisms of the Flesh by those of the Spirit. . . . [In justification] it is not a matter of uniting ourselves with an unmerited justice, thanks to the merits of Jesus Christ. In faith, what happens for the first time is that the Spirit, confronted with the mechanisms of the flesh, may take on the principle of a completely new existence—one that is capable of the creative audacity that alone is appropriate to sons and daughters.[56]

In summary, these biblical perspectives on the theme of justification demonstrate that one of the principal reasons to approach the theme from a broader perspective is to mark the greater or lesser importance of the aspect of social justice that may or may not be in it. That step is important if one is to overcome the individualism and subjectivism that permeate the life of faith of the churches, and that prevent the practice of an effective faith.

In addition to going to the Bible to rediscover liberating perspectives on justification, several theologians have worked at rereading the entire Protestant tradition through this same lens.[57] For example, Vítor Westhelle analyzes a text of Luther dealing with usury, in order to show that Luther does not make a methodological leap from a particular instance of sin to its universal condition. "The good news is not presented as a forensic 'yes' to all believers and sinners *(simul)*, independently of the particular content of their sins." According to Westhelle, Luther's theological reflection is founded on a particular historical experience, in which justice and sin meet in an antithetical relationship.

> This antithesis, discovered in the socio-economic arena of history *(sub specie mundi)*, certainly encounters in the doctrine of justification its dogmatic unfolding on the level of universalities, in an encompassing and eschatological dimension that Luther calls *"geistliches Regiment."* But the history of the struggle between oppression and justice cannot be disguised by a universal understanding of the relationship between sin and justification. That relationship explains the historical struggle, but without the struggle no doctrine of justification will be anything more than a formal and theoretical abstraction.[58]

The usurer, then, cannot be *simul justus et peccator* according to Luther's understanding (as *totus justus et totus peccator*), since that definition, according to Westhelle, can only be affirmed eschatologically as a profession of faith. By faith it is possible to know that grace, in the totality of the creative and redemptive activity of God, overcomes all condemnation. The totality of sin does not take away from the totality of grace.[59] In addition to the concern about the practice of justice, the question of the relationship between human and divine involvement in the event of redemption must be addressed. At this point the emphases arrived at by the various theologians diverge. All of them affirm the unlimited and freely given initiative of God: Of that there is no doubt. However, the event of justification itself is conceived in different ways by different authors. For some the practice of justice is seen as a consequence of justification (which is an act of juridical declaration), thus separating theology and ethics. For others, the act of justification by God implies a transformation of the human being into someone who does justice.[60]

Based on this discussion, José Míguez Bonino proposes an approach in which the relationships between God and humankind are not taken as "symmetrical and opposing," since the tendency is always to affirm God, diminishing the importance of human participation. He proposes the covenant as a point of reference for a new approach.

> The relationship that God has desired and initiated toward creation is that which we call a covenant. [In the covenant there is] a cooperation of the human being with God, maintained by the constant grace of God, which never reduces God's "partner"—even an unfaithful partner—to an object. Rather, the covenant directs itself to the human being, invites that being to

respond and to act, and in that way holds open permanently the door to human collaboration in God's purpose.[61]

In this sense Míguez Bonino sees the differentiation of human and divine justice as a matter for concern, because a number of distortions have derived from that dichotomy.[62] He concludes that it is necessary to speak of the two expressions of justice in such a way that, while affirming the grace of God—protecting the absolute prevenience of Jesus Christ—the unity of justice would be clear. For, in the final analysis, Christ is justice, "as origin, as power, as guarantee, as goal, as norm, and as human praxis."[63] Elsewhere, Míguez Bonino affirms this same more theocentric perception of justice as follows:

> The biblical notion of justice is neither an inference from God's nature or attributes nor an ethical reflection on human virtue but a notion descriptive of Yahweh's liberating action experienced from within a situation of oppression. That, I would claim, continues to be the only way in which we can today encounter and be involved in God's justice.[64]

In the Bible the justice of God and human justice within the relationship of the covenant are two sides of the same reality. This applies to the New Testament as well as the Old, since in both we meet the same God, the same justice, and the same demand for faithfulness to the covenant.[65]

Human Dignity and Justification

In the search for a rereading more appropriate to the Latin American reality, we encounter a number of different accents that nevertheless are not antagonistic. They can be affirmed as compatible because the principal concern expressed by each of them is the obvious injustice that affects the concrete life of human beings in our context, and the action of God toward them. Therefore, those theologians who emphasize the forensic aspect do so also from a liberating perspective, based on the socioeconomic context. Thus, for example, the dignity of the human being conferred by grace in justification is affirmed as vital and especially pertinent in our situation of marginalization, which tends to turn persons into things. Walter Altmann mentions two aspects that qualify as "liberating possibilities" of the traditions of the Reformation, one with respect to the oppressive ecclesial structures and the other concerning the dignity of the human being.

> Primarily, the doctrine of justification by faith is critical of the institutional church and the way it interposes itself between the action of God and that of

human beings. When this happens, human action ceases to be a liberating process in the midst of the concrete necessities of a marginalized and exploited people, in order to be the response to demands imposed by the institutional church. Justification by faith (and by faith alone!) unmasks the ecclesiastical demands with which the church ceases to be an instrument of salvation, in order to transform itself into yet another system of domination.

In the second place, it will not be difficult to trace a path from justification by grace (and by grace alone!) to the inalienable value of every human being. The ideology of human rights may not have arisen directly from the Christian faith—much less from Protestantism—but rather from a humanistic rationalism. But in truth we can say that justification by grace in fact *radicalizes the respect for human dignity*, by attributing it to the free will of God and not to a natural right. Faced with multiple ideological and social demands, such as those of production and property, or of culture and power, the valuation of the human being through what he or she is (especially in his or her own deficiencies, weakness, impotence, and marginality) returns us to the path that leads to Jesus of Nazareth, born in a stable and killed on the cross.[66]

Tomás Hanks, in turn, concludes that justification by faith has profound anthropological and psychological implications in contexts of oppression and poverty. Hanks refers to the humiliation of the poor, to the destruction of their dignity:

> The most devastating and *irreparable* effects of poverty are not the external physical deprivations, though those are terrible. The most unbearable problem of the poor is that they are continually submitted to affronts, humiliation, and insults—a treatment that crushes all of their sense of dignity, self-esteem, and self-valuation, and that eliminates systematically every basis for a hope that things will change.[67]

Justification by Grace and Spaces of Freedom

This vision of grace is found in other writings as well, although to a lesser degree. In each case, the author attempts to rediscover meanings of grace that might help to withstand or relieve the burden of the demands of the struggle for justice on the one hand, and those of the utilitarian and meritocratic society on the other.

The work of Rubem Alves is important for an understanding of the scope of the struggle for justice, which is a fundamental concern in Latin America.[68] When he compares the language of humanistic messianism with that of messianic humanism, he indicates that, though there is certainly a great similarity between them (for example, both maintain that the vocation of the human being "is to create history, in one way or another"), there is also a big difference: "But against messianic human-ism, which acts because it hopes, humanistic messianism hopes because it acts."[69] Although he does not name the doctrine explicitly, justifica-tion by faith contributes the affirmation that "humanization is primarily a gift of grace, that man is free to relax because his future is not his busi-ness only."[70] According to Alves, the problem with the Protestant tradi-tion is that, given the affirmation of justification as a gift, it has deduced that there is no place for human creativity. Consequently, work is "not a tool to be used in creating the new, but rather an expression of obedi-ence to the command of the One who was the only creator."[71] Neverthe-less, Alves insists that messianic humanism finds it necessary to preserve the notion of grace as creativity. In the context of the politics of God, grace creates the possibility and the necessity of human liberation. "Sal-vation is achieved through a politics in which God makes man free to create."[72] Human beings, recognizing the world, the present, and life itself as the gift of God, are freed from "anxiety about tomorrow." They recognize their capacity to enjoy life—without losing the erotic meaning of that phrase—even though they live in captivity, since they are not dominated by a messianic obsession with respect to their power to create history.[73]

Faced with a capitalistic, utilitarian, and meritocratic society, Sílvio Meincke analyzes justification by faith in relation to the open spaces of life that are constantly being increasingly restricted by our society. He shows how justification by grace and faith opens those spaces in order that peo-ple can live life, and how, at the same time, it motivates them to promote the same kind of open space for their neighbors as well. According to Meincke, this dimension of justification is important for human beings in our present society, which creates anxieties, self-justification, self-condem-nation, and the need for acceptance. In the urgency to create spaces for life in a society in the process of transformation, justification by grace and faith—not by works—presents itself as a liberating gift, because it presents life as a gift to be lived. In this way, free from the exaggerated concern to construct our own acceptance, "We have both hands free for the other."[74]

JUSTIFICATION AS LIBERATION

In Latin America the word "liberation" best encompasses the various emphases or approaches to the rereading of justification by faith pre-sented here. Certainly justification includes being liberated by God "from sin, the law, and death"—in all of their concrete manifestations—in order to engage oneself without fear in the practice of justice that our peoples need so greatly. The new dimension of this rereading of the doctrine is not in the well-known formulation, "freed from . . . , for . . . ," which already involves a big step if it is taken seriously. What is novel for us is the consideration of justification and liberation from a historical perspective of oppression, poverty, and struggle. In the present moment, the doctrine of justification is being confronted radically by the reality of injustice, whose products are the deaths of thousands of innocent people, and the loss of humanity for thousands more. Those products of injustice constitute the principal challenges of the Latin American reality to a rereading of the doctrine of justification by faith.

CHAPTER TWO

CHALLENGES
FROM LATIN AMERICA
TO JUSTIFICATION BY FAITH

To address the subject of justification by faith in Latin America requires having as a starting point the present life of the poor and excluded people of that continent, and then relating the life of the rest of the people to that of the poor.[1] The "poor" are the oppressed, the weak, the hungry, the marginalized, the rejected, the unworthy, the humiliated, the impotent, the insignificant—all people who are without social, political, or economic legitimacy in their society. Today in Latin America and other parts of the Third World the "excluded subject" has both economic and cultural dimensions.

CONDEMNED TO DEATH
BY AN ECONOMIC SYSTEM THAT EXCLUDES

The principal challenge is the *growing* exclusion of large sectors of humanity from access to the basic necessities required for them to live with dignity.[2] Such inhuman exclusion signals the crisis of an economic system that needs constant readjustments in order to be able to survive.[3] That crisis faces the capitalist system, brought now to its limit by the hardening of the rules of the game, with the prevalence of neoliberal politics and economics in recent years.[4] Factors that contribute to that crisis include free market pricing, the minimal role allotted to the state in the economy (seen, for example, in the privatization not only of commercial companies and utilities, but also of such service-oriented institutions as hospitals and schools), and the centrality of concerns for economic efficiency and personal merit.[5] In those societies governed by the laws of the marketplace, all have the freedom to participate in the economic system, but obviously not many have the means to do so. The rest, who constitute the majority, are excluded, and their life hangs always in the balance.[6]

The foreign debt is an aspect of the crisis of the international financial system and of the dominant economic order. The consequences of the debt, which is unpayable according to the economists, have been fatal for the poor and for large sectors of the middle class. Two particularly devastating consequences of the debt for countries of the Third World have been a reduction in social services and the relegation of internal markets to secondary importance.[7]

The social cost of this system is so great that theologians and economists speak of its "idolatrous" character that demands the sacrifice of human lives.[8] The society governed by the market rejects laws that control the market, and it affirms a freedom from laws regulating production and prices. The market, however, follows a logic of self-regulation that does not permit interference, and in societies under a market economy, laws are passed against those who seek the regulation of the market. Thus when popular movements arise with a cry of protest against the scarcity of goods and services that sustain life, against the lack of satisfaction of basic human necessities, against inflation, or against the lowering of salaries and unemployment (all of which are a product of the economic system), those movements are repressed by the armed forces or "forces of order," according to the requirements of policies of National Security.[9]

Laws oriented toward justice, such as the eight-hour workday (for workers who are lucky enough to have a job), become a dead letter, since workers have to work ten, twelve, or even fourteen hours in order to earn enough to survive.[10] Economists concerned with the real production of life for human beings seek a system whose logic would serve the majority, a system that excludes no one.[11] Franz Hinkelammert welcomes this logic as granting primacy to human rights in the hierarchy of social values.

> The logic of the majority only says something new if it is understood as a criterion for the formation of social relationships of production and, consequently, of the system of property and of the conduct of the economy itself, in the sense of *a society that does not allow any to be excluded*, be those majorities or minorities. In such a society no one is marginalized. . . . No one can satisfy his or her own needs by sacrificing the life of another. The satisfaction of basic necessities of each person must be encompassed in a human solidarity that excludes no one from the meeting of those needs. "Thou shalt not kill" is transformed into "thou shalt respect the life of the other in the framework of the satisfaction of the basic necessities of life."[12]

Thus, the satisfaction of the basic needs of all people (such as work, food, shelter, and education) is considered to be an indispensable requirement for a system that does not exclude anyone. However, those basic necessities are not separate from the dignity of the person as historical subject. In fact, according to Hinkelammert, the recognition of the human being as a historical subject is the very root of the respect that mandates the satisfaction of basic necessities. Mutual recognition between human beings who are subjects acting in history is the root of all values, and not an additional value.[13] It is against the background of that affirmation that one must consider another aspect of this challenge, that of the non-person.

CONDEMNED TO "BARGAIN AWAY" HUMANITY:
THE NON-PERSON

Latin American philosophy, especially that of Leopoldo Zea, insists that Latin Americans have been obliged to "bargain away" their humanity. In order to be able to legitimate themselves as human beings, they have taken a foreign "word" *(logos)* for themselves. That borrowed *logos* is the Western *logos*.[14]

Their humanity has been called into question ever since the arrival of the European conquerors, both Spanish and Portuguese, who legitimated their plundering and massacres of the indigenous inhabitants by maintaining that they were less than human beings. Subsequently, the majority of our thinkers became accustomed to expressing their world view using an alien *logos* that was never assimilated to the new context.[15] It was as though by using that logic they wanted to affirm their worth as human beings equal to the norm of "human" created by Western philosophy. For that reason their own manner of expressing themselves seemed alien even to themselves, to their history, and to their reality. It is in that sense that Enrique Dussel affirms the importance for the Latin American sense of identity of recognizing "alterity"—otherness in the sense of the difference of the other that enriches one's life and forms the basis for relationships of mutuality. The lack of that recognition expressed in the alien *logos* results, finally, in the Latin American experiencing himself or herself as a nonbeing.[16]

According to Zea, Latin Americans have to begin from their own negated humanity. This implies thinking philosophically beginning with their concrete humanity, their particular situation as oppressed people. From that base their own *logos* would be born. Then, with freedom and without misgivings, they would be able to take up, to reinvent, and to assimilate philosophical contributions from other latitudes.[17]

Latin American theology explicitly assumes as its interlocutor the non-person. Using language that arose in the development of the well-known

Puebla Document, Gustavo Gutiérrez defines non-persons as those not considered human beings by the present social order. They include exploited classes, marginalized races, and scorned cultures, in which the women of each group are doubly exploited, marginalized, and scorned.[18] In this analysis by Gutiérrez, the oppressed subject takes on color, sex, and cultural identity. We then touch other dimensions that go beyond the economic, and that relate to the dignity of the subject and to the meaning of life. Experience teaches that often a life of marginalization gnaws away at the intimate spaces of a person to the point of making him or her feel unworthy and insignificant in his or her own eyes, in the eyes of others, and even before God. The meaning of life disappears from the horizon. Marginalization and the consequent negation of significant participation by the human being—be that a poor person, an indigenous person, a Black, or a woman—in all spheres of life diminishes the humanity of those persons. Therefore Raúl Vidales affirms that significant participation of persons is the "structural root" of the meaning of living.[19]

African American theologians in the United States also take as their starting point the illegitimacy attributed to them because of the color of their skin. "How are we going to survive in a world which deems Black humanity as an illegitimate form of human existence?" is the question James Cone asks himself when he postulates Black theology as a theology of survival.[20]

It is thus clear that the means of obtaining basic necessities, a sense of human dignity, and the meaningfulness of life must go together if life is to be affirmed. When Vidales speaks of the "dawn of the Indian," he feels compelled to affirm the intrinsic relationship between basic material necessities and the meaningfulness of life:

> To have bread is not all of life, but all of life is born from bread guaranteed to all. Spirituality is linked to the meaningfulness of life. However, the meaning of life never can exist outside of life. It is lived life that itself is the meaning of life. A meaning of life outside of life is as impossible as a being outside of being. To give meaning to life in fact cannot take place except by living life as fully as possible and not reducing it simply to the lowest common denominator that sustains life.[21]

In recent years women, indigenous peoples, and Blacks (sectors doubly discriminated against by class as well as by race or sex) have mobilized to demand their right to be recognized as worthy subjects.[22] There is a large variety among the faces of the poor. The degrees of their oppression and marginalization vary according to the color of their skin, their sex, or their cultural history. This is the other challenge, or the other face of the challenge, for a reading of justification from the perspective of oppressed and humiliated cultures: the demand for recognition of the human worth of every person as a Latin American historical subject, in all of the rich variety that term encompasses.

Latin American history has been forced to march to a foreign drummer in its own lands, in which its own children are powerless to choose their own destiny, except for a very few brief moments. The first colonization and the dependence experienced ever since persist in marking the destiny of these peoples. Thus, we meet as brothers and sisters—human beings of various colors and cultures: Blacks and indigenous peoples, and people in whose body is mingled the blood of two cultures and two opposite histories—the Mestizos.

The faces of women are found in all communities and cultures. Women are discriminated against gratuitously, not for anything they have done against others. They are discriminated against mercilessly solely because of their sex, just as the Black and the indigenous person are discriminated against because of who they are, because of their color. If women's faces appear in every portrait of a poor community, the exact degree of their oppression and marginalization varies according to their color and social location. Women's histories repeat the histories of every one of the communities discussed, but on an even lower level. The Black woman is thus more discriminated against than the Black or indigenous male, because she suffers the marginalization not only of the racist environment, but also that imposed on her by the males of her own racial community. The same can be said about the other communities. A woman struggles for an identity not imposed by the androcentric society in which she inevitably lives. In such a society she is obliged to justify before others every action or attitude, in order to establish herself as a person not inferior to the male.

The faces of the Latin American poor—indigenous, Blacks, Mestizos, and women—share to some degree the experience of discrimination and humiliation, in addition to the experience of the hunger that threatens life.[23] Many of them today are rising up to demand their right to be *persons*, that is to say, human beings recognized as historical subjects. By the very fact of their living on this continent, all of the people who are poor and discriminated against have been created as brothers and sisters. They have shared that identity from the moment they first trod on the earth, ate from it, and struggled on it and for it. If in the past, before the conquest of Latin America, they did not really share their history as sisters and brothers, the present and the future make them truly siblings: Both their threatened life and their hope for the future unite them. The majority of

41

those groups are excluded by the international economic and financial order or by a tradition of discrimination or both. And all, without exception, are under the shadow of an uncertain future. The hope of a new society and a new humanity is setting in motion in a critical way the brotherhood and sisterhood of all people at the heart of the popular movement.

In summary, then, in the Latin American context two aspects of the life of the poor—both of which are products of economic and cultural marginalization and exclusion—challenge the doctrine of justification by faith. One is physical hunger and the lack of the basic necessities of life. The other is the experience of insignificance.

TOWARD A RECONSTRUCTION OF THE DOCTRINE OF JUSTIFICATION BY FAITH

Justification by faith must be oriented toward the affirmation of life—real life for real persons. When what is at stake is the life of the poor, the theme of justification must necessarily be read according to a logic different from the usual one that affirms that God justifies the sinner. This different reading is necessary because the poor introduce a concrete life and a history in which they are the primary victims of sin. They are of course not the only victims, but they are definitely the primary and most visible ones.

The existence of the poor also indicates that there are people responsible for their being poor, and that the sufferings of the poor are not arbitrary or gratuitous, but the product of a historical motivation that gives rise to them. For that reason it is not possible to speak directly or abstractly about justification by faith. Human beings have a face, a social location, color, and sex, and justification intersects that specific social and cultural reality.

Today we are not able to continue engaging in a universal discourse, without taking into account the particularity from which it is pronounced. By not touching on the realities of life of the distinct subjects who live in history, any discourse loses its force. In the present, however, there is no visible human reality that manifests the power of the gospel of which Paul was speaking and was not ashamed (Rom. 1:16). Therefore, to speak of justification as the affirmation of life implies that life as it now exists is touched and transformed on the concrete plane of experience and praxis. To speak of justification as the affirmation of life also entails calling attention to the negation of the life of concrete subjects who are called to live out their humanity. This historical mediation of concrete life prevents universal affirmations (such as that God justifies by faith) from falling into a void or into mere personal subjectivity.

We are clearly not claiming that the poor are not "sinners." Practice teaches us that people who experience themselves justified always recognize themselves not only as sinners but also as responsible for the structure of relationships of sin. An approach oriented toward the affirmation of the person turns out to be indispensable in a context where the faces of human beings have been deformed by poverty, by the violation of their rights, and by humiliation. We find ourselves confronting situations of depersonalization and dehumanization of masses of poor people. The poor themselves, however, are not the only people who are affected. The irrationality of repression and oppression by those who occupy power in many countries whose governments are dictatorships or have only a facade of democracy demonstrates the complete lack of humanity in the agents of those governments. To reflect on justification today in Latin America implies discerning with clarity the various expressions of dehumanization by sin, in order to fall neither into "cheap grace" nor into an ahistorical reconciliation. But it requires above all accentuating the good news for the poor: the affirmation of life.

What threatens the life of human beings is sin, which today can be recognized as an indestructible power. Paul saw it that way in his historical context as well. He identified sin as a mechanism woven according to patterns of injustice. That mechanism makes all human beings its slaves, both those who (without God) direct the destiny of history, and those who are led by them. Sin is a system that threatens the life of many, a mechanism built by specific people, by their practices of injustice guided by their greedy hearts. But in a given moment all people are slaves, and by not being masters of themselves, they have been dehumanized. Here the good intentions of individuals do not count, but only the effectiveness of the solidarity of all, in the search for a new way of living, oriented by the firm conviction that the right to a life of dignity belongs to all.

The study of justification as the affirmation of life must have the particular face of the poor. That study must address not only their economic oppression, but also their dignity as human beings, which has been denied by insignificance, by the color of their skin, or by their sex. Such breadth of perspective is required because the theme of justification touches both the identity of the person as a human being in his or her past, present, and future, and the power of sin that negates his or her humanity. The doctrine of justification by faith leads us to look simultaneously at the destinies of both God and humankind.

Justification as the affirmation of life has as its background the meaning traditionally attributed to justification. That doctrine must then be reread through a liberating lens, and in the context of the challenges of injustice and humiliation experienced by men and women of our continent and of the rest of the Third World.

PART II

JUSTIFICATION BY FAITH:
A LIBERATING THEOLOGY
IN PAUL

CHAPTER THREE

PAUL AND HIS CONTEXT

INTRODUCTION

A quick reading of the letters of Paul and of the book of the Acts of the Apostles introduces us to a world in motion. The scenes change from one place to another: Antioch, Jerusalem, Philippi, Thessalonica, Ephesus, Corinth, Athens, Rome. We are confronted with the important cities of the Greco-Roman world.

But this world in motion is far from being ideal for Paul; much to the contrary, conflict and pain are present at every step. The apostle speaks often of his constant tribulations, stresses, dangers, needs, persecutions, and struggles (1 Thess. 1:6; 2:2; 1 Cor. 15:31-32; Gal. 6:17; Phil. 1:17, 29; 2:17; 2 Cor. 4:8, 12; 11:23, 29). These conflicts take place on the economic, social, and theological planes, both within the Christian community and outside it.

The study of the theme of justification by faith in Paul must be carried out against the background of this troubled and conflictual situation of the first century of the Common Era in which his letters arose. His literary production must be understood against this larger social reality and against the details of Paul's own everyday life: his constant sufferings, persecutions, and abuses; his labors in the workshop as an artisan; his experience as a traveler; his terms in jail as a prisoner; his discussions on the periphery of the imperial center, with friends and with authorities of every type; and his celebrations in the company of his brothers and sisters. There is a restlessness in Paul: The world in which he lives must change, and that change is only possible thanks to the justice of God, which makes of human beings "instruments" (or, literally, "weapons") of justice in the service of God (Rom. 6:13). His desire is for a community in which there will be no discriminatory differences (Gal. 3:28), such as those that characterized his society. The Pauline proposal of justification by faith, then, must be situated in the historical context of the middle of the first century. In that way it will become clear that the theme of justification acquires a meaning beyond the theological dispute between Paul and the Jewish Christians who supported the law.

This study begins with an examination of some important aspects of the life of Paul as a Jew, an artisan, and a prisoner, against the background of the socioeconomic context of his time. From that beginning point we can examine specifically how justification by faith responds to that situation.

PAUL, A "PLURAL SUBJECT"

As the author of a literary work, Paul of Tarsus does not represent an individual isolated from his surroundings. As Lucien Goldmann has observed, the author of every literary creation is a collective, transindividual speaker who gathers together the aspirations, desires, and needs of a group and conveys them in a coherent discourse, with the intention of responding to the needs of the group.[1] Thus, in Paul we have to do with someone who came from a situation of privilege, who wrote well and with a variety of motives, and who was able to perceive coherently the underlying structures of the reality in which he lived. Paul, as such a "transindividual individual," was a collective author with a collective consciousness. We encounter Paul's collective consciousness as it was formed through a series of social relations that began in his childhood with his friends in Tarsus, the city of his birth, and that continued through his life. They included the Jewish community; the artisans who shared his trade; his companions in the study of the Scriptures (Pharisees); the Christian communities he founded; his companions in prison; and finally the great number of beggars, unemployed, and slaves that proliferated in the cities, and to whose lives he was an eyewitness. In addition, Paul's own letters and the testimony of Luke in Acts identify Paul as a traveler, rubbing shoulders constantly with other travelers of every sort: sailors, slaves on the way to be sold, fugitive slaves, traders, teachers, and soldiers, among others. Persecution, torture, exhaustion, and anxiety were sometimes Paul's own lot, but often others were the victims, such as Onesimus, whose story is conveyed by the letter to Philemon, or Prisca and Aquila, the artisan couple who were expelled from the city of Rome by the Emperor Claudius (Acts 18:2).

A literary analysis of the letters is not sufficient to understand Paul's theology. It is necessary also to establish the context in which his writing originated, and that context cannot be explained solely by the internal dynamic of his work. In the letters themselves there are a number of indications of what motivated each writing: responses to opponents (in 2 Corinthians, for example), special petitions (Philemon), the social and economic reality of the middle of the first century, and the spiritual and pastoral experience of Paul in his immediate context (2 Cor. 4:10; 11:24-25; Gal. 6:17). It is not the same thing, however, to establish the frequency with which Paul asked the brothers and sisters not to value themselves more highly than others (Rom. 12:13), as to try to explain why Paul appealed to that behavior in a society as highly discriminatory as was Greco-Roman society. How can one affirm for no reason at all, "For freedom Christ has set us free" (Gal. 5:1), without taking into account the context of the slaveholding society?[2] How can one speak about the justice of God without alluding not only to the injustices of an imperialist society, but also to an inequitable legal system?

Nor should one seize upon a single fact of the apostle's life to explain his thought. His personal experience of conversion in Damascus does not provide the key to understanding Paul's theology,[3] nor does Tarsus where he was born, nor Jerusalem where he may have been educated, nor the Jewish tradition that he received from his ancestors. It is the conjunction of all these profound experiences—including especially his occupation as an artisan, his ethnicity, his experience in prison as a convict, and his permanent contact with the common people of the cities of the provinces under the Roman Empire—that constitutes the place where Paul experienced God and the reservoir from which he constructed his theology.[4]

But this affirmation that his theology arose from his concrete experience still seems too generic. To be more precise, his vision of the world, which was a product of an environment that was oppressive and difficult for the poor, was markedly utopian: Paul longed for a society of equals where solidarity would reign.[5] If he had problems with his society, it was precisely because his gospel required a practice that did not agree with the pattern of life of Greco-Roman society, where equality was almost inconceivable. The saying of Pliny the Younger (62–114?) is well known: *Nihil est ipsa aequalitate inaequalius,* "Nothing can be more unequal than ... equality" (*Letters* IX, V).[6] As Schüssler Fiorenza notes, "The conversion of women, slaves, and young people who belonged to the household of an unconverted *paterfamilias* already constituted a potential political offense against the patriarchal order."[7] Among the aspects of Paul's life that nourished his collective consciousness and delimited his theological horizon, priority should be given to his ethnicity, his employment, and his time spent in prison, as constituting the nuclei of vital experience that is fertile ground for the creation of theology.

49

Paul the Jew

Paul's experience as a Jew emerges more from the Diaspora than from Jerusalem. According to Paul himself, he was in Jerusalem only a short time (Gal. 1:17-23; 2:1-10). His world, therefore, was the unique world of a Jew of the Diaspora—a blend of two forms of ancient culture: Judaism and Hellenism.[8] Born and reared in Tarsus, Paul probably owed his intellectual formation to that city known for its universities. Tarsus, capital of the province of Cilicia, was the residence of the proconsuls of Rome as well as a center for the production of linen, and a commercial hub as well. Through Dio Chrysostom (30?–117), we know of various disturbances provoked by the linen workers *(linourgoi)* of that city. Those workers were viewed negatively by the surrounding society. For example, Dio referred to them as the seditious and restless mob that does not enjoy the pleasures of the city. In order to calm their spirits, Dio further recommended the inclusion of the lower classes into full citizenship for a price of five hundred denarii. Disturbances also took place among some of the managers, and among the governors of the city and the procurators *(Discourses* 34.9, 15-16, 21-23).[9] The geographical position of Tarsus was clearly advantageous. It was the point of intersection of important routes between east and west, and thus commercial traffic was constant. Moreover, the city was known as a center for eastern religions, especially the cult of the goddess Isis. Cynic and Stoic philosophers abounded. It has been said that Paul's preaching and theology reflect something of this background of his youth.[10]

According to André Paul, the Jewish Diaspora was a large and solid system that determined statistically and ideologically the global form and character of the Jewish world.[11] The Jews of the Diaspora acquired certain privileges during the rule of the Greeks and Romans, and despite the uprisings of the Jews of Jerusalem, those in the Diaspora continued to enjoy many privileges. They were allowed to follow their own traditions and to govern themselves according to their own jurisprudence—as long as the laws of the state were not affected—and they were exempted from military service because of their strict Sabbath law.[12] They lived in community, and in several large cities where the Jewish population was sizable, such as Alexandria, they constituted what was called a *politeuma,* a term denoting a state, body of citizens, corporation, or colony of foreigners organized internally according to their own norms and customs.[13]

The Jews belonged to all social strata and carried out various kinds of work: They were farmers, military colonists (in Egypt), tradespeople, and artisans. In the Greek cities they were not able to own land because they were foreigners. Usually the Jewish communities did not include people who possessed great wealth. According to Saulnier, the cases of Philo and of Murashu, a banker of Alexandria, are exceptions.[14]

The fiscal politics of the empire affected the economic situation of the Jews in the Diaspora. In Egypt, for example, the government imposed the tax called *laographia,* "enrollment of the people." According to A. Paul, it was "a personal tax . . . that had to be paid by everyone who was not citizen of a Greek city or of Rome (except for a privileged few, like certain priests)."[15] With Augustus, the imposition of the tax caused a triple negative effect among the Jews:

1) Economic oppression. The villagers, deprived of money, were the ones most greatly harmed.

2) An insulting discrimination. The *laographia* constituted a barrier that destroyed any desire for emancipation. Moreover, it lumped together as taxpayers both the Jews and the native Egyptians.

3) The social and ideological stratification, within the Jewish group, into two distinct and occasionally opposing layers. On one side was the minority of citizens more favored and less harmed, who continued paradoxically to be open to Hellenism and to coexistence with the Greeks (a group of which Philo would later serve as an example). On the other side was the majority of the rural population, impoverished by the taxes, resigned to isolation, and then led to a nationalistic reaction by the influence and with the help of the first movements of resistance of the Jews of Palestine (after the death of Herod, and until 70 C.E.).[16]

This Jewish world was linked to Jerusalem by its ethnic and religious identity, but at the same time it was not separated from the Greco-Roman world. The Jews would pay the tax to the Temple (the cycle and a half),[17] and, if their economic conditions permitted, they would make festival pilgrimages to the Temple in Jerusalem. In their neighborhoods, they observed the customs of their country, relying on their synagogue and holy books (principally in the Greek of the Septuagint). They communicated easily with the native people of the city or with other peoples, using the "common" *(koinē)* Greek, which had become their own language.[18]

Paul affirms that he was educated as a Pharisee (Phil. 3:5). In Palestine, the Pharisees constituted closed communities and distinguished themselves by their zealous fulfillment of the religious commandments, especially those concerning the tithe and the purity laws. They believed themselves to be the true Israel among the Jews (their name means "separated"), and, as such, they maintained a separation between themselves and the great mass of people who were unable to follow all the requirements of the law, especially those concerning the tithe. Curiously,

51

the members of the Pharisees' communities came sociologically from the common people, which was not the case for the Sadducees. According to Joachim Jeremias, the masses saw in the Pharisaic communities their protection against the Sadducees' movement, which was composed principally of the old hereditary and conservative nobility.[19]

Paul's tendency to see everyone, both peoples and individual persons, as equal through faith in Christ (Gal. 3:28) may be related to his own experience prior to his conversion. As a Pharisee, he participated in a separation between peoples (between Gentiles and Jews) and within the people (between the masses and the Pharisees). Before his conversion Paul was proud of being a Jew (Phil. 3:5; 2 Cor. 11:22; Rom. 11:1; Gal. 2:15), and moreover, was very satisfied to belong to "the chosen and elite race of his people, sure of realizing in his religious observance an ideal that would make him without reproach before God, before human beings, and in his own conscience."[20] His apostleship among the Gentiles made him change that perspective.

However, the apostle never ceased to be a Jew. According to Davies, his national and religious heritage formed a single fabric that can be recognized in his Christian theology.[21] But the change in his perspective is also a fact. Sanders notes two important breaks with Palestinian Judaism in Paul's pattern of religious thought. One is concerned with the election of Israel, and the other with the place of the law. Paul explicitly denied the salvific efficacy of the covenant between God and Israel, a confidence that was the heart of "covenantal nomism." Furthermore, the election of Israel was transferred to Christ, and through him to Christians. The law, then, is not the condition for participation in the people of God, because, thanks to Jesus Christ, one participates in it through faith.[22]

In Christ, then, the people of God is fulfilled, since all who believe are included in it, not only Jews by birth. One becomes part of the people of God through Christ, and not by the law. Thus, in Paul one can observe a participationist eschatology, over against a covenantal nomism.[23] In this sense his concern was for the inclusion of Gentiles in the salvific plan of God through Christ, a concern that E. P. Sanders sees as Paul's principal contribution to the history of Christianity: "In denying the Jewish privilege as the elect of God, Paul makes the church in theory universal; it is God's intention to have mercy on all."[24] Stendahl even concludes that "the doctrine of justification by faith was hammered out by Paul for the very specific and limited purpose of defending the rights of Gentile converts to be full and genuine heirs to the promises of God to Israel."[25]

Exclusiveness, then, is precisely one of the keys to supporting a rereading of justification from the perspective of those who are poor and those excluded by race and sex. Another factor that may have allowed Paul to

52

give consistency to his theology was his experience in the artisan's workshop and his social position that resulted from that way of earning a living.

Paul the Artisan

Paul's life appears to have been framed by the ambiguous combination of social privilege and economic need. By birth and education on the one hand, and by sympathy and circumstances of life on the other, Paul belonged both to the middle and to the lower classes.[26] Paul was neither a slave nor a freed slave. To all appearances, he was a freeborn artisan, independent, but of modest means. According to Luke, he had the opportunity to be educated academically in Jerusalem (Acts 22:3). In other words, he was not one of the freeborn but unemployed or unskilled and therefore poor people, of whom there were many in the urban environment.[27]

His social position was a bit more favorable than that of persons on the lowest rungs of his society. But this difference should not be exaggerated by suggesting that he belonged to an upper or upper middle class, or that he moved with freedom among rich people in the city to impart his messages in their houses.[28] According to Paul himself, he endured hunger (1 Cor. 11:27), and he had to work day and night (1 Thess. 2:9) to support himself. Roland Hock presents a study on Paul as an artisan—specifically a tentmaker *(skēnopoios)*—based on information from Luke (Acts 18:3) and from references by Paul himself to his manual labor. The picture presented is fairly realistic, and very close to what might be the life of artisans of antiquity, who, like Paul, earned their living by their labor. In that context, it is likely that Paul learned his craft of tentmaking in a domestic setting, possibly through his father, as was common not only in Jewish families, but also in Hellenistic society.[29] The daily life of most artisans was difficult. While some prospered, the majority, who hoped only to earn their daily bread, spent hours and hours in the workshop and still suffered want. Paul's claims that he worked day and night (1 Thess. 2:9) and that he often suffered from hunger, thirst, and cold (2 Cor. 11:27) are not exaggerations, but rather simply reflect the experiences common to many artisans.[30]

On the other hand, artisans suffered scorn and marginalization by their society. They were stigmatized by the aristocracy as slaves, uneducated, and useless. They were treated like slaves, because the majority of them in fact were. They were assumed to be without education because they spent all their time locked in the workshop, without the possibility of educating themselves. They were viewed as useless, because the products of their craft were usually articles "of luxury and extravagance."[31] In Greco-Roman society generally, manual labor—that is to say, manufacturing and commerce—were seen as forms of labor without dignity. The only labor considered to be dignified was related to agriculture. According to Thomas Wiedemann, the status of the artisan varied in the different Roman and Greek societies, but in all areas such labor was considered inferior to that of people who produced "natural" wealth through agriculture.[32]

If Paul spent all day working in his workshop, it is very probable that he occupied his time also reflecting on the gospel, sharing it, and discussing his ideas with his companions at work, clients, or visitors. In Acts 17:17, Luke tells us about Paul's daily conversations in the *agora*, or marketplace, which is where artisans normally established their workshops.[33] Thus, despite the fact that the aristocracy saw in the artisan a person who was uneducated, the workshop served sometimes (as in the case of Simon the cobbler, who was a Cynic[34]) also as a social setting for a certain intellectual activity. Sometimes one person would read while another worked. At other times the workshop was the scene of philosophical discussions.

Therefore, on the one hand, the privilege Paul enjoyed from having been born free and from working as an independent artisan is undeniable.[35] On the other hand, the fact that he spent entire days working, talking, and listening to the slaves and freed slaves who very probably worked in workshops adjacent to his (as was the custom for practitioners of the same trade), and the fact that he suffered the scorn of his society because of his employment, situated Paul to a large extent on the side of the poor who struggled for subsistence. Paul would not have suffered the same exploitation as that of the slaves who worked the land or in the mines, but he was far from enjoying a life of leisure.[36]

Thus, one of the factors of Paul's life that inclined his theological discourse toward a community of equals and solidarity that favored the marginalized was his experience in the workshop. That experience not only reflected his own personal life, but it was also enlarged by what he could hear, feel, and judge from the other artisans who did not enjoy the status of "freeborn" (but rather were slaves or freed slaves), or who did not enjoy the welcoming friendship of the sisters and brothers of the churches, who often shared their lodging with Paul (see Acts 18:3; Rom. 1:12; 15:32). Paul's experience was also enlarged by his contact with clients. Among those clients would have been travelers, including traders and sailors, for example, who needed serviceable tents for their stopovers in the ports or for the plazas of the marketplace. Paul may well also have had private clients—rich people who bought tents of luxurious fabrics to use on the beach on summer days or for shelter during huge banquets.[37] These contradictions or contrasts could not have passed unnoticed by Paul.

If there was an element of "social mobility" and of "status inconsistency" in Paul, as appears to have been a common phenomenon in the first centuries of the Common Era,[38] for him it would have entailed a move from a higher to a lower social status. Perhaps that movement downward was by deliberate choice, reflecting Paul's determination not to be supported economically, in a systematic fashion, by the church as a missionary,[39] or perhaps it reflected a tendency inherent in the historical juncture in which he lived. This ambivalent reality that allowed Paul to "know what it is to have little, and . . . what it is to have plenty," as he expressed it to the Philippians (Phil. 4:12), is one of the elements that allowed him to discern "the justice of God" that is central to his gospel. Many in the community and beyond it knew only what it was "to have little." The christological hymn of Philippians 2:5-11 systematizes theologically Paul's life of commitment as a follower, imitator, and preacher of Jesus Christ. The spontaneous and freely given solidarity of the believers, made concrete in economic aid and hospitality that were not considered payment for his ministry (Acts 17:10; 18:3; Rom. 16:22-23; Phil. 4:18), had to have been for Paul a significant gesture that reinforced the vision of an egalitarian community that was so central to his theology. On one occasion he spent more time in prison than the law required. If Paul had offered money (a bribe) to the Roman procurator, possibly he would have been set free (Acts 24:26).[40]

Paul the Prisoner

Paul's language referring to justice and justification has a forensic tint, though not exclusively so. He speaks of judgment, condemnation, sentence, punishment, justification, and liberation.[41] Current studies on the justice of God and its forensic aspects always send us back to the traditions, whether of the Hebrew Bible or of late apocalyptic Judaism.[42] However, it appears that until now, no one has considered the fact that this forensic tint of justification does not simply come from the traditions, but is also motivated by one who is familiar with the language of justice in its legal sense because of his time in prison and his experience of personal suffering.

In fact, Paul was arrested and brought into court more than once, and received a prison sentence as well as suffering the punishment of Roman flagellation. According to his own testimony in 2 Corinthians 11:23, he was imprisoned many times *(en phylakais perissoteros)*. The expression is surely superlative, but it underlines the undeniable fact that he endured the experience of being a prisoner. In Philippians 1:13, 14, 17 and in Philemon 1, 13, he speaks of his chains or imprisonment *(desmoi)*. From Luke we know that he was imprisoned in Philippi (Acts 16:16-38; see also 1 Thess. 2:2), Caesarea (Acts 23:23–26:32), and Rome (Acts 27–28), and that he appeared before the courts in Thessalonica, where Jason had to pay a fine to the magistrates (Acts 17:6-9). Apparently he was also imprisoned in Ephesus (see 1 Cor. 15:32; 2 Cor. 1:8), or at least there is a strong

55

hypothesis suggesting that Paul wrote the letters to the Philippians and Philemon from there.[43]

Little is known of the conditions in the prisons of that time or of the daily treatment of the prisoners.[44] There was a double system of prisons, and both a state prison and a private prison were located in the house of the magistrate of the city. According to Theodor Mömmsen, the prisons in private houses were more secure and provided better conditions than those of the state. Nevertheless, the prisoner had always to be shackled to a soldier to be guarded.[45] Paul apparently experienced both types of prison (see Acts 28:16).

As for the treatment of the prisoners, there was always a bias in favor of the prisoner with influence, power, status, or wealth. Peter Garnsey has identified both *de iure* and *de facto* inequalities. The *de iure* ones were due to the bias of judges and Roman officials. For example, the very practice of relying on two types of court (one in which normally—though not exclusively—those of low status appeared, and the other for people of high status) and the class-determined differences in the punishments meted out to those sentenced in each type of court, itself pointed to discrimination against those from lower social ranks.[46] The double penal system was begun in the first century and reached its maturity in the time of Hadrian. With the introduction of the *cognitio* (which accorded to the judge all the decision-making power of the court to determine the penalty) came the variation in penalties: very severe ones for the poor and those of low status (like slaves, freed slaves, and poor freeborn people), and light ones for nobles and the rich. Capital punishment was rare in this second group, who normally suffered exile (*deportatio* or *delegatio*) or expulsion from a governmental position (such as the senate or council). The most common lesser sanction was the payment of a fine. For the unprivileged groups, punishment for capital crimes was the *summum supplicum*—the death penalty, whether by crucifixion (*crux*), being thrown to the wild beasts (*bestiis dari*), being burned alive (*vivus uri, crematio*), or fighting as a gladiator. Another penalty for this group was forced labor in the mines (*metallum*) or in public works and services, a less severe penalty. Torture was generally reserved only for slaves, although in the second and third centuries poor freeborn people also suffered it.[47] Unlike *de iure* inequality, *de facto* inequality was not openly recognized by judicial and political authorities. In practice, for example, there were Roman citizens (without power or influence) who suffered corporal punishment or torture, even though that was prohibited by law.[48]

On the basis of such data, Mömmsen, a specialist in Roman law, concludes that the treatment of a prisoner clearly depended, on the one hand, on the personality of the superior or of the deputy in charge of the case, and on the other hand, on the power and influence of the prisoner. For wealthy prisoners or those who had the support of friends, the sentence was reduced or was never carried out, while those who were poor or insignificant ended up in the most horrible misery.[49] Paul himself spent two years abandoned in the prison in Caesarea. Felix, the Roman procurator, allowed some leeway in Paul's case, in the hope that he would give him money as a bribe (Acts 24:26).[50] Moreover, the maximum duration of preventive detention was two years,[51] a fact that Felix did not take into account. With the arrival of his successor, Porcius Festus, Felix continued to hold Paul prisoner simply because, according to Luke, he wanted to ingratiate himself with the Jews (Acts 24:27).

With the law or without the law, injustices come to light. The fact that the life of the prisoner did not necessarily correspond to legal justice can be seen also in Luke's account (whatever the literary genre of the passage) of the incident in which—threatened by shipwreck—the soldiers proposed killing the prisoners on board the boat in which they were being transported, for fear that the prisoners would escape by swimming away (Acts 27:42).

Paul wrote Galatians and Romans prior to his experience in the prisons of Caesarea and Rome. However, he had already experienced the burden of an inequitable legal system. The letter that he wrote from prison to the Philippians carries the voice of a prisoner-narrator who is anticipating a verdict of death even though he is innocent. It is about someone who today would be called a political prisoner, for Paul was arrested for provoking the crowds by speaking of another Sovereign, another reign, and another justice inaugurated by an innocent person who was crucified—one judged by Roman law and condemned to the maximum penalty reserved for slaves: crucifixion. As far as we know, Paul was not arrested for indebtedness, nor for robbery or another crime, nor for being a fugitive slave.

The forensic language so abundant in the theology of justification could thus have been rooted not only in the theme of judgment as portrayed in the biblical tradition, but also in Paul's experience in the courts and in the prisons, in which he lived in anguish awaiting a verdict. The Roman authorities condemned him even though he was innocent. But God justified him by grace. In Roman law, grace did not count, but rather only the merits—social status, power, and wealth—of the accused. The penal code of the principate acknowledged social differences, and the punishment, which depended on the crime, was only applied in all its rigor to the slave, the poor person, and the foreigner. The aristocrat, who was free and a citizen with considerable power, was governed by gentler norms. In contrast to this state of affairs, Paul recognized that in God's justice there is no favoritism: All are sinners and all receive the grace and the gift of God's saving, liberating, and re-creating justice.

Thus far we have encountered Paul as a transindividual subject with a collective consciousness nurtured by his experience in Roman society as an artisan, as a Jew, and as a prisoner. Clearly his daily experiences of relationships with others and with God, framed in a socioeconomic and political context hostile to persons excluded from that society, constitute an element of capital importance for understanding his theology and the theme of justification by faith in particular.

THE ROMAN EMPIRE

The concrete experience of Paul was a central point of reference for understanding the destructiveness of sin and the revelation of "the wrath of God . . . against all ungodliness and injustice of those who imprison the truth in injustice" (Rom. 1:18, author's trans.).[52] Speaking in less theological terms, we can ask ourselves how his contemporaries in the first century of our era imprisoned the truth in injustice. Many who write about this epoch mention the peace and security (a policy inaugurated in the "new order" proclaimed by Augustus [14 B.C.E.–29 C.E.]), the prosperity, and the economic energy. These qualities are seen by the majority of these writers as benefiting those to whom this Roman peace, concord, and security were granted.[53]

It is likely that Paul witnessed huge building projects in the cities he visited, but very probably the many hungry people did not go unnoticed by him either. Paul lived in the Pax Romana, but he knew equally the movement of troops and the military bases on the borders of the provinces of the empire. The Romans were proud of their laws, but poor people and slaves felt the laws turned against them.[54] Paul himself was arrested unjustly. Dignity and wealth were in vogue, but not even a freed slave could overcome the stigma of slavery, for his or her exploitation did not cease. Civilization, peace, the law, and dignity for the privileged signified for many people poverty, submission, injustice, and humiliation. These contrasting experiences of the same reality were supported by both the economic and the social factors of this period. The economic factors made physical life virtually impossible for the poor, and the social factors denied their human dignity.

The Truth About Civilization

One of the events that attract one's attention in this period, when Augustus established himself in power as the emperor, is the dawn of urbanization. The number of new cities was increasing, old ones were being reconstructed, and the urban population was growing. Together with Rome, Alexandria, and Antioch, which were the three most famous cities, the cities of Corinth, Athens, Philippi, Thessalonica, Smyrna, Ephesus, Tarsus, Pergamum, and Laodicea were either founded, increased in size, or renewed in this period. In addition, especially in the time of King Herod, the cities of Palestine grew at an astonishing rate. Everywhere were construction projects for new buildings such as gymnasia, baths, temples, or stadiums. An increase in the number and quality of communication routes, both new and rebuilt, is another factor that highlights the progress of urbanization.[55]

Roman art, Latin literature, and philosophical knowledge also mark this as a period of progress and civilization. A number of famous poets praise the greatness of the empire—which Virgil, for example, calls "eternal"— and of the emperor, his reign, wealth, and power.[56]

However, the cost of this advance of civilization and urbanization during the first centuries was high for those who had to bear the brunt of it. That cost was borne especially by the conquered provinces and by the poor in general, whether they were from the provinces or from the imperial city, and whether they were slaves or freed, citizens or foreigners, peasants or urban dwellers. Of those poor people, some suffered more than others, but all suffered.[57]

The origin and distribution of wealth account for why this historical period was experienced so differently by the various sectors of the population. Wealth arrived in Rome from various sources. In the beginning it came as a result of wars. If the military investment was large, the burden of its payment was unbearable for those from whom it was exacted. Plunderings of national treasures, destruction of temples, indiscriminate pillaging, the taking of prisoners of war who were made into slaves, and various forms of confiscation of the wealth of the conquered were the principal components of the booty.[58] To that initial profiteering from wars were added the tributes exacted over the long term from provinces that were conquered or that surrendered voluntarily, and taxes of every sort. According to Garnsey and Saller, the provinces were responsible for supplying the Roman government with food and other articles, in addition to the money exacted in taxes and tribute.[59] Poor people were those most greatly affected by this fiscal policy, since a larger tax burden fell directly or indirectly on those who worked the land—peasants or tenant farmers.[60]

As far as the economy was concerned, the most important means of production was the land. According to Salvioli, the story of the formation of the *latifundia* (large landed estates) summarizes the important points of the economic history of the Romans:

> Enriched by the Punic and Asian wars, the Patricians appropriated for themselves fertile territories both from the colonies and from what were "public lands." By means of the interest on the money lent to them, they took from

free peasants the fruits of their labor, and having augmented their mass of capital, they sought to invest it in the purchase of real estate. It was useless and impractical to continue lending to small free landowners who never produced an appreciable surplus. They failed to make money because the increased cultivation of wheat and other cereals lowered the price, and marketing the grain was difficult. As a result, the debtor could never free himself from his obligations. Then expropriation comes into play: The free laborers were expelled and replaced by slaves. Thus a part of the free agricultural population was reduced to the condition of employees.[61]

In that way, at the beginning of the Common Era land was concentrated in the hands of a few wealthy landowners, not only in Italy but also in the provinces.[62] With this step from a peasant economy to one of tenant farmers came a tendency to change from the cultivation of grains to crops that produced greater profits, like grapes and olives.[63] That political decision affected especially the poor people, whose diet was based on grains.

Surplus production was an important source of income. De Ste. Croix analyzes that surplus in the ancient Greek world, where conditions and practices similar to those of the Roman period prevailed. He concludes that two principal ways existed to extract the surplus of production from the workers, one direct and the other indirect. The landowners extracted profit in a direct way by forced labor, that is to say by the labor of slaves or of those who because of indebtedness were (supposedly temporarily) placed in indentured servitude to their creditors, until they had paid their debt by their labor. To this direct kind of exploitation must be added tenant farmers and those day laborers hired sporadically. Other ways of getting access to the surplus came indirectly by means of rent if the land was leased, or by the price of manumission if a slave was able to pay it. Indirect exploitation was also used by the state for the collective benefit of the land-owning class of freeborn status. It took place by means of taxation (in cash or kind), military conscription, and forced service. The most important of these methods, of course, was taxation—a burden that increased during the period of the Roman principate. Those affected by this indirect extraction of profit were, among others, the small landowners, artisans who worked on commission, and tradespeople. But the majority were peasants.[64]

This form of enslavement (in the sense that it was compulsory) was gradually changing in the first three centuries of the Common Era. During that period a strong pressure was exerted on the free poor population, such that at the end of the second century C.E. the majority of the peasants were subject to forms of servitude or near servitude.[65] In Asia Minor and Syria, like other parts of the empire, compulsory exploitation often took the form of indentured servitude as a consequence of debts.[66] The free or partially free peasants were exploited through rents, charges of tribute, and compulsory service. With the necessity of paying tribute to Rome came an important new form of oppression.[67]

Together with acquiring a monopoly of ownership of agricultural lands, the Romans employed usury to multiply their wealth. When Rome began to conquer the provinces, according to Kavaliov,

> oppressions of a usurious sort increased greatly . . .; many allied and unallied states were weakened to such an extent that they were obliged to surrender to Rome. The rate of interest on borrowed money greatly exceeded the "legal" level, reaching and even exceeding 48-50%.[68]

Furthermore, the Romans took advantage of speculation in commercial goods and real estate (both rural lands and city buildings), frequently in order to lease them for high rents to poor people.[69]

It was not only the empire itself that was involved in domination and oppression. The Romans often found fertile ground for the support of such practices among their provincial allies as well. With the politics of the empire a number of changes also took place in the cities of the provinces, especially in the arena of social and economic structures. Those changes favored primarily the local aristocracy, for the strongest ties of the Roman administration were with that group. In general, those authorities became richer and more powerful with the arrival of the empire, in exchange, certainly, for their submission to the policies of the imperial administration, which sometimes cost them greatly.[70]

Civilization thus had a negative effect on the provinces of the empire.[71] In general, civilization was dedicated primarily to the progress of the cities. The rural communities continued living in very primitive conditions, which led to the growth of profound hostilities between cities and rural areas.[72] But urbanization also harmed the poor people of the cities. In Ephesus, Nicea, Claudiopolis, and Nicomedia, there were tensions because of the misuse of municipal funds. The authorities dedicated huge quantities of money to lavish building projects, which diminished the usual donations to the populace. Tenny Frank, who affirms that the study of the cities in Asia Minor in the first two centuries of the empire is the study of both the progress of urbanization and the growth of prosperity, recognizes that there was discontent on the part of the poor, and that progress deepened the social contrasts between poverty and wealth.[73]

The Truth About Dignity

The truth about dignity in the Roman world is that only a few could qualify as "dignified" or "worthy." That designation was restricted to the upper class. The most important criteria for belonging to that class are summarized by Alföldy: to be rich, to have a high position and to exercise power through it, to be considered to have more prestige in the society than everyone else, and to be a member of one of the three famous "orders": senator, equestrian, and decurion. That sector of society was the beneficiary in the distribution of wealth obtained from the various sources already mentioned.[74]

An "order" was a juridically defined social category. In order to be a member of one of the orders, one had to have prestige or dignity. To possess prestige, one would have to have been born into a noble family, to possess wealth, and to enjoy a good moral reputation. Clearly it was a privilege or a right that circulated among the families of the aristocracy. The law was supposed to clarify and define the distinctions of privilege. The emperors were pressed to distinguish clearly among the differences of status, or what Pliny (62–114?) called the differences between "the little ones" and the "great ones" (*Letters* X.5).[75]

In addition to this main distinction, there were also various categories of rich people. The delineation of those distinctions responded to a wave of new candidates for membership in the orders who were people of dubious origin, such as officers of the army. They had reached the prestigious position where they might apply for such membership because of their military service to the regime. The aristocracy lodged various protests against the acceptance of this sort of person, especially those coming from the provinces of the empire.[76] In effect, with the advent of the empire two sectors of the population found themselves able to ascend to nobility: soldiers (officers) and a special category of slaves, namely those of the imperial household. This fact greatly annoyed the aristocracy. In reality, the concern to preserve the purity of status expressed only the nostalgia of the elite nobility for the past they remembered.[77]

From the perspective of the poor, these distinctions probably did not amount to much. For them there were only two categories that mattered: the rich and powerful nobles on the one hand, and the poor on the other.[78] In fact, for the populace in general, the real division fell into two large and unequal sectors, which by the time of the emperor Hadrian (76–138) came to be labeled formally *honestiores* and *humiliores*—the "worthy" and the "humble." The former were the members of the three orders, and the latter were the rest of the people—clearly the majority. In the time of the apostle Paul, the large majority of the inhabitants of the empire were poor or of a despised status, that is to say, not "worthy." They included slaves, freed slaves, freeborn poor people, and foreigners.

Of all of these, the ones who suffered the greatest scorn and marginalization, as well as often outright exploitation, were the slaves, especially all those who lived in the rural areas.[79] Roman law denied everything to those slaves, the "excluded" par excellence. The slave was not a person but an object, and as such was not a subject but the object of law, even to the point of not being allowed to contract a marriage or legally have a family. Similarly, a slave had no right of inheritance, could not own property, could not be a creditor or a debtor, and could neither sue nor be sued in a court. A slave could also not make a will or leave heirs of any sort. An owner could receive payment for any damages caused to a slave, as was the case for damages to other property belonging to the owner. If an owner abandoned a slave, that did not mean that the slave would be free, but rather that he or she would simply become a *servus sine domino* ("servant without a master"). Like any other goods that the owner might lose or abandon, a slave also might become the property of whoever might wish to take possession. In principle, the owner could do with the slave whatever the owner wished: sell, give away, punish, and even kill him or her.[80] Legal attenuations were added little by little, such as, for example, prohibiting a slave from being fed to the wild beasts (*lex Petronia,* 19 C.E.), or forbidding an owner from killing a slave who was sick.[81] In practice, the slave of rich owners was often granted the authority to administer the owner's fortune. There are also examples of slaves (especially domestic servants) who enjoyed a better lot in life. However, with or without the law, in practice most of the time the injured party was the slave vis-à-vis the master.[82]

There were variations in the social circumstances of the different categories of slaves. For example, marked contrasts existed between city workers and those in the fields. Those from rural areas lived in worse conditions than those in the city. In Italy and in other provinces, for example, the slaves who constituted the majority of workers in the mines and agriculture were brutally exploited and despised, while the slaves within the city who worked in households lived in better conditions. The latter at least were able to aspire to manumission at the age of thirty, while the others were not.[83] In any event, being a slave constituted an unbearable stigma for the rest of one's life. Even when a slave somehow achieved manumission, the past condition of slavery remained an obstacle to living a life of dignity or worth.[84]

Slaves were not the only people who suffered in this social arrangement. Closely parallel to the situation of agricultural slaves was often that of freed slaves and freeborn persons who, because of their extreme poverty, found themselves obliged to work under the same conditions and to endure the same suffering as the slaves.[85] In some provinces, such as Asia Minor or Egypt, those who worked the land were not slaves in the traditional sense of the term, but rather dependent peasant servants obliged to

63

work because of their debts. Their treatment was even worse than that of the household slave (Philo, *De specialibus legibus* III.159-62).[86] The freeborn poor of the cities were able to receive a share of the donations—wheat, normally—that rich citizens (or, in Rome, the emperor himself) sometimes offered, generally to gain prestige and social power.[87]

Because of their gender, women suffered additional restrictions in their freedom as human beings of dignity and worth. Considered in ancient times a dependent being, a woman was always under the domination of the *pater-familias*, whose powers were extensive over the members of the household, which often included a number of family clusters. The woman was under his tutelage until she was transferred by a legal marriage to the tutelage of her husband *(manus)*.[88] In the Hellenistic era, Greek and Roman women (and especially the latter) achieved some significant degrees of equality with respect to the male. In the beginning of the empire, however, there was an attempt to restrain women's emancipation by means of the Augustinian legislation. According to Catherine Salles,

> Augustus, who wanted to preserve the number of Roman citizens of old lineage, promulgated laws that favored marriage and large families. Adultery was severely punished and the state supported the husband by banishing the woman and confiscating a portion of her goods.[89]

Salles concludes, however, that the legislation of Augustus had little influence. Obviously slave women, freed women, or freeborn poor women suffered a greater oppression than women of the upper classes, for to their marginalization on the basis of gender one must add the burden of their socioeconomic condition and status.

THE SOCIAL CONTEXT OF PAUL'S LETTERS

This brief look at the political, social, and economic context of the Roman Empire sets the stage for an examination of Paul's letters, and especially the letter to the Christians at Rome. How can we read Romans without listening to the voice of an innocent prisoner? Or without feeling the pain and the rage of the thousands of slaves crucified unjustly by human laws that hid the truth in injustice? Or without seeing the thousands of persons disadvantaged by the "progress" of civilization? Or without hearing the cries of a country destroyed by Roman invasions? The letter that has been the object of abstract discussions, sometimes without specific, concrete meaning, presents itself to us now with a new message concerning the revelation of the justice of God, realized in justification by faith as an affirmation of life.

CHAPTER FOUR

JUSTIFICATION BY FAITH IN PAUL'S LETTERS PRIOR TO ROMANS

INTRODUCTION

Paul, the missionary of Jesus Christ—artisan, Jew, and persecuted man—confronted a world that had to take a different course. The concept of justification by faith allowed him to manifest that reality and that hope. Although this study focuses on the letter to the Romans, in which Paul produces a clear and coherent statement of his theological thought, that letter builds on an entire lifetime's worth of experience and reflection.[1] Paul's earlier letters sketch out that history, which, in turn, gives specific historical substance to the letter to the Romans. Romans must be interpreted in light of the earlier letters and not *vice versa*, as is often done.

In order to relate Paul's theological propositions to his immediate context, each letter is introduced by an exploration of the socioeconomic context in which it arose, and by a discussion of the various tensions that can be identified through the letter. Paul's letters present only implicitly their relationship to Greco-Roman society. The clues and implications in all of the letters must be carefully gathered, woven together, and placed against the background of the socioeconomic situation of the first century. Once that is done, the patterns of relationship of the letters to their contexts will become clear. Once those relationships have been sketched, it will be possible to identify the theological concerns that arose from those contexts. Formulas considered to be pre-Pauline (1 Cor. 1:30; 6:11; 2 Cor. 5:21; Gal. 3:28; Rom. 3:25-26; 4:24-25; 8:34; 5:1-2; and others) will be read within the logic of Paul's theological discussion, for they acquired different meanings once they were incorporated into that structure. Each letter is approached differently,

65

depending on what the letter offers to the study of the theme of justification. The following categories of texts will be examined: (1) texts that allude directly, even in a marginal way, to justice, the just person, or justification; (2) texts that do not allude directly to those themes but that contribute important elements to that study (such as the themes of resurrection and judgment); and, in one case, (3) an entire letter (Galatians) dedicated to the theme of justification.

1 THESSALONIANS

In the first known writing of Paul (with Silvanus and Timothy), written in approximately 50–51 to the Thessalonians, neither the noun "justice" or "justification," nor the verb "to justify," appears. The adverb *dikaios*, "justly," is used when Paul recalls the holy *(hosios)*, just *(dikaios)*, and irreproachable *(amemptos)* manner with which he, Silvanus, and Timothy conducted themselves when they were in Thessalonica (2:10). The adverb refers simply to the way a person behaves in concrete practice. However, shaped by the strong eschatological tone of the letter, various elements are introduced that relate to Paul's understanding of justification: the concrete practice of faith, its link to faith in the God who raises the dead, and the believer's hope of being destined for salvation.

These three dimensions of religious experience of the young Christian community of Thessalonica can be understood only within the context of the great suffering they were experiencing.[2] Thessalonica was the capital of Macedonia, a province of Caesar, and the seat of the proconsul. Its strategic geographical position on the great Ignatian Road that united the West with the East connected it to the markets of the Danube and Central Europe, which allowed it to become a prosperous city from every point of view, especially through commerce.[3] A majority of the Christians who formed the community of faith in Thessalonica were probably humble artisans and poor and illiterate people.[4] Many came from paganism, but there were among them some "God-fearers," or Gentiles attracted especially to the moral principles of Judaism, but who did not become full converts to life under the Mosaic law.

The intense eschatological accent and the repetition of the word *thlipsis* (tribulation, oppression) suggest that the Thessalonians themselves, as well as Paul and his companions, were living in extremely difficult times (1 Thess. 1:6; 3:3-4) and were experiencing acute suffering. The letter assumes that an important part of the suffering of the believers in Thessalonica was due to persecution by "their compatriots" *(symphyletai)*—that is

66

to say, the people with whom they shared daily social life—and not by the Jews.[5] Paul can therefore identify parallels between his suffering and that of other brothers and sisters from Judea who were persecuted and abused by their *symphyletai*, the Jews (2:14). The tribulations of the Thessalonians, however, could also have been aggravated by the economic poverty resulting from urbanization. According to Ronald Russell, it may be that the members of the church were suffering from unemployment or from what was a common lack of enthusiasm for their work. In the cities, including the ports, there were not many opportunities for work, and salaries were low for what jobs did exist. Consequently, discouragement in the workplace was high.[6] In this context, Paul insisted on working with his hands (4:11) and reminded them that he himself worked day and night in order not to be a burden to them (2:9).

Paul himself, along with his coworkers, endured sufferings and injuries while they were in Philippi. Even after that, they had "courage . . . to declare to you the gospel of God in spite of great opposition" (2:2) in Thessalonica. Both Paul's own letter and the witness of Luke in Acts 16:19-24 and 17:1-9 testify to the powerful ideological control exercised by the Roman authorities of that time.[7] Though Luke places these arguments against Paul into the mouths of the Jews, the forsaking of idols demanded in 1 Thessalonians 1:9[8] (which probably targeted also the cult of Caesar that apparently played an important role in Thessalonica) and the option for another king, namely Jesus (Acts 17:6-7), might be interpreted as a strategy against the empire.

The Christians of Thessalonica, as imitators of Paul and of Christ, began to live a different life-style, one that brought tribulations down upon them. Exactly what those tribulations entailed is not clear, but the repetition of the word *thlipsis* indicates a context of oppression and physical suffering. One can assume hostility, marginalization, and contempt both from groups outside the church and from the forces of order. There may also have been economic implications for Christians—great difficulty in obtaining access to education and employment, or a change in their legal status. Such experiences endured by the Thessalonians and other communities that imitated their behavior (1:7) constituted a fundamental element in Paul's subsequent theological reflection. As Daniel Patte observes, "According to Paul's faith, it is in the believers' experience that the convictional pattern is established for them."[9]

The content of that faith might be expressed as follows: They converted from idols to serve the true and living God, and to await the coming from the heavens of the Son whom God raised from the dead, Jesus, who rescues *(ruomenon)* us from the wrath to come (1:9-10). The sentences preceding and following these theological affirmations, which contain such expressions as "we know," "we have proved to be," "you yourselves know," and "you remember" (1:3, 4, 5; 2:1, 5, 9, 11), underline the significance of experience. From this close connection between their experience and the content of their faith, one can recognize that faith or believing is related to events and situations that fulfill the pattern already introduced in the experience of Jesus, of Paul, and of others.[10]

The Practice of Faith

In 1 Thessalonians, Paul underlines the dynamism of the faith (1:3; 2:13) of the Thessalonians. That faith is both in and before God, and it can be seen through their praxis. Therefore it is known beyond Macedonia and Achaia (1:8). The author links the word "faith" (pistis) to other active attitudes that mark in a visible way the new Christian way of being: love (agapē; 1 Thess. 1:3; 3:6; 5:8) and hope (elpis; 1 Thess. 1:3; 5:8). Moreover, this trilogy that Paul will take up again in other letters (e.g., 1 Corinthians 13) is reinforced with nouns in the genitive case that denote clearly the praxis of faith. The quality of faith is active (tou ergou tēs pisteōs; 1 Thess. 1:3), love is expressed in works that imply even sacrifice (tou kopou tēs agapēs), and hope is sustained with a heroic tenacity (tēs hypomonēs tēs elpidos). These attitudes and behaviors issue from the Lord Jesus Christ (1:3) and are characteristics common to him and to his imitators (mimētai; 1:6). The trilogy of faith, hope, and love appears again at the end of the letter, where the author emphasizes the militant quality of faith that is indispensable for the believer in a context of pain and conflict. In expectation of the "day of the Lord," Paul exhorts them to "put on the breastplate of faith and love, and for a helmet the hope of salvation" (5:8).

The participation and solidarity of the triune God with humankind is clearly evident in the life and faith of the believers of Thessalonica. The first person of the Trinity is the one who raised Jesus from the dead (1:10), who therefore will raise the believers as well when Christ returns (4:14), and who takes vengeance on God's enemies on that Day (4:6). The power of the Holy Spirit is a gift from God (4:8) that strengthens the praxis of faith, love, and hope (1:3, 5) in the midst of suffering. And Paul points to the example of the life of Christ whom one must imitate (1:6),[11] the one who died, was raised, and frees us from the wrath to come (1:10).

Faith in the God Who Raises the Dead

Paul tried to comfort the new believers with the affirmation that God raised Jesus from the dead and will likewise raise those who have followed his way—those who have died in him (4:13, 14, 18). This assurance from Paul forms part of the content of the faith expressed in 1:10. Thus in this letter the focus of the message of the gospel is not on Jesus' death on the cross, but rather on the believers' conversion from idols to the living and true God, and the hope that awaits the return of the Christ whom God raised from the dead. The context of suffering of this Christian community grounded their encouragement and confidence in the God who loved them, chose them (1:4), and destined them for salvation through Jesus Christ (5:9), and who has the power to raise the dead.

Chosen for Salvation: Free from Wrath

In order to help the young community withstand with courage the difficult situation it was experiencing, Paul returned to the concept of the wrath of God. That concept is the well-known message of the prophets referring to the day of the Lord, who is drawing near in order to avenge God's victims and grant mercy to God's agents. Those who serve the living and true God, and not false idols, have been freed by Jesus from the wrath to come (1:10). In this first letter Paul is radically judgmental against both pagans (here the Romans) and Jews, because they are the ones who are causing the suffering. The Romans are presented as deceitful (like their idols), announcing "peace and security" (5:3).[12] They will come to ruin, along with all those who, like them, live in darkness (5:5). They are the ones who reject God ("do not know God"; 4:5), and prefer to live an impure life (*porneia;* 4:3), allowing themselves to be guided by covetousness (*epithymia;* 4:5), profiting from and taking advantage of their neighbor (*hyperbainein kai pleonektein;* 4:5, 6).[13] According to Paul, the Jews also have fallen under the wrath of God for persecuting those who preach the gospel to other peoples (2:15-16). Those who suffer persecution by these agents, and who lead a life of militant faith, full to overflowing with love and hope, are far from the wrath and destined for salvation, "through our Lord Jesus Christ" (5:9). They are the children of light and of the day (5:5, 8).[14]

The principal objective of the apostle was not to focus on the destruction of those who cause the sufferings, but to comfort the young Christian community recently founded in Thessalonica (4:13, 18; 5:11). He accomplishes that by emphasizing that their sufferings will have an end, because God is intervening in history in favor of the "children of light." Despite their suffering, it is worth living as Jesus lived. He is the risen one, and through him all the dead will be raised. By his life, death, and resurrection he has freed the believers from the wrath that is imminent, for God, through Jesus Christ, has destined them to salvation.

1 CORINTHIANS

Corinth in the time of Paul was a flourishing city. It was the seat of the governor of the province of Achaia, a senatorial province. It had been completely destroyed in 146 B.C.E. for having been one of the last cities to resist the Roman invasion. Julius Caesar rebuilt it in 44 C.E. as a Roman colony, assigning land to veterans and other groups from outside the city. As the capital of the province it enjoyed a number of benefits, and in the early years of the first century a building program was initiated.[15] In Paul's day, the population consisted mostly of freed persons, but there were also veterans and slaves. The geographical position of the city was strategic both militarily and economically. Situated between "two waters," it could be glimpsed from afar. Corinth was renowned as a producer of bronze articles, and it was a city frequently visited by foreigners who arrived for the famous Isthmian Games as well as to buy bronze and other products.[16]

The following text of Alciphron provides an acerbic glimpse from below of the wealthy classes of Corinth:

> I did not enter Corinth after all; for I learned in a short time the sordidness of the rich and the misery of the poor. For example, at midday, after most people had bathed, I saw some pleasant-spoken, clever young fellows moving about, not near the dwellings, but near the Craneum, and particularly where the women who peddle bread and retail fruit are accustomed to do their business. There the young fellows would stoop to the ground, and one would pick up lupine pods, another would examine the nutshells to make sure that none of the edible part was left anywhere and had escaped notice, another would scrape with his fingernails the pomegranate rinds (which we in Attica are accustomed to call *sidia*) to see whether he could glean any of the seeds anywhere, while others would actually gather and greedily devour the pieces that fell from the loaves of bread—pieces that had by that time been trodden under many feet.[17]

Although Murphy O'Connor warns that behind this text might be the zeal of the have-nots, the situation indicates the precarious condition of the underprivileged, which stands in stark contrast to God's option for the poor and ignorant that Paul himself affirmed (1 Cor. 1:26-28).[18]

Paul wrote this letter to the Corinthians from Ephesus between 53 and 56 C.E.[19] Contrary to 1 Thessalonians, in this letter we do not find the community suffering persecutions by the Romans because of the gospel, even though they lived in a Roman colony. Instead, the Corinthian community appears to have been suffering from a number of internal problems. In various parts of the letter Paul directed himself to certain members of the church who continued in a life-style common to that society, that is to say,

70

JUSTIFICATION BY FAITH IN PAUL'S LETTERS PRIOR TO ROMANS

community life marked by divisions according to status, dinner parties given by rich pagans,[20] and the prostitution frequent in ports like Corinth. In fact, the immediate problems to which Paul alluded were principally internal to the life of the Christian house-churches—communities well known for the conflicts among the members and with Paul himself. Those conflicts were of several types: social (between poor and rich), theological (against enthusiasts and Gnostics, who were bordering on heresy), ecclesial (disorder in the worship service [14:1-39] and the question of the appropriate style of leadership for women [11:2-16]), and moral (incest [5:1] and fornication [6:16]). In addition, Paul's own apostleship was questioned (chap. 9). In 1 Corinthians the terms "justify" or "justice" appear infrequently. However, the times they do appear—the verb twice (4:4 and 6:11) and the noun once (1:30)—suggest the following emphases: (a) the relationship among justification, humiliation, and the practice of justice; (b) the action of judging justly as belonging to God; and (c) Paul's affirmation about faith in the resurrection of the dead.

Justification Versus Humiliation (1:10-31)

In this letter and the following ones to the Corinthians (collected in the canonical letter known as 2 Corinthians), Paul manifested his profound annoyance and worry about this community that he had founded. Although his ideal was to see among Christians a community of equals in which no one considered himself or herself better than any other, in Corinth the opposite attitude prevailed. Perhaps the slaves or other workers of Chloe (1:11) were those who reported that situation to Paul.[21] Probably they, together with other poor people of the community, were those who saw themselves as despised by some who thought of themselves as superior, even though (as Paul observed) the majority of the community was poor, and it was as the poor, despised, and ignorant that they were called and chosen by the Lord (1:26-27).

In the first chapter of the letter, the apostle related weakness to the cross and identified the poor and ignorant as God's chosen ones. One of his motives may have been to counteract the power of certain leaders of the church of Corinth.[22] Paul demonstrated a knowledge and power that differed from those commonly recognized, and that opposed self-glorification.[23] He explained that if God chooses what is base and despised in order to reduce to nothing things to which value is accorded, God does so in order that no one boast in oneself in the presence of God (1:29). For it is through God that one is in Christ Jesus, "who became for us wisdom from God, and righteousness and sanctification and redemption, in order that, as it is written, 'Let the one who boasts, boast in the Lord'" (1:30-31).[24]

Paul directed these words to those members of the congregation who considered themselves wise. They were the people he felt obliged to remind that it is through the action of God, and not by such human merits as wisdom or power, that one is in Christ. It is God who made Christ wisdom, justice, and redemption for "us." For that reason there is no room for glorying in oneself instead of in the Lord.

In this section of the letter the mercy that God has for the poor can be seen in the dramatic inversion of values on the social level: The foolish confound the wise and the weak the strong. This idea, which is also typical of the message of the prophets, is grounded in Paul's theology of the cross. The crucified Christ is a scandal for the Jews and folly for Gentiles. But from God's perspective, the divine foolishness and weakness visible in the crucified Christ are the source of the power of God.

The difference of emphasis from that in the message directed to the Thessalonians is noteworthy. Because of their sufferings, the Thessalonians needed the inspiration of faith in a God who has the power to raise Jesus and his followers. In Corinth, on the other hand, perhaps because of the arrogance of some leaders of the community, Paul considered it important to proclaim as the true source of a greater wisdom and power (1:25) the weakness and foolishness of a crucified messiah. Later in this same letter (chap. 15), the author took up again the theme of the resurrection of the dead, but from the angle of a militant faith.

Only God Judges Justly (4:3-5)

In 1 Corinthians 4:4, the apostle affirmed that although his conscience encountered nothing reproachable in himself, that was not the reason for his justification. The Lord alone is his judge. The context is circumstantial: One can see a Paul disturbed by the criticisms brought against him by some leaders of the community of Corinth. Paul again attacked those who considered themselves to be wise and who were boasting to other people. They were the ones who were judging him, and Paul rejected their judgment. Therefore he said to them: "But with me it is a very small thing that I should be judged by you or by any human court. I do not even judge myself" (4:3).[25] Note the metaphor of the courtroom, and of God as the only judge on the day of judgment. Here Paul portrays a God who judges according to the designs of the heart of each person (4:5), and not according to what is accomplished through special privilege or achieved by a particular merit (prestige accorded because of one's nobility, wealth, power, or wisdom). This fact, along with Paul's anguish at being judged and finding his authority challenged a number of times by the various circles in which he moved (some of the leading members of Christian communities, or authorities among the Jewish people or in the Greco-Roman society), helped to clarify his subsequent formulation about justification by faith, God's gift through grace.

Justification and the Practice of Justice (6:1-11)

In 1 Corinthians 6:11, the verb "justify" (dikaioō occurs together with the verbs "cleanse" (apolouō) and "sanctify" (hagiazō). The context of this passage is Paul's criticism of certain members of the Corinthian community who were committing injustice (adikeō) and fraud (apostereō) against others in the church (6:8). He brought two charges against them. First, they had recourse to judges outside the Christian community—that is, to Roman courts, whose judges Paul called "unjust" (adikoi; 6:1) and made up of unbelievers (apistos; 6:6).[26] Apparently the Corinthians were appealing to Roman judges so that the decision would go in their favor, since they were protected by Roman law. Paul does not explain the nature of the case. Probably it was a civil matter, not a criminal case. Perhaps it concerned property or debt, for those were common, everyday cases for the courts of the first century.

Paul's first charge is related to the second: Not only did they have recourse to Roman courts, but apparently some of the wealthier members of the Christian community of Corinth needed the protection of the "unjust" Roman law in order to commit injustice and fraud. Instead of putting themselves in the place of the defrauded and oppressed, they perpetuated the same offenses that characterized the courts' own injustice. Paul, then, had to remind them that the unjust will not inherit the realm of God (6:9).[27] After a list of negative behaviors (introduced by the word adikoi)—perhaps behaviors common in Corinthian society (6:9-10), he also reminded them that some of them had followed the same practices. However, in the name of the Lord Jesus Christ and in the Spirit of God, they had been cleansed, justified, and sanctified. For that reason it was inconceivable that they would continue to practice injustice. Concerning the doctrine of justification, Orr and Walther observe:

> Here is the other side of the commonly emphasized Pauline doctrine of justification by faith. It is not correct to conclude that justification by faith eliminates the basic need for a righteous life; it rather provides a true basis for it. Those who inflict injustice upon each other exhibit that they do not believe in forgiveness or in reconciling love. Thus they have really not accepted the love of God for themselves, and thus they have rejected the justification offered by God.[28]

In the three cases just mentioned, the dispute over whether justification is by faith or by works of the law does not appear. The opponents in these three cases are not Judaizers, but Christians who wanted to follow a way of life contrary to that of the justified person, parading their knowledge and their power.

Faith in the Resurrection of the Dead (Chapter 15)

In chapter 15, the theme of the resurrection (of Christ and of the dead) is related to the theme of faith. A similar connection is drawn among the themes of death *(thanatos)*, the law *(nomos)*, and sin *(hamartia)*. Although Paul says little about those themes in this letter, it is worth noting his discussion of them, for they appear again as central themes in Romans.

The theme of the resurrection is linked both to faith and to sin, and faith in the resurrection of the dead is linked to the power that it gives in the daily struggle in the cause of Christ.[29] Paul links faith in the resurrected one to the general resurrection of the dead. The latter depends on the resurrection of Christ. One confesses the resurrected Jesus because one believes in the resurrection of the dead (15:12). The resurrection of Christ affirms and guarantees the hope of the believer in life beyond death, because Christ's resurrection is the down payment on that hope.

In order to emphasize the effective reality of the resurrection in human history, Paul returned to the example of the two prototypes of humanity with opposite functions: Adam who introduces death for all, and Christ who conquers death and introduces life for all (15:20-22). Faith in the resurrection of Christ is fundamental, for in the final analysis, salvation depends on it: "If Christ has not been raised, your faith is futile and you are still in your sins" (15:17). But faith in the resurrection of the dead is equally indispensable, for in it is power and confidence for the struggle in life and for life (15:31-32). Therefore Paul was capable of struggling even to the point of putting his own life in danger. That struggle without faith in the resurrection would have no meaning: "If with merely human hopes I fought with wild animals at Ephesus, what would I have gained by it? If the dead are not raised, 'Let us eat and drink, for tomorrow we die'" (15:32). The expression "wild animals at Ephesus" is no casual saying, but refers to serious difficulties that the apostle confronted in that city.[30]

Paul ended chapter 15 with the anti-life triology par excellence: death, sin, and law—concepts he does not develop, but only introduces. In 1 Corinthians Paul limited himself to talking about the victory over death that God grants us through Jesus Christ.[31] In this last theological reflection prior to the final recommendations (chap. 16), Paul sought to strengthen the hope of those members of the community who were experiencing difficulties. At the same time he explained certain theological concepts to

74

those who were seeking an easy and pleasant life, thinking they already lived in the fullness of the Spirit or of the realm of liberty.[32]

GALATIANS

Sometime between 50 and 55 C.E. Paul wrote his letter to the churches of Galatia in Central Anatolia, which had been a Roman province since 25 B.C.E.[33] Its agrarian history in that period appears to coincide with that of Pergamum, Pontus, Bithynia, and Cappadocia. Throughout the empire at the end of the republic and the beginning of the principate, the lands of local kings passed into the hands of the Romans. In the case of Galatia, they came to be the direct possession of the emperor. According to the hypothesis of the economist Rostovtzeff:

> The royal land *(gē basilikē)* and the private estates *(ousiai)* of the Pergamene kings, and also those of the kings of Bithynia, Pontus, Galatia, Cappadocia, Commagene, etc., became *ager publicus* when these regions were transformed into Roman provinces. Subsequently those parts of the land which had not passed into the ownership of Roman citizens were united in some way with the private patrimony of the Roman emperors (in some parts of Asia Minor, for instance in Galatia, the crown-lands may have passed directly into the hands of the emperors).[34]

The passage of military troops through those regions was devastating for the provinces. In the time of Trajan, rich people saw themselves obliged to provide financial help to the province so that it could support the army during its transit through the region.[35] The prominence of the military may also be reflected in the fact that Galatia was known for its slave markets, for many people apparently became slaves through being prisoners of war.[36]

Most probably the weight of the Roman presence was felt as a burden. It cannot be coincidental that in this letter more than in others Paul used images of slavery and freedom. As Betz has observed, "Paul's message of 'freedom in Christ' must have found attentive ears among people interested in political, social, cultural, and religious emancipation."[37] According to Betz, "freedom in Christ" summarizes the gospel of Paul, and this "was not only a 'religious' and 'theological' notion, but pointed at the same time to a political and social experience."[38]

In Galatia the native language persisted. However, according to Betz, Paul's strategic use of rhetoric to accomplish theological ends through the letter leads one to suppose that its addressees came from a Hellenized and

Romanized city. The intricate rhetorical patterns of the letter also suggest that "these people also had some education and at least modest financial means."[39] Many of the members of the Galatian churches to which Paul wrote may have been Christians who had converted from world views and belief systems of Hellenistic religions that Paul considered enslaving (Gal. 3:9).[40] This letter reveals the powerful theological tensions between Paul and his manner of conceiving the gospel, and that of others who were promoting among the Christians the practice of circumcision and the fulfillment of the law.

In no other letter did the apostle Paul speak as convincingly of freedom as in this one, and in no other letter prior to Romans did he develop more fully the concept of justification by faith. Liberation and justification by faith are inseparable experiences. Paul sees in the churches of Galatia the imminent danger that they would submit to other forces capable of obstructing the freedom that Christians had obtained by faith in the gospel that Paul proclaimed.

> They regarded themselves as free from "this evil world," with its repressive social, religious, and cultural laws and conventions. They had left behind the cultural and social distinctions between Greeks and non-Greeks, the religious distinctions between Jews and non-Jews, the social systems of slavery and the subordination of women.[41]

They had already been freed from powers that enslaved them to the view that the purposes of their lives and of society were fixed and immutable, because of both cosmic powers and changeless laws. Now they were running the danger of falling under submission to another gospel (3:1).[42] Overwhelmed by the bad treatment he received in his body—at the hands of both Romans and Jews—for the cause of Christ (6:17), Paul felt forced again, as in the case of the Corinthians, to recall and explain the power of the gospel of the cross. From this man, persecuted, tortured, and criticized, the call to freedom was sounded.[43]

The tone of the letter is highly polemical. Sanders criticizes the popular caricature of Paul's position toward Jewish law, for it does not take into account the fact that the polemic itself led Paul to make violent pronouncements against the law of Moses, for which almost the only positive function suggested is as "pedagogue."[44] For Sanders the discussion of the law in Galatians (and Romans) must be seen in the context of the question of the access of Gentiles to salvation or to the promises. Paul's fundamental point is that such access is through faith (Gal. 4:18).[45] Sanders's word of caution is important, but it cannot mask the fact that Paul's affirmation in Galatians that one is justified by faith and not by works of the law points also toward an important truth about human existence: To live in Christ is to live in freedom, while to submit oneself to the law is to return to a condition of slavery.

The entire letter to the Galatians is shaped by the theme of justification by faith. For that reason it is important to read the letter in its entirety instead of focusing on particular texts. Such a reading will lead to a better understanding of the meaning of justification in the Galatian context, especially the meaning of justification as liberation from a law that excludes.

Justification and Liberation

Freedom from slavery is the thematic axis that captures our attention in this letter. Beginning with the introduction, Paul spoke of liberation from this "present evil age" through the redemptive act of Jesus Christ (1:4). That age was the one in which they were living under the domination of the Roman Empire with all of its enslaving religious beliefs. It included the principalities and powers, both of the society and of the cosmic order. For that reason Paul was surprised by the ease with which the believers had fallen into the net of submission thrown by some Judaizing preachers who demanded that they fulfill the law. Those preachers were demanding circumcision and the observance of days (5:2; 4:10) if people wanted to be truly justified and true members of the people of God. The Galatians had already received, by faith and not by law, the gift of the Spirit (3:2), which is freedom. In Paul's eyes, with the return to the law they were invalidating the death of Jesus and treating the grace of God as useless (2:21). Therefore Paul saw himself obliged to emphasize that justification (being "just" before God and human beings) is granted not by works of the law but by the faith of Christ (*dia pisteōs Christou;* 2:16). The only requirement is that a person live in justice and freedom. Since that is the case, the law is shown to be limited in its power. If the law were able to justify, that is to say, to make human beings truly able to do justice, it would not have been necessary for God to take any further liberating action, for "justice would indeed come through the law" (3:21, author's trans.).

Paul declared that they were distorting the gospel, or that they had exchanged it for another (1:7). If he denounced anyone who was proclaiming another gospel, he did so not out of sectarian concerns, but because the freedom of the Christian granted by the death and resurrection of Christ (1:18-19) was at stake. Whenever one denies freedom, one denies Jesus Christ. Paul could not conceive of one without the other, for Christ came to liberate *(exagorazein)* those who were slaves to the law, in order that they could become children of God (4:4-5) and truly free.

77

Thus, he insisted: "For freedom Christ has set us free. Stand firm, therefore, and do not submit again to a yoke of slavery" (5:1).

In his dispute against his adversaries (in this case, the Judaizers), Paul criticized the law as limiting the freedom of Christians (2:4), who live "by the faith of the Son of God" (2:20, NRSV note 1).[46] Paul concluded that when the law rules over people, they run the danger of becoming slaves again (2:4), even though in fact the event of Jesus Christ frees slaves, making them into free children and heirs (4:4-7). To submit oneself to the precepts of the law when one is already in the Spirit was equivalent to continuing to submit oneself to the idols of Hellenistic cosmic religion.[47] It was to fail to trust that God had justified them by faith, and that their practice was the manifestation of the redemptive love of Christ. The apostle reminded them that the Spirit they had received made the Christ-event a present reality whose concrete manifestation was in the fruits of the Spirit. Christians, who participated in the Christ-event by means of baptism, were the agents through whom the Spirit was manifest, and that, in turn, was the manifestation of freedom.[48]

Critique of the Law That Excludes

With the arrival and revelation of faith (3:23)—that is, with the coming of Christ—came freedom from submission to the law. At that moment the Christians passed from the category of slaves, or of children with tutors (4:1), to the condition of children who were free and without distinction, marginalization, or oppression of any sort (3:28). Therefore, with faith they entered a new stage of life. In the first place, every privilege was overcome that had previously been granted to those who had the law and denied to those who did not.[49] Since justification is by faith and not by the law, salvation was extended to other peoples as well as to the Jews. The promise that in Abraham all nations will be blessed (3:8) is fulfilled with the arrival of Christ.

Being justified by faith, then, opens a space for freedom in order that men and women might realize their full humanity. In this free space exclusion and discrimination are eliminated, and justice reigns. For although Paul began the discussion of justification by faith with the proposition that Gentiles also form part of the salvific plan of God, the logic of his thought concerning freedom led him not only to transcend the barrier of ethnicity, but also to affirm the social and sexual justice that arises from this new creation in Christ: "There is no longer Jew or Greek, there is no longer slave or free, there is no longer male and female; for all of you are one in Christ Jesus" (3:28). These are not merely rhetorical phrases if they arose in the socioeconomic context of the principate, when only the aristocracy had access to the power and prestige reserved for freeborn sons and heirs. According to Dennis R. MacDonald, Galatians 3:28 should be seen as a dominical expression that Paul took over and interpreted in his vision of the new creation: "The new creation must raze the walls protecting the privileged—whether Jews by dint of Torah obedience, or the 'free' by dint of legal status, or men by dint of XY chromosomes—and excluding the disadvantaged—whether gentiles, slaves, or women."[50] For the believer, exclusion on the basis of privilege reaches its end with Christ.[51] Moreover, with this new dimension of faith Paul also removed the binding authority of church rules, for precisely when he spoke of such rules or directives, he indicated that in God there is no partiality (1:11; 2:6). We can say that for the apostle, through his new, free, and just way of conceiving and living life, to justify meant to enliven. Faith enlivens, and, therefore, "the just will live by faith" (3:11, author's trans.).

In summary, the fact that God "snatched" *(exaireō)* them from the power of idols (or of "this present evil age")—through the event of Jesus Christ was an act of liberation from submission to every sort of slavery, including the slavery that can come from the Mosaic law. To be justified by faith and not by Jewish law makes all who have faith members of the people of God. The right granted to all by grace opens a space for new manifestations of human community and overcomes distinctions of race, class, and sex. Circumcision and uncircumcision are reduced to secondary conditions, because since Christ no such quality is of value for justification. For what is important in this new creation is the love that grows out of faith or (what amounts to the same thing) faith that is enacted through love (5:6; 6:15).

PHILIPPIANS

Philippi was known for its strategic geographical location on the famous Ignatian Road. Augustus founded a Roman military colony there. As happened in Corinth and Thessalonica, that meant not only a boom in commerce and construction through the process of urbanization or reurbanization, but also a military presence and the frequent sight of troop movements.[52] It meant, moreover, that veterans displaced local authorities from their administrative functions, that the efforts of the populace at economic production were dedicated to the veterans, who had displaced the local authorities, and that, apparently, any sign of an uprising was immediately put down. Paul and his companions were no strangers to problems with the Roman authorities when they were accused of going against

Roman policy (Acts 16:12-40). Paul himself confirmed the fact of having endured sufferings and injuries in Philippi (1 Thess. 2:2).

Paul wrote to the Christian community of Philippi—for which he felt a special affection (1:8)—from prison, possibly from Ephesus.[53] According to some exegetes, the letter to the Philippians is composed of fragments of three letters, identified for convenience as A (4:10-20), B (1:1-3:1), and C (3:2-4:9).[54] Aspects of B and C are of particular interest for this study, though in A there is a glimpse of the economic solidarity that existed between the Philippians and Paul (4:14). Letter B provides clues to the Philippian context and contains the exhortation that alludes to justice (*dikaiosynē*).

The Price of Grace

Paul was suffering from being unjustly imprisoned. He was imprisoned not for committing a crime, a robbery, or even for having a debt he could not repay. Rather, he was a prisoner for a cause to which he had entrusted his life. That cause was seen as a threat by those charged with safeguarding the order of the empire (Acts 16:9-20). Like any political prisoner in repressive nations, he feared for his life, for he did not know what the verdict would be. Paul was fearful about the pending sentence, which would literally determine whether he lived or died. In that context he needed the certainty of the accompaniment and solidarity of Christ. That need was particularly intense for Paul, to the degree that for him the body of Christ and his own body had become one, whether in death or in life (1:20).

Paul called the experience of unity with Christ "grace" (*charis*). Thus, he thanked the Philippians for their "solidarity in grace" (*synkoinōnous mou tēs charitos*), which they expressed as much in their chains as in their defense and consolidation of the gospel (1:7). Paul again referred to the idea of grace in shared suffering in Philippians 1:29-30. This line of reasoning is not unusual in Paul's letters. On the contrary, the centrality of his gospel of the cross touches not only the redemption of Christ as a past event, but also the way or path of the disciple who—precisely for being Christ's follower—is nailed to the cross together with Christ, and who therefore bears in his or her body the marks of Christ (Gal. 6:17).

Paul saw in his own life the path of martyrdom of Jesus Christ, who freely abandoned all privileges, assumed all human weaknesses, became a slave, was humbled, and obeyed the will of God even to death under the most humiliating torture of the cross (2:6-8). But just as Christ was exalted, so Paul also awaited exaltation on "the Day of Christ," when his "fruits" would be seen, and it would be recognized that the race he had run and his resulting weariness were not in vain.[55] This interpretation of the experience of suffering explains Paul's fervor in the exhortation to joy.[56]

The author of letter B did not speak of justification by faith, but clearly that is the experience of the justified person: to have the eschatological certainty of the triumph of life over death. This vivid conviction allowed Paul to affirm in Romans that he was not ashamed of the gospel, because it is the power of God for the one who believes, and because in it the justice of God is revealed (Rom. 1:16). Thus, grace is present even in suffering, but specifically in suffering resulting from the cause of the ministry of the justice of God (2 Corinthians 3-4; see the discussion of letter C, which follows).

Justification with Works of Faith

The Fruits of Justice in the Day of Christ. In Philippians 1:11, we encounter the phrase "fruit of justice" *(karpos dikaiosynēs).* In 1:9-11, Paul prayed[57] that the love of the Philippians would continue to grow ever greater in recognition *(en epignōsei)* and in sharpness of perception or perspicacity *(aisthēsei),* to the end that they would be able to discern well *(dokimazein)* between what is correct and what is incorrect and to opt for the better.[58] This is "in order that they be transparent and without offense on the day of Christ, full of the fruits of justice that comes from Jesus Christ for the glory and praise of God" (1:10-11, author's trans.).

Paul explained that the fruits of justice proceed from God. However, in the two previous verses he spoke clearly of how important it was for the Philippians to develop and deepen the love between them. Paul considered it indispensable that the love practiced by the Christian community of Philippi be intelligent, knowledgeable, perspicacious, and sufficiently perceptive to be able to make good decisions in difficult contexts. The importance of these verses is in this quality of concrete love shown by the believer, which, in turn, produces the fruits of justice. Such love is clearly not the sort of uncritical and sentimental love that does not know where to direct itself. Concrete, discerning love will be valid on the day of Christ, when God will judge according to their hearts (2 Cor. 5:10). Note that it is the practice of the Christian who loves effectively that glorifies and praises God.

The Praxis That "Suffices" for Salvation. Paul spoke in his immediate historical context about "working out one's salvation" (2:12) and about what suffices for salvation (1:19).[59] The expression "this will suffice for my salvation" (1:19, author's trans.) is a phrase from Job 13:16 (LXX), which Paul cited in the context of a dispute between preachers of the gospel. Accord-

81

ing to the apostle, some of them were preaching "from envy and rivalry" (1:15), believing that they were augmenting Paul's sufferings in prison. Paul chose not to be upset by the fact that Christ was being proclaimed in a variety of ways, both false and true (1:15-18).

It is at that point that he inserted the sentence, "I know that this will suffice for my salvation thanks to your prayers and the help given by the Spirit of Jesus Christ" (1:19, author's trans.). There are two ways of interpreting the expression. One is to interpret it in the sense of literally freeing or "saving" him from prison. However, it is difficult to understand how those who preach out of selfish ambition are going to liberate Paul in that literal way. It is more likely that Paul would think that the prayers and the Spirit of Jesus Christ would help him to obtain his freedom, but the syntax of the sentence (with *touto* appearing first) does not allow that to be the meaning here. The other interpretation would be to interpret the phrase in a theological sense, namely as referring to salvation before God. In that case, what would have been "sufficient" was Paul's own testimony and his conduct that brought him to prison and placed him in a judicial process in which the preachers who were proclaiming the gospel as his rivals believed themselves to be augmenting his pains. This latter interpretation appears more appropriate, for it is precisely the context of Job. In the midst of his deepest pain, Job enters a judicial process in which he silences his friends Eliphaz, Bildad, and Zophar. They judge Job to be guilty of some crime, and he appeals to God to be allowed to defend his conduct before God. If Job succeeds in appearing in God's presence, he will be saved—considered "just"—for, says Job, "An impious person does not appear in God's presence" (Job 13:16b, author's trans.). Paul picked up the language of Job with the certainty that the believers were already proclaiming the Word courageously and fearlessly and had already been inspired in the Lord by Paul's chains—that is, by his testimony (1:14). That would "suffice for salvation" even though Paul might be condemned to death by the Roman Praetorian, and even though he was criticized by enemies. The concrete experience of Paul in the cause of Christ was sufficient for his salvation because his practice was directed and motivated by Christ. Therefore he could affirm that to live is Christ and to die is gain (1:21).

Again in 2:12 is the idea of "working out one's salvation," or, as others prefer, "putting salvation into practice."[60] Following the christological hymn with which Paul identified himself as an obedient imitator of Christ, he then exhorted the Philippians, who had excelled by their obedience, to work out their salvation with fear and trembling.

Paul did not object to the use of this phrase, because he took for granted the fact that God is not only the author of salvation but also the one who promotes the good works that the believer accomplishes as the fruits of his or her faith.[61] Thus, for the apostle, "working out one's salvation" is possible because God is the one who is effective in both the desire and the deed, "for God's good pleasure" (2:12c-13). One characteristic of Paul is that he was always careful to attribute to God the initiative in all things (2 Cor. 3:5). Thus, in this same letter to the Philippians (3:12-16), the apostle wrote about his effort to achieve the stature of Jesus Christ by following the "goal," always throwing himself into whatever lay ahead. But he was able to do so "because Christ Jesus has made me his own" (3:12c). Paul affirmed clearly that salvation is not something static, but rather that one progresses in it.

The Justice of God and the Justice of the Law

Letter C (3:2–4:9) touches explicitly on the problem of the justice that comes from God, in contrast to the justice of the law. Paul did not use the verb "to justify," but simply contrasted justice in the traditional sense, which is related to the fulfillment of the law, with the justice that arises from the faith of Christ, that comes from God, and that is supported by faith (3:9). The context was a polemic in which the opponents cannot be readily identified. It is very probable that they were Jewish Christians (3:17-19).[62] But Paul might also have been referring to other adversaries who (like the later Gnostics) were living a lax moral life, thinking only of their own interests (3:19).[63] According to Paul such conduct is not proper for people who count on citizenship in heaven,[64] and who base their vision of utopia on the expectation of a Savior who will transform their bodies from miserable to glorious because he has the power to bring all things into submission to himself (3:21). Those who do not live under this communitarian hope are enemies of the cross of Christ (3:18), not only because they diminish the value of his death and make his grace vain, but also because they do not recognize that grace in moments of persecution (1:29). Whether the phrase "their god is the belly" (3:19) refers to dietary laws or to libertine behavior that ignores the difficult way of the cross, it is clearly not the announcement of the liberating faith in Christ for the good of others!

Paul inverted the critique of his adversaries. Those who believe themselves to be the circumcised are really the uncircumcised, they are "dogs"—a term by which Jews referred to Gentiles. The true circumcised are those who do not place their confidence in "the flesh," which means in circumcision as a summary of the entire system of the law. They place their confidence instead in their lack of any privileged status (such as being of the lineage of Israel, a Hebrew, or a descendant of the Hebrews, or demonstrating conduct irreproachable under the justice of the law), in order to gain Christ (3:8-9). Thus Christ is won by renouncing every privilege—all "gain"—before others.[65] And if one is "found in Christ"[66] by this attitude of despising the gain, one is the product not of justice in the traditional sense, but rather of the knowledge that one has of Christ (3:8). That knowledge allows one to know where true justice comes from. True justice does not come from the law but arose from the faith of Christ. It is precisely the justice that comes from God that was sustained by that faith.

Paul divested himself of all his privileges in order to be found in Christ and in order to know Christ (3:10). Once again there is the connection between knowledge and justice that can be observed elsewhere in Paul's writings. Here it is apparent that knowledge does not have to do with a greater accumulation of information, but, as in the Hebrew Bible, with an intimate relationship or an interrelationship. Paul emptied himself in order to be united with Christ in the way of death and resurrection.[67] Insofar as he knew the power of Christ's resurrection, he entered into communion with Christ's sufferings, to the point of making himself like Jesus in death, with the hope of participating in the resurrection of the dead (3:10). That experience gave Paul the power to endure the struggles and confrontations with his adversaries (1 Cor. 15:32; 2 Cor. 4:7–5:10). Paul did not consider identification with Christ a static achievement, but a dynamic state always in process of moving forward (Phil. 3:12-16).

2 CORINTHIANS

Like the letter to the Philippians, 2 Corinthians is understood to be composed of fragments of several letters.[68] These would have been written by Paul over a short period of time, motivated by a strongly polemical context, just as in 1 Corinthians. Letters A and B were probably written from Ephesus and letters C and D from Macedonia. They were written between 55 and 56 C.E., after Paul had endured great suffering in prison in Ephesus, the capital of Asia, where he was almost at the point of death (2 Cor. 1:8-11; 1 Cor. 15:32). He may have been freed by the prayers of many believers from Asia (1:11). The assassination of the proconsul of that region, Junius Silvanus (a direct descendant of the family of Augustus), between 54 and 55 C.E., also may have contributed to Paul's release, for that assassination would have disrupted the judicial administration of that province.[69]

The polemic that can be seen in all of the letter fragments is very sharp. The underlying argument, in which Paul reacted harshly to being the object of direct criticism, related not just to a question of personal choice about life-style. Rather, for Paul the argument pointed toward the life-style that a Christian should follow under the mandate of the cross of Christ and in the hope of the resurrection of the dead.

Of the five letters that make up 2 Corinthians, only letter A, and especially 2:14–6:13, is directly relevant to the issue of justification by faith. Paul developed the argument of that letter in reaction to an opponent or, more probably, to a group of opponents. Their precise position is not clear, but perhaps they included some of the preachers who brought letters of recommendation from other communities where they had ministered, resulting in the criticism of Paul by some leaders of the community because he did not offer such letters himself (3:1). Paul responded to the community, indicating that the community itself was his letter of recommendation—a living letter, written not with ink but with the living Spirit of God. The following sections of the letter are specifically connected to the theme of justification by faith: the ministry of justice (chaps. 3-5), the new creation (5:16–6:1), and the judgment of Christ according to works (5:10).

The Ministry of Justice for All, Contrary to the Ministry of Condemnation (Chapters 3–5)

Here Paul found an opportunity to remind the Corinthians of the quality of life and freedom proclaimed in his gospel, in contrast to the law of Moses written on tablets of stone. The Corinthians are the product of Paul's ministry, "a letter of Christ . . . written not with ink but with the Spirit of the living God . . . on tablets of human hearts" (3:3). Paul hastened to explain that this "living letter" had arisen not from his own ability, but because God enabled him to be the minister of a new covenant that set forth a new way for human beings to live together. That covenant differs from the one followed by protectors of the letter of the law or of legalism, for such a covenant kills (3:6). The new covenant, on the contrary, is a covenant made upon the horizon of the Spirit that gives life (*zōopoieō*, 3:6).

The life-giving ministry empowered by the Spirit is the ministry of justice (3:8-9). The law was unable to grant justice, though it had its glorious moment (the Israelites were not allowed to look at Moses' face because of the glory of God that shone there [3:7]). However, Paul attributed to the law a ministry of death (3:7) and of condemnation (3:9). The apostle was empowered by God to announce a superior covenant, not temporary but permanent. The ministry of justice allows one to know true freedom, for with the experience of conversion, the

85

veil that covers the heart when the law of Moses is read is pulled away (3:15, 17). And now not only a privileged person like Moses can reflect the glory of the Lord, but all people, with their faces uncovered, continue being transformed in that same image, by the action of the Lord that is the Spirit (3:18). In summary, to enter the new covenant of the service of justice (of the Spirit or of Christ) is to pass from slavery to freedom, and from the privilege of some to the privilege of all, as beings transformed into a more perfect image of God in Christ (3:18). The ministry of justice goes against the law that excludes and opens the horizon to a new existence that leads to fullness of life.

But in order not to be misunderstood as meaning that one can already live this life in all its fullness, Paul again hastened to identify what carrying out this ministry of justice would entail: bearing in all ways "the death of Jesus." That means being afflicted in every way, perplexed, persecuted, struck down, but never crushed, in despair, abandoned, or destroyed (4:9), because it is from there—from a place where it would appear that nothing can be salvaged—that an extraordinary power appears, which is the power of God.[70] If they are continually being given up to death for the cause of Jesus, it is so that the life of Jesus can be revealed in their bodies. The servant of justice dies so that the beneficiaries of that justice might live (4:12). Here Paul identified himself again with the earthly life of Jesus—his way of life, his death, and his resurrection. Paul accepted death in order to give life to others, affirming that living in Christ is living not for oneself, but for the one who died and was raised for them (5:15). Paul accepted death because he had faith in the resurrection. He believed that the one who raised Jesus from the dead would also raise him (4:14).

A New Creation: the Justice of God (5:16–6:1)

Life according to the Spirit of Christ marks a new life, a new creation, and a different way of perceiving the world and one's relationships (5:16 and 5:17 should be seen as parallel).[71] This new beginning is due to the reconciling action of God through Christ, and to the ministry of reconciliation that God entrusts to us (5:18). This same idea of the reconciling action of God in human history, and of the ministry of reconciliation that we have because of that action, is repeated in three subsequent verses.

In 5:19 Paul recalled the reconciling activity of God in Christ, which now includes the whole world: God was in Christ reconciling the world to Godself. "By the present participle and by the imperfect tense, the apostle indicates the duration of the concrete history of Christ in which and through which God intervenes personally."[72] This reconciling activity that does not take into account human transgressions put within us the word of reconciliation, namely the cross. In this section of letter A, the fact of not taking account of human transgressions is secondary. The primary purpose of the passage is to manifest the ministry of reconciliation that the human being now enjoys because of the reconciling action of God in Jesus Christ.

In 5:21 Paul explained the work of God in Christ and the purpose of that work. For our sakes God "made him to be sin who knew no sin." That is to say, in Jesus God entered into solidarity with humankind, and with all the fragility that characterizes human beings. Particularly as an innocent victim himself, Jesus stood in the place of all weak, innocent victims of sin. The purpose of that solidarity was to make human beings instruments of God's justice: "so that in Christ we might become the justice of God" (5:21, author's trans.). The aim is to be the justice of God in human history, to be God's collaborators (6:1). That justice is related to the ministry of reconciliation assigned to each human being—a ministry that is in turn equivalent to the ministry of justice, of the new covenant (3:9).

Within the texts that speak of the reconciling activity of God and of the reconciling task of God's creation (5:18, 19, 20), Paul made clear the motivating interest of his theological discussion: that the Corinthians be reconciled with God, with Paul, and among themselves, and that they live as new creatures in Christ. With all the authority of an ambassador of Christ (5:20), of an agent of reconciliation (5:19), and of an instrument of the justice of God (5:21), Paul begged them, in the name of Christ, to be reconciled.[73]

The Judgment of Christ Conforms to One's Works (5:10)

Paul's interpretation of the eschatological judgment again uses forensic language in the image of the courtroom in which Christ will judge each person in accord with his or her practice (5:10). No one will be exempt from this ultimate judgment. All must appear before the judgment seat. Paul may have had in mind not only those who reject the gospel of Christ, but also those who say they belong to Christ, but whose behavior contradicts them. The theme of the judgment at the end-time clearly was important for Paul, for it occurs again (albeit without explicit use of the courtroom image) in what is called the "tearful letter." In that letter also the verdict meted out corresponds to a person's works. The verdict, according to Paul, would be especially harsh against his adversaries, whom he called "false apostles," unprofitable workers, servants disguised as servants of justice: "Their end will match their deeds" (11:15). In this text and other similar ones, it is clear that the eschatological judgment of God was always a part of Paul's thought. Neither salvation by grace, nor justification by faith, eliminates the requirement of an honest practice of justice, appropriate to the justified person.

Paul concluded this letter (A) to the Corinthians by returning to the question of the letter of recommendation (6:4-10). He demonstrated that his life of surrender to the other, as a servant of God, served as both his true recommendation and the authentic mark of apostleship.[74] Throughout the letter it is clear that Paul attached great importance to the concrete practice of the servant of God's justice, a practice oriented not by the letter of the law but by the Spirit of the Lord.

SUMMARY: JUSTIFICATION BY FAITH IN THE EARLY LETTERS

Already in the early letters Paul introduced a number of elements that have a bearing on the meaning of justification by faith as that theme would be developed in Romans.

1) In the midst of theological disputes and socioeconomic difficulties, Paul occasionally discussed the new faith and its implications based on the event of Jesus Christ—his entire earthly life, death, and resurrection. Even though in his discussion Paul focused on the cross and resurrection, the earthly life of Jesus was always present in those two dimensions, and in the fact that Paul explicitly assumed Jesus' historical life in his own concrete life (2 Cor. 4:10-12).

In his theological discussions Paul spoke about justice and justification[75] with varying intensity. In one group of texts he dealt briefly with these concepts, sometimes picking up on pre-Pauline formulas, especially when Judaizers were not present in the community (e.g., 1 Cor. 1:30; 4:4-5; 6:11; Phil. 1:10). In a second group of texts he presented the theme in a more extended manner, but without its being the fundamental theme of the letter, correcting positions of both Judaizing and Gnosticizing opponents (e.g., Phil. 3:2–4:9; 2 Cor. 3:3-18; 5:11-21). Finally, justice and justification emerge as the central theme of the letter to the Galatians, as an argument against Judaizers.

In the first group of texts Paul dealt with the practice of justice by the justified person. In the second group he contrasted the justice of God with that of the law or with justice proper (Philippians). He also contrasted the ministry of justice with that of condemnation or of the law, as in 2 Corinthians, in order to underline the quality of life, freedom, and commitment proclaimed by his gospel even in the context of suffering. In Galatians Paul developed an apology against those who posited circumcision as a requirement for justification. For Paul that would be the same as returning to another slavery, slavery to the world distorted by the require-ment of the law and of circumcision. Against the background of a discus-sion of slavery and freedom, Paul contrasted works of the law that enslave with the faith that liberates.

2) From the way he presented his theological propositions one can see that Paul's chief concern was the present life of the Christian, in which dif-ficulties and conflicts of every sort abound. He was not concerned to pre-sent or elaborate upon a systematic reflection. In every letter, one encoun-ters difficulties and conflicts of a different type. In some communities there are problems between the members themselves—discrimination, injustice, and divergent theological opinions. In other communities one can observe with greater clarity problems in the interactions of Christians with Roman society. In all the letters the author presents himself as a man who suffered in his own flesh, physically and emotionally, both within the communities and outside them, because of his preaching of the gospel. His suffering was due both to the way he formulated the gospel in the con-text of Jewish traditions he considered limited, and also to the place where he was spreading his gospel, namely the Roman Empire. In both contexts his theological propositions upset customary behavior and chal-lenged his addressees to a new way of living.

3) The theme of justification by faith and not by works of the law appears even more explicitly in the polemic against Jewish Christians or Judaizers who were affirming circumcision and other observances of the law as a condition for belonging to the people of God. However Paul's interest was not simply to persuade people that Christ justifies and the law does not. Among his concerns was to include among the people of God the large sector of humanity who did not have the privilege of the Jewish law. By the faith of Jesus Christ, Paul places Jews and non-Jews on an equal plane: The Christian faith welcomes all without exception. Another of Paul's concerns was to show that the horizon of faith leads to a human existence that is more just, free, and mature. The law, in this sense, was limited. Paul referred explicitly to the Mosaic law, in order to contrast it with the gospel of faith. But his vision of the law was broader than that, encompassing every type of law, logic, system, or mechanism that tends to reduce the human being to slavery. Therefore the logic of his theology of justification by faith led him to speak out beyond the boundaries of reli-gion, and he took up other aspects of human history as well (Gal. 3:28). This fuller meaning of "law" underlies the theological reconstruction of justification as an affirmation of life.

4) One of the important purposes of the preceding rereading of Paul's earlier letters was to identify a variety of elements that are interrelated with the event of justification by faith. Each of the distinct components

present in the Pauline concept of justification appears in relation to a particular incident that happened to Paul or to one of the congregations. The most significant of these components is the new creature born "in Christ." Being "in Christ" indicates a practice that is just and honest (1 Cor. 1:29; 11:6), mature and free (Galatians, Philippians, and 2 Corinthians), and reconciling (2 Corinthians). It points to the fact that God justifies in order that justice be done, or in order that the human being be the justice of God (2 Cor. 5:21). To that end, Paul constantly related justification by faith to the participation of the believer in the death and resurrection of Christ (Phil. 3:10).

Being "in Christ" likewise implies another aspect of the same justifying action: Given that one is renewed, one's sins have been forgiven (2 Cor. 5:19). Paul never placed a heavy emphasis on the forgiveness of sins, and when he did refer to it, he never did so in isolation from justification (1 Cor. 1:30; 6:11; 2 Cor. 5:19-25). Moreover, he never omitted mention of the judgment of the end-time, which is always presented as being in direct relation to the present practice of the believer, of the justified person (1 Cor. 11:34; 2 Cor. 4:4-5; 5:10; Phil. 1:19; 2:12; 1 Thess. 2:4; 4:6).

Another element integral to justification by faith is freedom from all slavery (Galatians). Paul alluded to the Mosaic law as a way that leads back to slavery when one's life is not conformed to the Spirit. Justification, he said, is by faith and not by works of the law (Gal. 2:16). But for the apostle justification by faith refers not only to the Mosaic law, but also to every type of logic or mechanism (such as "the elements of the world") that enslaves the human being who has been constituted as a free child of God (Gal. 4:7).

The element of exclusion is another factor addressed by justification by faith (Gal. 3:14, 26). Faith, through Christ, opens the way for all who want to belong to the people of God and to receive the gift of the Spirit, independently of the Mosaic law. What was the exclusive privilege of a chosen people is broken open to include all people in a ministry that leads to life (2 Cor. 3:12-17). Finally, the person who belongs to the people of God is ultimately the one who does God's will, independently of circumcision, election, or law (Phil. 3:1-16).

Paul also connected justification by faith to the loving solidarity of God through Jesus Christ in his death on the cross (Gal. 2:19-21; 1 Cor. 1:23-29; 2 Cor. 5:19-21). The resurrection thus constitutes another component of Paul's discussion of justification. It is closely connected to faith, such that without the resurrection one would remain in the reality of the earlier life that one had already abandoned (1 Cor. 15:17; 1 Thess. 1:10). When life is hard, the power of the promise of the resurrection and of life is what sustains and gives power to whoever receives the justice of God by faith

(1 Cor. 15:31-32; Phil. 3:7-11). The same theme is found in Romans, in the affirmation that we are justified by the resurrection of Jesus Christ (Rom. 4:25).

Paul also related justification to reconciliation between God and humankind. He mentioned it only once in the early letters, when he exhorted the Corinthians to be reconciled, and it occurs again in Romans 5:10. His theological argument is that in the new creation God reconciled the world in God's Son (2 Cor. 5:19-20).

5) Finally, several other motifs should be noted that appear frequently in both the early letters and Romans: the connection between justice and knowledge, the negative attitude of boasting in one's own merits (be it in relation to circumcision or to wisdom), and the gracious divine initiative in all things.

CHAPTER FIVE

JUSTIFICATION BY FAITH
IN ROMANS

THE SITUATION IN THE CITY OF ROME

The Socioeconomic Context

Rome was the capital city and the center of the empire, from which administrative, political, economic, judicial, and military policies arose. Paul was aware of Rome's importance, for he did not live in a narrow world that ended on the boundary of a ghetto first Jewish and later Christian. When he wrote the letter to the Romans, he had traveled a great deal and was acquainted with many types of people. He had witnessed the Roman economic and military might that proclaimed "Peace and Security" everywhere they invaded, but only in exchange for non-negotiable submission to Roman authority.[1]

Roman wealth is legendary. Many scholars of ancient history praise the flourishing economy and culture that accompanied imperial rule. Commercial traffic flourished, especially on the seas. More goods were imported than were exported, for Rome was a city of high consumption.[2] The goods came from every corner of the then-known world: food, clothing, furniture, and construction materials. Unfortunately, however, poverty did not disappear. On the contrary, much of this boom provoked or accelerated the migration of peasants to the city after the theft of their lands that had occurred with increasing frequency since the time of the Republic.[3] This mass of impoverished people joined the already crowded poor neighborhoods of the city. Included among the poor were thousands of slaves, especially foreigners, many of them prisoners of war who arrived in waves each time a rebellion was smothered in one of the provinces.[4] In addition, the frequent famines hit the poorest sectors of the city especially hard.[5] The desperate situation of the poor can be seen when after the great famine of 6 C.E., Augustus had the city purged of a portion of the slaves, gladiators, and foreigners (except doctors and professors), in order to reduce the number of mouths that had to be fed.[6] In summary, Rome was an overpopulated city where contrasts abounded, and, as a result, so did social problems. It was not in vain that a force of about twenty thousand armed men was needed to maintain order in the city at the beginning of the empire. Juvenal describes without comment the vandalism and vices that flourished.[7]

The fact that Paul did not know personally either the city of Rome or its Christian communities poses no significant problem. Though he had not been there, and therefore would not have known firsthand the internal theological problems of the communities, his letter immediately takes the reader back to the historical context of Rome in the first half of the first century. That context was shaped by the concrete experiences of human beings with whom he shared his life, as well as by the theological disputes of the other communities with which he was in close touch. Their common ground included not only such specifics as the tension between the "weak" and the "strong" concerning food (Romans 14), or Paul's posture toward the Roman authorities (Rom. 13:1-7). The theological proposal emerging from Paul's eschatological horizon was much more radical, and more deeply rooted in their reality. On the other hand, Paul was not entirely unfamiliar with the situation and events of Rome itself. He knew personally various Christians from the Roman community (Romans 16), and he even lived with Aquila and Priscilla (Acts 18:2-3), who surely told him about Rome and their experience of life there. Thus when Paul wrote his letter, he did not write to an utterly unknown place.

The Christians in Rome

According to a recent study by Peter Lampe of the Christians of Rome in the first two centuries, a majority but not all of them in Paul's day lived and met in the district of Trastevere and on the Appian Way (on both sides, from Porta Capena to the Almone River).[8] Those are known to have been the unhealthiest areas of the city, densely populated and with heavy traffic. People lived in tenements or shanties. Merchants from the orient and sailors from the ships that docked near Rome made those neighborhoods their home base while in the city. The area amounted to a *barrio* in which people with very few resources eked out a living.[9] Paul must surely have heard of those neighborhoods.

If the majority of Roman Christians lived in such sectors of the city, most probably they were poor too, and they would have held their meetings in houses rented from some member.[10] There were of course people in the community who were less poor, and thus able to help those who were needier.[11] The Roman Christian community or communities (there were several) appear to have been economically diverse, including people who were very needy and others who could be asked to help the poor. In Romans, as in the majority of his other writings, Paul again preached solidarity among the brothers and sisters, in keeping with his vision of the church as a community of equals (12:1-13).

Theological Conflicts

Paul wrote the letter to the Christian community in Rome in 56–57 C.E. from Corinth.[12] He had been a prisoner not long before in Asia, and he had been set free. He traveled to Macedonia, returned, wrote the letter of reconciliation to the Corinthians (2 Cor. 1:1–2:13; 7:5-16; chaps. 8 and 9), and then returned again to Corinth. His intention was to go to Spain, but before going to that country he had to go to Jerusalem to deliver the money he had collected in Macedonia and Achaia for the poor among the saints of Jerusalem (Rom. 15:24-26). His plans included spending a short time in Rome on his way back from Jerusalem, in order to experience among the sisters and brothers in Rome the mutual encouragement of their common faith (1:12; 15:28), and also to get some needed rest before continuing on his journey (15:32).

The apostle was very concerned about his relations with the brothers and sisters in Jerusalem, as can be seen from the solemn language with which he asked his addressees to pray for him (15:30-31).[13] Paul sought to gain the support of the Roman Christians in his struggle to defend a gospel that includes all the peoples of the earth. Therefore he insisted that the gospel of Jesus Christ is received by faith and not by the law. That theme can be seen several times in his earlier letters, but it is expanded in the letter to the Romans. For example, Romans 15:30-31 points to the seriousness of the problems Paul had in being accepted by the leaders in Jerusalem. Paul had gone too far for the most conservative ones, who were attached to Jewish tradition. At the same time, Paul wanted to maintain the unity of the church—hence his interest in the collection. He would not give up anything of his gospel, but he also did not want to cause needless divisions.

Finally, he wanted to win the sympathy of the Christians of Rome, not only because he planned to visit them after going to Jerusalem, but also because the Roman community, perhaps by being situated in the capital of the empire, had a certain prominence among the primitive Christian communities (1:8). Moreover—a fact important for Paul's immediate future—the Roman Christians had a close relationship with those in Jerusalem, indicating their attachment to a tradition somewhat different from that of Paul. In fact, despite a large number who came from paganism, it appears that the Roman Christians were themselves faithful to a large part of the heritage of the law, without imposing the requirement of circumcision on others.[14]

This fact helps to clarify not only some of the contents of the letter, but also the manner in which the letter was developed. Its principal message is the justice of God that had revealed itself in that moment—a message explained and clarified with respect to how that justice is received, and especially with respect to the role of the law and of Israel (chaps. 9–11). The letter was written with great courtesy and a certain formality, in contrast to Galatians and portions of Philippians, where all traces of diplomacy are lacking.[15]

From the way Paul developed his theology in Romans, it is possible to identify two fundamental motivations in his theology of justification.[16] The first was to include in the people of God those who do not have the privilege of the law. The second was to strengthen the hope of Christians in a new, more just life for all, giving thanks to "the God . . . who gives life to the dead and calls into existence the things that do not exist" (4:17). In order to accomplish this, Paul developed the theme of the gift of the justice of God, which includes both judgment and mercy. Because of God's love for the marginalized, who suffer because of sin and the law held captive by it, God's justice is given to make all human beings without exception (whether because of class, ethnicity, or gender) new creatures in Christ. As new creatures they are transformed into subjects related as sisters and brothers, who practice justice in a world where there had not been a single person capable of doing so. These new creatures empowered to do justice are the people justified by faith.[17]

THE READING OF JUSTIFICATION IN ROMANS

There is a consensus among interpreters that Romans 1:16-17 is Paul's thesis statement. That conclusion must be expanded, however, to recognize that Paul elaborated that thesis under challenges from the socioeconomic world of the Roman Empire, as well as from one or more groups of Judaizing Christians who were tending to exclude people who did not fulfill all the requirements of the law.

Even the thesis statement is built on a conjunction of historical context and theological agenda. The phrase, "I am not ashamed of the gospel" and the reiteration and importance of faith *(pistis)* lead precisely to the historical context. The definitions of the gospel as the power of God for the salvation of all, and of the justice of God as revelation of the gospel, lead one to the central theological point that Paul wanted to develop in that historical context. "I am not ashamed" is equivalent to affirming "I confess," "I declare fully." It is a confessional sentence.[18] The fact that Paul chose the negative form of this formula suggests the connotation of resistance to his message on the part of his world (1 Cor. 1:21), and also the connotation of valor, for the one who takes up the gospel has to be ready to defend it and to resist pressures to adapt it (1 Thess. 2:14-16; Mark 8:38).[19]

The insistence on faith in Romans 1:16-17 introduces Paul's theological polemic against those of his contemporaries who assign to the law an essential role in justification. Paul insisted, supporting himself by the Scriptures, that justification is achieved by faith and not by works of the law. Given this fact, there can be no exclusion of other peoples who are not under the Jewish law. But Paul's basic interest was to extend to everyone, without exception, the message that the gospel is the power of God for the salvation of all, because in it is revealed the justice of God. The element of faith is central, but it stands on the base of this premise.

Paul contrasted the power of God with the power of sin manifest in the concrete injustices of history. The gospel is a force in which the justice of God is manifest, and for this reason it is gospel—that is to say, good news—for those who thirst for that justice in a world plagued by injustices. God's justice has transforming power. God, as the Creator, has the power to transform victims and victimizers into brothers and sisters who, oriented by the logic of God's Spirit, do justice in order to transform their unjust world.[20]

Justice of God and Injustice (1:16–2:29)

The great news that Paul insisted on proclaiming is the arrival of the justice of God that comes to humankind as a gift. He announced that gospel first in the thesis of his letter (1:16-17), and he stressed it again with an additional explanation in 3:21-26. Between those two summaries of the gospel, Paul emphasized that the justifying intervention of God is not coincidental, but rather it is required by the concrete actions of all men and women without exception. More precisely, the revelation of the justice of God in this kairotic "now" (3:26) is a response to the injustices of human beings. Paul had in mind the same God known in the Hebrew Scriptures. The interventions of God in history with God's people were always like that: The clamor of the oppressed because of the injustices of other people attracted the intervention of God. Though Paul did not say that directly, it is implied. Miranda is correct when he says that it is not fidelity to a covenant that is the precondition for God's intervention as a just God, but simply God's compassion for those who suffer injustice and cry out to God. Before any covenant had been established, God was quick to hear the cry of the oppressed.[21] It is for this reason that injustices emphasize the justice of God (3:24-26). Of what, then, does that justice consist, and what is its relationship to the theme of justification?

Immediately after affirming the good news of the revelation of the justice of God (1:17), Paul posited, in a virtually parallel construction, the revelation of the wrath (orgē) of God against all impiety (asebeia) and injustice (adikia) of human beings (1:18).[22] He presented the simultaneity of the two revelations of God—God's wrath and God's justice—as two aspects of the same process.[23] The justice of God has made itself present, and the wrath is already breaking forth: It has permitted men and women who practice injustice to fall to their own destruction (1:24-32).[24] The wrath of God, then, is provoked by the unjust actions of every human being.[25] Those actions are summarized by the term "sin" (hamartia), the interpretation of which must be seen in conjunction with that of "injustice" (adikia), which is the way Paul identified those actions in Romans 1–2. Paul then proceeded to give concrete consistency to these actions, and to make clear that all human beings, Jews and Greeks alike, have the same capacity to commit them. In 1:18, Paul indicated that the wrath of God, inevitable, immediate, and proceeding directly from God, breaks forth because of the gravity of those actions that imprison (katechontōn) truth in injustice.[26] It is a serious perversion, the inversion of the order of creation desired by God.

When Paul arrived at the conclusion that people had imprisoned truth in injustice, it was because in his eyes, in the imperial Greco-Roman society, injustice had usurped the place of truth. By juxtaposing injustice and truth, Paul characterized injustice as a lie and justice as the truth (see also 3:5-7). The seriousness of the case was that injustice was presenting itself as truth, that is to say as justice, preventing the truth from manifesting itself as such. For that reason, the empire's rallying cry of "Peace and security!" meant for the poor and oppressed only a lie intended to cover up injustice.

Paul stressed the fact that all human beings have the potential to commit impieties and injustices and to imprison truth in injustice. Those who believe themselves to be just and who sit in judgment over others are not exempt—not even the Jews, who see themselves as holding a special privilege as the chosen people with their law to illuminate their practice.[27] For Paul that exception does not hold. The relationships of Jews and pagans alike with other human beings reveal the real knowledge they have of God.[28]

The affirmation concerning knowledge and practice is developed in 1:18-32. In that section the author set forth the present reality of his world, including both Jews and Gentiles. In 2:1-16 and 2:17–3:19, Paul explained that it is people's practice and entire way of being that concerns God. There are three movements in 1:18-32: (1) God makes Godself known (1:19, 20); (2) human beings reject or distort that knowledge (1:21, 23, 25); and (3) human beings do what is inappropriate (1:21, 22, 24, 26, 27, 29-31). In order that no one would be able to present any excuse, Paul announced in the first point that God has made Godself known to all people through God's works since the creation of the world. Intelligence (nous) is capable of perceiving God's power and divinity (1:19, 20), but human beings lost the ability to use it adequately.[29] They consciously (that is, having known God) decided to act according to another logic that does not correspond to the knowledge of God. In three ways that are different yet have the same meaning, Paul described the way he perceived this exchange that human beings made (1:21, 23, 25).

At issue is the theme of idolatry, with which his readers would have been familiar.[30] In fact, the scriptures and the prophets of the Hebrew Bible were not foreign to them (note 3:21 and the frequent citation of the Hebrew Bible in Romans). Very probably Paul also had in mind the divinization of Caesar, something that was abominable to him.[31] Romans 1:23 expresses it clearly: "They exchanged the glory of the immortal God for images resembling a mortal human being." That meant exchanging one God for another, but the other is not the true God. The test of whether one is worshiping the true God or a false god is the practice in which one engages. Insofar as the focus of one's worship is not the true God, it is an idol—something created, and for that reason a lie. Therefore Paul said that people were exchanging the truth of God for a lie, worshiping and serving the creature instead of the Creator. In making this exchange, they saw themselves obliged to present arguments that would lead other people to recognize their god as legitimate. At that point they became confused in their reasoning, boasting of their wisdom (1:22).

The fundamental problem is not simply a difference in divinities at the level of ideas or of devotion. As Gustavo Gutiérrez observes, in the entire Bible idolatry always bears the mark of death and of blood unjustly shed.[32] Both true knowledge of God and a true relationship with God are manifested on the level of interhuman relationships. The wrath of God is not revealed simply against those who do not glorify or give thanks to God. It is revealed against the impieties and unjust deeds of human beings who imprison truth in injustice (1:18).

99

The practice of those who neither glorify nor give thanks to God but rather get lost in their own rationalizations, who exchange the truth of God for a lie, who exchange the glory of the incorruptible God for a corruptible human representation, and who invert the knowledge of God, is a practice full of interhuman injustice (1:29-31). It results from opting not to hold fast to the knowledge of God (1:28-31), for the knowledge of God demands the practice of justice. At the end of each of the three affirmations in 1:21, 23, and 25, Paul interspersed references to these interhuman behaviors in dialectical relationship with the rejection of the knowledge of God. He presented the facts as if they were inevitable and irrefutable, all three times using the formula, "God handed them over" (*paredōken autous ho theos;* 1:24, 26, 28).[33]

In 1:24-32, Paul described the reality to which the lack of knowledge of God leads. The author dramatized the situation, explaining that the whole society ends up being affected when it is far from the knowledge of God. In the structure of social relationships that embody sin, the corrupt desires of the hearts of both individuals and couples came to light, as did social injustices and depraved attitudes of every sort—the long list headed and summarized by the word *adikia* in 1:29-31.[34] Paul concluded the first chapter by making the reader recognize the gravity of the situation: "They know God's decree, that those who practice such things deserve to die— yet they not only do them but even applaud others who practice them" (1:32). The circumstances of Paul's society gave him the sense of no possible escape. The truth had been held captive to such a degree that one could no longer discern it. Everyone was responsible for that situation, and even those who sat in judgment over others (2:1) would not escape the judgment of God.

In 2:1-8, Paul referred to those persons who believed themselves to be just because they judged others, but in practice committed the same crimes as those whom they condemned. He was not simply issuing a general warning about not judging others lest the judger be judged by the same standards. Rather he was speaking about social institutions, possibly having particularly in mind the judges of the urban tribunals that he had come to know at close hand, many of whom were corrupt. By judging the accused, they condemned themselves: Because of their incoherent practice, Paul seated them in the same dock as the accused (2:1).

Once again Paul picked up themes central to 1:18-32. Those who judge and commit "the same things"—that is, who shut up truth in injustice—do not escape the judgment of God. Their heart is hard and impenitent (2:5a), or unfeeling and cast into shadow (1:21). Therefore they have stored up wrath for themselves "on the day of wrath, when God's righteous judgment will be revealed" (2:5; see also 1:18). With this declaration, Paul juxtaposed the judgment of God with the judgment of human judges. The judgment of God is just because God is just and true, and because there is coherence in God's acts: God gives to each according to his or her works (2:6). The judges of Roman society, on the other hand—or even all those in that or any society who assume the function of judge—are often corrupt and unjust. In an inverted society, judgment favors the unjust and condemns the innocent. Truth is imprisoned in injustice. Paul knew that well, not only because he knew the experience of the people of Israel through the Scriptures, but also from his own experience as an innocent offender who more than once had to abide by the verdicts of the courts.

Romans 2:8 closes the section that refers to the situation of the society in general. Key words from the beginning of the section reappear. That is, the words *alētheia, adikia,* and *orgē* from 1:18 appear again at the end of the first part of the section, in the form of condemnation to death for those who practice injustice (1:32).

Paul might well have been able to end his analysis of the perverse inversion of reality here, and to begin to develop the theme of justice and the justification of God. However, because of the burning heat of the theological discussion with some groups who appealed to the privilege of election, and who insisted on imposing on others the fulfillment of the law as a condition of justification, he saw himself obliged to make it clear that the law had lost whatever function it originally had. Furthermore, the justice of God is a free gift and, as such, good news for all human beings. On the legal plane, God's justice came as good news particularly for the poor, for it was different from both the Roman and the Jewish legal systems. In contrast to them, the justice of God was incorruptible, equitable, and compassionate. Thus one was justified by grace and not by merits, as was the case under the laws of that time.[35] Those who believed themselves to be just, whether pagans or Jews, deceived themselves if their practice demonstrated the contrary.

The Jews are the focus of 2:9-29. The previous section supposed that all those who persevered in doing good and who did not do "such things" would achieve eternal life (2:7). Paul thought that the Jews saw themselves as fitting in this category because they possessed the privilege of the law granted to them by God to illuminate for them the way of justice. But the apostle insisted that there is no favoritism before God: Eschatological judgment will be determined by one's practice, whether or not one has the law (2:9-11). As Paul's readers knew well, the people who are just before God are those who practice the law, not those who hear it. Those who do the law are the ones who are found justified on the day when "God, through Jesus Christ, will judge the secret thoughts of all" (2:16).[36]

What is important to God is that the truth not be imprisoned in injustice, independently of the law or of circumcision.

Paul began to attribute greater importance to the actions of human beings than to their formal relationship to the law, thereby making relative the same law that had held absolute authority. If the Gentiles, who do not have the law, persevere in doing good, it is as if they have fulfilled the law. Conversely, if those who have the law work evil, it is as if they did not have the law (2:14-15). The same thing happens with those who consider circumcision useful before God—as a sign of the chosen people. They consider that the validity of this sign is rooted in the act of circumcision itself. However, according to Paul, if a person transgresses the law, circumcision accomplishes nothing (2:25-26).

For Paul, then, the Jews also were responsible for the inversion of values that prevailed in that society. The incoherence of their practice condemned them (2:21-23). To demonstrate that fact, Paul resumed the discussion of the problem of the rejection of the knowledge of God already addressed in 1:18-32. But the new point of entry to the subject was their false knowledge of God due to their perversion of the law. Any Jews who rest in the law and boast in God apparently believe that they know the will of God, that they can use the law to discern what is best to do, that they can serve as the guides and educators of the ignorant, and that they possess in the law the full expression of knowledge and truth.[37] However, their own actions that do not correspond to the law denounce them as transgressors (2:17-22). For this reason, God judges independently of the law. For what God judges are "the secret thoughts of all," according to the gospel, through Christ Jesus (2:16). Therefore, for Paul neither the law nor circumcision is important, but rather the actions motivated by the heart, which is the source of the practice of both justice and injustice.

In 1:21, Paul declared that those who opted to become "futile in their thinking" instead of glorifying God, and whose heart fell into the shadows, found that their deadened minds turned them toward the practice of injustice. He noted that some say that they glory in God, but their practice turns out the same as that of those who get lost in their own reasonings. A Jew who takes refuge in the law and focuses all of his or her confidence on it, out of a longing for human praise from other human beings, transgresses the law. For Paul such an attitude before God on the part of Jews is worse than when the same attitude is held by others, not only because by transgressing the law the Jews dishonor God (2:23), nor because by their action "the name of God is blasphemed among the Gentiles" (2:24), but also because they prove to be no different from the pagans in justifying their injustice.

[They] take possession of religious revelation in order to serve their own interests; and its character of "sacred ideology" continues to pervert their judgment even to the point of using unconsciously what is religious in order to justify injustice in their relations with their peers.[38]

Since the practice of the Jews is like that of the pagans, their hearts too are "hard and impenitent," and for that reason the wrath of God and the revelation of God's just judgment devolve equally against them. Their hardness of heart and their impenitence can be seen in their practice of injustice. That practice, however, is made even worse by their habit of hiding it behind their preaching of the need for obedience to the law (2:21-22). What Paul wanted to make them understand was that their identity as a privileged people must be demonstrated through a way of life that is both honest and coherent with justice. That was the purpose for which they were chosen and had the oracles of the prophets entrusted to them (3:2). But the law is incapable of making them fulfill its assignment. Therefore Paul affirmed that the true Jew is a Jew on the inside and not on the outside, and the true circumcision is that of the heart, engraved by the Spirit and not by the letter (2:29).

In summary, the law, on which the Jews pride themselves, does not make them just. Any Jews who boast in the law, imprison truth in injustice and convert the law into an accomplice of injustice *(adikia)*. The fact that there were Jewish people in Paul's society did not guarantee the existence of justice. On the contrary, their being known as transgressors of the law they said one had to obey, not only provoked a more flagrant rejection of "the name of God . . . among the Gentiles" (2:24), but also falsified the truth of God. In order to be justified by their words, the Jews also had to recognize that they were practicing lies and injustice (3:4). The justice of God had to be entrusted to someone who truly fulfilled God's design: Jesus of Nazareth, the one called Son of God.

Justification by Faith and the Practice of Justice

In the inverted society described by Paul, no one is capable of doing justice. Therefore there is no one who succeeds in doing justice, even an individual who has good intentions. Despite the presence of persons of goodwill, or who might judge others with sincerity, or who might try to fulfill the law, in concrete terms the result is the same: The perverted society remains perverted, and innocent victims multiply. No one is able to discern the truth—not the Gentiles, not the Jews, not even the innocent victims who find themselves utterly abandoned.

That situation led Paul to recognize in his society something more than simply the fact that injustices were being committed between human beings. In Romans 3, he began to name that prevailing situation as "sin." From then on he began to personify it. He described it metaphorically as a power that dominates human beings, and that seems to be born out of their practices of coveting (*epithymia*). That power then acquires autonomy and comes to dominate those who produce it,[39] in such a way that it encompasses everything: interhuman relations, relations with God, relations with the natural order, relations with oneself—the very heart of the human being and of the natural order. Therefore, Paul insisted, there is no escape for anyone; "All, both Jews and Greeks, are under the power of sin . . .: 'There is no one who is righteous [just], not even one'" (Rom. 3:9-10; see Pss. 51:4 LXX; 116:11).

And what about the poor? Paul's categorical affirmation makes one think about the innocent victims, the poor, and the oppressed: Are they also under the wrath of God? Paul affirmed that indeed all people are, and that there is no one who is just. But are not perhaps the injustices committed by human beings what provoke God's wrath, and is it not perhaps to the cry of the oppressed that the justice of God responds? This is very clear in the Scriptures, even in most of the cases when Paul cites the Hebrew Bible to show the absence of even a single just person. However, Paul persists in affirming that there is no one who does what is good, that all have sinned and are deprived of the glory of God (3:23).

Before answering the question about justice and the poor, it is necessary to make clear that Paul was emphasizing equality among peoples in the matter of their unjust practices that provoke the wrath of God. But although his theological elaboration touches anthropologically[40] the weakness of the human being dragged down by desire, one is obliged to ask about the sin of the victims. Paul makes a subtle and important selection when he quotes the psalter to affirm that there is not even one just person. It is important to look not only at the word "just" (*dikaios*), which he substituted for "the one who does what is good" (*poiōn agathon*),[41] but also at the texts he chose to cite. Psalms 14:3 and 53:4 (LXX 13:3; 52:4), which Paul interwove with other biblical texts to support his affirmation that there is not even one just person, are both introduced by references to the foolish ones who say in their hearts that there is no God, who are corrupt and perverted, who devour the people of God as one devours bread, and who do not call upon YHWH (Pss. 14:1-4; 53:1-4). Whereas the evil ones make fun of the plans of the wretched, YHWH is the refuge of this devoured people (Ps. 14:6). God will save them because "God is with the company of the righteous [just]," and because of this, evil will tremble (Pss. 14:5-7; 53:5-6).

Psalm 14 in particular is very clear about the identity of the unjust and of the innocent victims of those "agents of evil." The resemblance in the first case to the analysis that Paul presented in the first two chapters of Romans is clear: The former are those who are foolish of heart and corrupt, who exhibit abominable conduct, who do not call upon God, who are perverted in disposition. They will tremble in terror, for, as they can read between the lines, they will get what they deserve.

Paul, however, did not make explicit the identity of the victims—the wretched, who are devoured by the powerful—nor did Paul make explicit the well-known solidarity of God with the destitute, which is an affirmation that one encounters outside the psalter. It is interesting also that Paul avoided the word "innocent" in Romans 3:15, even though it does appear in Isaiah 59:7. Paul was more concerned to emphasize the wickedness of the unjust that has made of the society a dead-end street. Therefore he incorporated other texts of the psalter and of Isaiah in order to affirm that some of the unjust are assassins, wretches, fighters, cheats, slanderers (Rom. 3:13-17). In all the texts he was careful not to mention the victims, even though the texts he cited may do so (e.g., Pss. 5:9-10; 140:3-4, 6; 10:7-14). The victims, of course, are implied, because *someone* is killed, ruined, abused. Paul, however, wanted to make clear, from his own concrete experience and as an eyewitness to his perverted and corrupt society, that sin had taken possession of every human being, including the poor and oppressed. Sin had enslaved human beings. Unfortunately, much current exegesis concentrates on the analysis of sin as a power and personifies it. The personification of that power diminishes the importance of the dynamic of the practice of injustice that dialectically gives birth to and nourishes sin as a power, and at the same time is provoked by it.[42] Interpreters often overlook the fact that the first two chapters of Romans, where the sinful situation of the society is described, speak of *adikia* and not of *hamartia*. The two words are not interchangeable synonyms, but rather the former "constitutes the qualitative characterization of what Paul understands by *hamartia* ['sin'] in the whole rest of the letter."[43]

The apostle could not have found a better example of the power of the dominion of sin or of the entirely inverted reality that it creates than the slave society in which he lived. That society provided the root metaphor that he elaborated in Galatians when he spoke of freedom in Christ. Paul appears to have been, however, the only one of the New Testament writers to make that connection. According to Luise Schottroff, the assertion that sin takes possession of all people and turns them into slaves is a genuine part of Pauline thought. Paul took the metaphor from the slave society in which he lived, in which the slave was not counted as a person, but rather as an object and the property of his or her master, without a will of his or her own, obedient in every detail to his or her owner.[44]

THE AMNESTY OF GRACE

Thus, in Paul's metaphor, all people are recognized as being enslaved to sin because their practice, voluntarily or involuntarily, is marked by impiety and injustice due to the dominion of sin. In chapter 7, Paul discusses this inconsistent relationship between will and practice. Human beings in their intelligence *(nous)* are able to do justice, but the logic of sin reigning in the society enslaves them, making them incapable of complying with justice.[45] Such a people are under the power of sin even before the act is committed.[46]

Now one can better understand why Paul discredited the law as a means of justification. In a society in which the truth has been imprisoned by injustice, no one can know God. Therefore there can be no just people. The Jews cannot be justified or present themselves as just before God through works of the law, for the law does not lead to the knowledge of God, which is the source of the practice of justice. The law only gives knowledge of sin (3:20).

The key to overcoming the apparent impasse is the good news, which is Paul's principal interest: the intervention of the justice of God by means of Jesus Christ for all who believe, and justification by grace through faith (3:21-26). Prior to this point there have been three places in Romans where Paul referred to how one is justified and just before God. First, he stated the matter outright in 2:13: "For it is not the hearers of the law who are righteous in God's sight, but the doers of the law who will be justified." Second, in 3:14 he set the stage by citing Psalm 51:4: In order for one to prevail in a trial and be justified, God must be proved true, even though every human being be a liar. Third, in 3:20 he stated the negative condition: No one will be justified before God by works of the law, for the law gives only the knowledge of sin.

Although these three affirmations have as their principal referent those who are under the Jewish law, the conclusions are not limited to them, but can be extended to all humanity. In Paul's society, the three affirmations demonstrated indirectly the utter powerlessness of all people to justify themselves or to be just before the judgment of God, not simply because of something innate in the human being (they had the capability of knowing God, who had revealed Godself to them, but they failed to do so; 1:19-20), but principally because of the impossibility of practicing justice in that perverted society.

The three statements about justification seem to contradict one another, but there is an internal logic that unites them, in which the praxis of justice takes priority. The first affirmation is true: Only those who practice justice, with the law or without it, will be justified. Furthermore, there would have been no need of another means of justification if it were not for the perverted reality that Paul described in chapters 1 and 2. But

Paul's experience in his society taught him the impossibility of doing justice in such a world and being declared just on that basis. Then, although the first affirmation is true, in practice it proves impossible. Because of the dominion of sin, no human being is able to act justly toward other human beings, not even the Jews by means of their law, which is holy, just, and good (7:12). On the other hand, according to the second affirmation, whoever seeks to be justified by his or her words and to triumph in a judgment must support his or her effort by the practice of justice and by giving an account of that practice (whether through the fulfillment of the law or by other means), because only the one who practices justice is just before God. However, since one's practice is unfaithful (2:2-3), in order to be justified one must recognize the veracity of God and one's own lie. But since humankind has lost the capacity of discernment because truth has been imprisoned by injustice, no one is capable of recognizing either the truth or a lie, and so no one is able to be justified. Just as it is impossible to do justice, it is also impossible to declare oneself innocent or guilty. Therefore, the third affirmation comes into play: Since it is objectively and subjectively impossible to practice justice in a world like this, no one can be justified, and none can justify themselves by their own works.[47]

Justification cannot be reduced to declaring the one who is guilty to be instead "just" or "justified." There are simply no grounds for affirming that the concern to which Paul granted first priority was the need for the human being to be declared just before God, or for his or her sins to be forgiven.[48] The fundamental problem for Paul was that there is not even one just person *(dikaios)* capable of doing justice in order to transform the reality characterized by injustice.[49] In order to be just and faithful to the creation, and faithful and merciful toward the weak, God must intervene with a justice and a power distinct from and superior to that of the sin that reigns, and God must establish God's own sovereignty in the face of idolatry, offering new alternatives of life for all. Only in that way can God be revealed as just, and neither forgetful of nor inattentive to the cry of the entire creation, especially of the poor—the most extreme victims of injustice.

There are, then, two principal difficulties in the situation to which Paul addressed himself: the power of structural sin that enslaved all humanity and, in a dialectical relationship, the impossibility for human beings to do justice, because it had been imprisoned in injustice. As a consequence, in the social, economic, and political reality to which Paul was responding, the poor and weak were completely abandoned to the perverted logic of injustice. Paul saw that logic, in turn, as connected to the lack of knowledge or rejection of God. Therefore God had to reveal Godself in order to be truly known.

107

In this climactic moment Paul announced the revelation of the justice
of God (3:21-26) as something that broke in from another "age" radically
superior to and different from the present. What happened was the eruption of God into history, an event mediated by the liberating life of Jesus
Christ.[50] If Israel with its law could not move forward the plans of God,
Jesus of Nazareth succeeded in doing so by his faith. It is in this context
that the event of justification took place.

Justification by Faith

Paul introduced the good news (3:21-26) with the phrase "but now"—
an eschatological phrase pointing to the contrast between the two ages
that leads to the proclamation of liberation:[51]

> But now, apart from law, the justice of God has been revealed, and is
> attested by the law and the prophets, the justice of God through the faith of
> Jesus Christ for all who believe. For there is no distinction, since all have
> sinned and fall short of the glory of God. (3:21-23, author's trans.)[52]

In this good news are three great reasons for rejoicing: The justice of God
has been manifested; that justice is feasible because it is a gift of God that
has already been revealed in history through the faith of Jesus Christ; and
it extends to all, not just to the Jewish people, because it is received by
faith independently of the law.[53]
Now the crucial question is how this justice is manifested. In the first
place, for Paul this justice was revealed, brought near, and made feasible
through the gospel of Jesus Christ (1:16). Jesus Christ was the revelation
of the practice of a just person, whose life of faith ensured the arrival of a
new humanity, a new aeon. In that capacity, Jesus believed until the end in
the faithfulness of God, even though they killed him. That is the foundation of God's justice. It is that faith-trust-obedience[54] of Christ that makes
possible the justification of every human being (Rom. 3:26; Gal. 2:16; Phil.
3:9) who receives the gift of the justice of God with the same faith as that
of Jesus.[55] Therefore Paul recognized that the justice of God is revealed
through the faith of Jesus Christ for all who believe.[56] God's raising of
Jesus of Nazareth, the one accused and harassed by the laws of his time,
not only justified him before every creature, but also justifies every human
being (4:25).[57]
In order to cut off at the roots any people's claims to exclusive access to
salvation, Paul introduced a cultic fragment already known to the primitive community (3:24-26a). That fragment speaks of the liberating work of
Christ and the forgiveness of sins, and with it Paul annulled any salvific
character that might be attributed to the Jewish law. In that fragment the

act of the death of Jesus is recalled in its redemptive and expiatory function. That soteriological tradition may have arisen among the Hellenists of Antioch who proclaimed Jesus as the reconciler, having in mind not only the tradition of Leviticus 16, but also the practice each year of marking the Day of Atonement in the Temple of Jerusalem.[58] Jesus is presented as *hilastērion*, which is a difficult and much discussed term referring both to the place of sacrifice and to the victim at the same time. It thus expresses God's expiation by God's own deed, once and for all, of the sins of all humanity. In that way the expiatory role of the temple functionaries was annulled, and with it the ritual law, and salvation was thereby extended to all nations.

With the ambiguous word *hilastērion* Paul invoked a sacrificial image that did not take into account the entire person and work of Christ. Maillot indicates that the error of many Western theologians is to have concentrated their research on 3:25: "to have attributed to the person of Christ this expiation for our sins, without being aware that it is a parable drawn from the Hebrew Bible and not a literal soteriology."[59]

This cultic fragment can be read, however, from the perspective of the Jesus of history. The death of Jesus Christ on the cross shows the fullest expression of sin in Paul's day. The Roman authorities had already crucified many innocent slaves, but their innocence was obscured by the untruth of the law, which became an accomplice in the injustices.[60] "For us to be free from the law it was necessary that the law crucify Christ before our eyes; only in this way could we understand that justice does not come through the law."[61] With the unjust condemnation and death of Jesus Christ—the clearly innocent person "who knew no sin" (2 Cor. 5:21), the Son of God—sin showed clearly its true nature and identity.

However, its power could, in the end, be destroyed: God destroyed that power in raising from the dead Jesus Christ, the condemned one. The Jewish law cursed all those hung on a tree, whether innocent or not. In its cursing of the Son of God, the futility of the law was manifest. Thus, Jesus' death on the cross in Jerusalem and Jesus' subsequent resurrection exposed the futility of both the Roman and Jewish systems of law, and both Gentile and Jewish ways of living—in short, the entire present age.[62] That death allowed Paul to discern the signs of the justice of God who is both just and justifier. By his life of faith, Jesus marked the end of the sacrifices of innocent people. He assumed these sacrifices for once and for all, and opened the possibility of a new way of living. The faith of the Christian consists in receiving and making his or her own the faith of Christ ("to live in Christ"). The Christian participates in Christ's death and resurrection (Phil. 3:10-11; 2 Cor. 4:11) because he or she believes that God raised Jesus.

But saying that the justice of God is revealed in this world by the liberating work of Jesus Christ does not change anything in the central problem of human reality. Paul had to interpret two very important elements relative to Jesus Christ that affect human beings in profound ways: the act of justifying that comes through the faith of Christ, and the need for faith in the human beings who receive the gift of the justice of God.

Paul said in 3:23 that all sin and all are deprived of the glory of God, and subsequently he affirmed that they are justified (*dikaioumenoi*) by the gift of God's grace, by virtue of the redemption-liberation (*apolytrōsis*) realized in Christ Jesus.[63] The verb "justify" here translates the Hebrew verb *ṣ-d-q* in its hiphil or causative form.[64] That is to say, God makes it possible for human beings to do justice. If the great calamity that Paul described was that there was not even one just person, no one who could do good, Paul then affirmed the opposite. Because of the manifestation of the justice of God in the faith of Jesus Christ, there are just people, for they have been justified, and all of that has been accomplished by God's grace.

The purpose of justification is to transform human beings into subjects who do justice, who rescue the truth that has been imprisoned in injustice (8:4). In the obedience of faith and not of the law, one enters into a new order of life, and those who opt for this life make the members of their own bodies instruments of justice (6:13). This is possible because, according to Käsemann, God gives God's very self in the gift of justice, and by that gift the human being recovers the capacity to do justice.[65] Paul doubtless had in mind the reality of a new creation (2 Cor. 5:17)[66]— not only of individual hearts but of the whole society and the entire world (8:19-21).

This is good news for all of society—principally for the poor, who suffer the impieties and injustices of the oppressors, but also for every human being—because the opportunity to practice justice is opened to all people, since by grace they have been made and declared just. From the forensic point of view, it can be seen that, because of God's gracious act of justification, men and women can present themselves before God and other people as just and worthy people. In the event of re-creation, God does not take into account sins previously committed (Rom. 3:25; 2 Cor. 5:19).

God, then, is both "just and justifier" (3:26), and (as is God's right) redeems God's creatures as sons and daughters so that they can transform the world, even though the world is under God's wrath and judgment and will be so until the end of time.[67] This last point is especially important for the poor, for the present judgment of God, which is in dialectical relationship with the also-present justice of God, guarantees to the weak (who are always threatened by the injustices committed by human beings) that justice will be done.

The fact that God graciously stepped into human history and revealed God's own self as both just and justifier by means of Jesus Christ presents another important piece of data. The knowledge of God had been rejected, mistakenly known, manipulated, or hidden, and that lack of the knowledge of God was reflected in the practice of injustice between human beings. Now, in Paul's view, with the revelation of God in Jesus Christ, and with the manner in which Jesus lived his life, true knowledge of God was finally achieved. Then, since the knowledge of God corresponds to the practice of justice, the opportunity arose for all who have faith truly to practice justice—that is, to live in accord with the knowledge of God.

This new possibility is relevant for all humanity. As for the Jews who were under the law, Paul proved that the law does not have a role as the driving force for justice in this new logic of God. It is faith that is the key for understanding this new reality. Moreover, it is the logic of faith that allows the law to fulfill its original function of doing justice (3:31; 8:4). Not only that, but faith is also the medium through which salvation is extended to all, circumcised and uncircumcised alike (3:21, 29).

Of what does the faith of the believer consist? In order to ground his argument that it is faith that justifies and not the law, Paul returned to the example of Abraham (Romans 4). By means of that discussion the apostle explained the content of the faith of the believer: Abraham was justified because he believed that God gives life to the dead and calls into being things that are not (4:17). Paul alluded here to a new creation, to the necessity of believing in what is impossible for human beings.[68]

With that concrete example, the apostle affirmed that Abraham transgressed physical laws (a man of his age could not father descendants), but Abraham believed against all hope (*hos par'elpida ep'elpidi episteusen*) that he would do so (4:18-19). Having heard the promise of God, Abraham emerged strengthened in faith (*enedynamōthē tē pistei;* 4:20), fully convinced that God has the power to accomplish whatever God promises (4:20-21). Immediately afterward, Paul drew a parallel to the faith of the believers he was addressing: The descendants of Abraham also believe in the one "who raised Jesus our Lord from the dead" (4:24).

In 10:10-11, the apostle again emphasized the intimate relationship between faith in the resurrection and justice. Jesus was raised for our justification (4:25) or (in other words also from Paul) Jesus was raised in order that we be fruitful for God (*hina karpophorēsōmen tō theō;* 7:4). When Paul compared the role in history of Christ and Adam, he underlined the life-sustaining character of the gift of justice through Christ (5:17, 18, 21). The same life-sustaining character was the focus of his discussion of the work of the Spirit of God or of Christ (8:6, 10, 11). The hope or faith of the believer in whom the Spirit of the Risen One dwells is hope or faith that the believer will receive life just as Jesus did, the first of many (1 Corinthians 15). But since resurrection refers to re-creation, transformation, and new life, one must agree with Miranda when he affirms that *"the foundation of hope consists in the fact that this justice of God is already on earth and that it is this which is going to transform the world* and all its civilizing structures—including bodies."[69] Human beings will bring about that transformation because they have been justified (made and declared just) by grace and faith.

THE AMNESTY OF GRACE[70]—THE LOGIC OF THE SPIRIT

In Romans Paul was writing to communities of Christians who supposedly had already been justified and believed in the one who raised Jesus from the dead (4:24). He was not "evangelizing" the Christians of Rome, but reminding them of and clarifying theologically what had taken place in the life of those communities. The heart of the specific message that Paul directed to the present reality of the Christians at Rome is found in chapter 8. That message served to strengthen the faith and hope of those who were suffering the domination and condemnation of the empire, as well as the anguish of having to submit to a law that enslaved and excluded. The particular message of Romans 8 must be understood against the background of a rereading of the rest of that letter and Paul's earlier letters with respect to the theme of justification by faith.

Romans 8 summarizes what has been said earlier in the letter. It begins by affirming that there is no condemnation for those who are in Christ Jesus (8:1) and concludes by affirming the absence of condemnation by God (8:33), by Christ Jesus (8:34), and by the logic of the socioeconomic system of his time (8:35-37). Between the beginning and the end of the chapter are the reasons for and implications of Paul's affirmation.

In order to accomplish that explanation, Paul interrelated two types of language. One type of language speaks about faith in God: the absolute certainty of the solidarity of God with the condemned, which is manifested in the love of God in Christ. No one and nothing will be able to separate us from that love (8:38-39). The other type of language speaks of the faith response in the human being: "In all these things we are more than conquerors through him who loved us" (8:37). Men and women recover the power and the authority to re-create their world because, when they are justified, their spirit and the Spirit bear witness that they are sons and daughters of God (8:15). At issue is the power that springs forth from those called to be conformed to the image of the Christ (8:29).

It is important to consider which type of language is being used in a particular instance, and its interrelation with the other type, in order not to accuse Paul of being a spiritualizer or of being naive. Without this semantic and historical consideration, language such as that of 8:37 is no more than a slogan. The interrelationship of the two types of language allows us to see the faith Paul had in the possibility of overcoming a context apparently impossible to conquer in a head-on confrontation. It was not difficult for Paul to observe that the poor were condemned to great poverty, the slaves (including freed slaves) to perennial humiliation, and the common people to submission to Rome. Paul, however, rejected that condemnation, arguing that God already condemned beforehand the logic of sin and its agents.

Here Paul introduced the necessary language of faith, which sometimes goes beyond scientific analysis and often is more effective than are objective and rational practice. Experience teaches that in the liminal moments between life and death, human beings feel compelled to appeal to a superior force beyond themselves in order to be able to get out of the impasse. For that reason and in that way, the language of faith becomes the language of the love of God.

According to Paul there is no condemnation that weighs on those who are in Christ (8:1)—those who have decided to participate by faith in another logic distinct from the one prevailing in the first half of the first century. Paul gave two reasons and a purpose for which people would make such a decision. The reasons are (1) "The law of the spirit of life in Christ Jesus has set you free from the law of sin and of death" (8:2 NRSV note z), and (2) God "condemned sin in the flesh" (*katekrinen tēn hamartian en tē sarki;* 8:3). The purpose is so that the justice of the law *(to dikaiōma tou nomou)* might be fulfilled in us through conduct oriented according to the Spirit (8:4).[71]

Three words help to clarify this different logic that the apostle proposes: condemnation, liberation, and justice. In them can be seen the complete solidarity of the triune God with those condemned to death in human history.[72] God condemned *(katakrinō)* sin in the flesh. Why? and how? The answer appears in condensed form in 8:3, after having been explained more fully in the first three chapters of the letter. For Paul it was impossible to continue living in the old way, and, tragically, there was no objective possibility of finding another alternative. Chapters 1–2 describe the practices of injustice *(adikia)* of human beings that are diametrically opposed to the will of God. Paul recognized that those practices generated a perverse logic that imprisoned truth in injustice, to the point of calling truth a lie and a lie the truth. That perverse logic condemned all men and women to submission to it. Paul began to name that logic "sin" *(hamartia)* in Romans 3. Therefore the wrath of God *(orgē theou)* was revealed (1:18), and so also was God's justice *(dikaiosynē theou;* 1:18), condemning sin in the flesh *(sarx)*—that is to say, condemning the perverse logic that, one way or another, had condemned the life of all people to submission.

And God accomplished all this by grace. Since God judged by grace and not by merits, God's love was extended to all creatures—those excluded by the requirement of the law and those condemned by sin. God's love reached especially those who were experiencing condemnation by oppression, hunger, nakedness, persecution, dangers, and the sword (8:35-37)—the very victims of the logic of sin manifested in the time of the principate.[73]

For Paul no human being was capable of condemning sin and at the same time eliminating it, nor was anyone even capable of doing justice. The law of the Jews, the gift of God so that justice could be fulfilled, had itself been captured by sin and "weakened by the flesh" (8:3). For this reason the law also failed to constitute an effective response. According to Paul, God alone—a God who is distinguished by divine love—was able to free the human being and condemn sin at the same time.

But God did not do this from outside the world of God's creatures. God did it through human beings in order that they too might participate with authority in the liberating event. The result that Paul glimpsed was the greatest possible solidarity of God with humankind, to the point of taking on their humanity, and even more specifically, the humanity of the poor, who in Paul's day were the principal victims of sin. It is for this reason that Paul perceived, in the life and death of Jesus, the God who assumed historical form. In the Son, God entered into the perverse and deadly logic of sin in order to condemn it, freeing humankind from the law of sin and death. "When before our eyes the law crucifies as an outlaw the only man who did not know sin, God destroys sin and the law forever. At this point the justice of God begins in history and the 'justice' of the law ends" as that which justifies.[74] The good news, then, is that the old logic has limits, and that there exists another logic that leads to life, namely the law of the Spirit.

However, it is not enough to repeat that Christ assumed human form in order to liberate us. Working in that way runs the danger of taking away all the dynamic energy of the law of the Spirit that gives life in Christ Jesus (1:2), and therefore of failing to take advantage of the opportunity made available to us to transform the concrete, perverted world. For although it is certain that there is no condemnation for those who are in Christ, the ultimate purpose of God was not simply the condemnation of sin, but "that the just requirement of the law *(dikaiōma tou nomou)* might be fulfilled in us, who walk not according to the flesh but according to the Spirit" (8:4). The ultimate purpose of God, then, is like that of Jesus, for it is by the faith, confidence, fidelity, and obedience of Jesus that human beings are established as just (*dikaioi katastathēsontai;* 5:19).[75]

According to Paul, the "law of the Spirit that gives life" has freed the creation from the logic of sin and death because, through the solidarity of God in the life of God's Son, another logic was inaugurated. That new logic enabled the justice of the law (which before had been reduced to being incapable of fulfillment) to be done by those who follow the logic of the Spirit and not that of the flesh or of sin. Such people are capable of following the logic of the Spirit because they were freed from the condemnation to following egotistical interests that would hide truth in injustice.

Paul believed that from that moment on, the Spirit of God dwells in "those who are in Christ Jesus" (*tois en Christō Iēsou;* 8:1)—those who opt for that logic of the Spirit that gives life. Those people, who apparently have no power (8:35-37), have the authority to overcome all condemnation to death and to proclaim a new economic and political order. The logic of that new order is based on the law of the Spirit that gives life, because its tendencies are life and peace (8:6), and because the Spirit is life since its interest is justice (*dikaiosynē;* 8:10). The practice and proclamation of justice are thus central in this new logic of the Spirit. Life (*zōē*), peace (*eirēnē*), and justice (*dikaiōma* or *dikaiosynē*) are three words that Paul used to speak from the horizon of that logic.

The result that Paul proposed to the communities of his day in order to strengthen their hope in a world that was threatening the life of excluded peoples and persons, was thus, on the one hand, to make them see that every system that follows a logic of sin has been condemned and has no authority to continue condemning its victims. On the other hand, the result was to stress the good news of another logic that tends toward the well-being in life of all persons and peoples because it is rooted in justice. That logic is the logic of the Spirit. The practice of that logic is the only one that liberates from sin and death (8:2). And one does not walk alone, individually, within that new logic, because one's own private interest is not being pursued. Paul unites human beings, reminding them of their relationship as children of a single divine Parent, and brothers and sisters of the firstborn Son (8:14-17).

This is already a big step toward opening up the awareness of those who feel alone and impotent in the face of the power of sin. But Paul went even further, appealing to the power of the divine in human affairs. One of his objectives was to make his readers recognize that those who live according to the law of the Spirit have no reason to fear. They have all the legitimate authority to reign (*basileuō*) in history (5:17), and not to be slaves of the law of sin. When they receive the gift of justice (*hē dōrea tēs dikaiosynēs;* 5:17), divinity forms a part of them: Their acts, attitudes, and thoughts are in accord with the logic of God. They are made like gods by the work of the Holy Spirit (of God or of Christ), and their divine identity is verified when they let themselves be guided by the Spirit.

For that reason Paul insisted on the gift of divine adoption. They are children of God, God's heirs here on earth and co-heirs with Christ. For Paul it was very important that that fact be taken into account, and he focused on it alone in 8:14-30. But it is important to understand that Paul was addressing those who were enduring times of great suffering.[76] In such contexts, there is no danger of misunderstanding this announcement of divine identity in the human being. The insistence that it is a free gift of God—in order that no one boast in oneself—also averts such a danger, as does the theological declaration that in Christ we are children of a single divine Parent and therefore siblings of one another. In this argument of Paul, there is no room for anyone to dominate a neighbor. Moreover, human history did not reach its fullness with the revelation of justice and justification by faith. In Romans 14:10, Paul reminded his addressees of their responsibility "before the judgment seat of God" where they will give an account of their acts (see also 1 Cor. 4:5; Phil. 1:10; 2 Cor. 5:10).

Paul's realism did not permit him to disregard suffering. He spoke of it in all of its harsh reality. Sin has not disappeared; the cancellation of its dominion over those who are under grace has been declared (6:14), but it remains present. "Sin itself is not implicated in personal existence, but personal existence necessarily establishes the conditions that make sin possible,"[77] and one must take responsibility for it.

Paul makes one recognize clearly that the power of the divine in the human being does not cancel suffering. The Son of God suffered on the cross because of the perversity of the inverted logic of Jewish and Roman law. If the creation waits eagerly for the revelation of the children of God (*tēn apokālypsin tōn huiōn tou theou*), groaning until now with the pains of labor, the children also, who possess the firstfruits of the Spirit, groan with longing for full liberation (8:18-25). To be children of God even implies that the sufferings can grow more severe. To enter into the logic of life in Christ is to suffer like him (8:17) and for his sake (8:36). But Paul tried to interpret the sufferings against the background of the proclamation of his certainty that a superior reality awaits us. Therefore, he strengthened the Christians by affirming that the present sufferings are not to be compared with the glory that is about to be revealed (8:18).

This should not be interpreted lightly as a "happy ending." Paul's concern for the present was very serious, and he tried to sketch out a new and feasible way to resist the unjust logic of the Roman principate. Those who

116

are baptized into Christ must recognize the power of their spirit, and of the Spirit that is united with them, to testify that they have the dignity of children of God (8:15-16). They do not feel alone in the struggle against that which condemns them to death, because the Spirit is prepared to be in solidarity with them whenever their own strength fails (8:26-27). Nor will they live in fear of making a mistake in the struggle for life. The experience of the gift of justification that is by faith and not by works of the law has made them children of God confident in the grace of God.[78]

Guided by the Spirit, then, they are children of God; being children of God they have received a spirit of freedom, not of slavery. Destined to "be conformed to the image of [God's] Son" (8:29), human beings who are joined in Christ as sisters and brothers and who persist obstinately in the Spirit can sustain the necessary conviction and courage to say, "In all these things we are more than conquerors through [the one] who loved us" (8:37). The one who raised Christ from the dead has the power to guarantee them life (8:11). Everyone who condemns a man or a woman to death has already been condemned by God. "Who is to condemn?" "Who will bring any charge against God's elect?" "Who will separate us from the love of Christ?" Paul answers with a hymn to the power of the love of God:

> For I am convinced that neither death, nor life, nor angels, nor rulers, nor things present, nor things to come, nor powers, nor height, nor depth, nor anything else in all creation, will be able to separate us from the love of God in Christ Jesus our Lord.

117

PART III

JUSTIFICATION
AS AN AFFIRMATION OF LIFE:
TOWARD A THEOLOGICAL
RECONSTRUCTION

CHAPTER SIX

FROM A BIBLICAL-HERMENEUTICAL READING TO A THEOLOGICAL REREADING

INTRODUCTION

A complete theological reconstruction of the doctrine of justification from the Latin American Third World perspective is beyond the scope of any single study, for clearly there are many angles from which one might undertake such a reconstruction in contexts of oppression and struggle. In this study I have approached the reconstructive task, as I did the foregoing study of justification in Paul, using the biblical key of exclusion. I have begun not with an abstract, generic "Human Being," but with those specific human beings who are the excluded. This key enables us to examine forms of oppression that, although they are reinforced by the economy, also transcend it. They include viewing the other person as insignificant because of his or her economic poverty, color, ethnicity, or sex—forms of oppression summarized by the terms classism, racism, ethno-centrism, and sexism.

Using the basic criteria developed in the preceding chapters, we examine justification as an affirmation of life from two perspectives: (1) justification and the threatened life of the poor, and (2) the gift of being subjects of history as the power of justification by faith. The discussion concludes with an exploration of the meaning of the sacrifice of Christ, judgment, and forgiveness. Before developing those dimensions of justification by faith, however, it is necessary to examine the step that must be taken from the reading of the biblical text to a theological reading contextualized in the present Latin American reality.

In the modern context it is not enough simply to repeat the same words that Paul used to address his communities. His experience of life and of God, his following of Jesus of Nazareth, his historical juncture, and the incipient Christian community all differ from our own contexts, experiences, and commitments. We are in another time, another situation, another ecclesial experience. However, God has not ceased to reveal Godself. The life of Jesus Christ, his death and resurrection of which we read in the Scriptures, and God's Word that continues to reveal itself through our realities remain sources of inspiration that must be reinterpreted with the purpose of giving life to every human being.[1]

The apostle picked up the kerygma and traditions already current in the communities to which he wrote (e.g., baptismal practices, cultic activities, dominical sayings: 1 Cor. 1:30; 6:11; Gal. 3:28; Rom. 3:24-26a; 4:24-25; 5:1-2; 2 Cor. 5:21), and then he reinterpreted them in his new situation. Similarly, we also need to pick up again central aspects of the thought of Paul about justification by faith and reinterpret them in light of our Latin American reality. Paul read the event of Jesus Christ from his own perspective. We have learned how Paul lived and interpreted his faith in Jesus Christ, and how he re-elaborated the theme of justification. It is our turn now to take up once again the kerygma—the life, death, and resurrection of Jesus—and, with the aid of Paul, to reinterpret, deepen, and try to move forward into our own context Paul's presentation of justification by faith. Without this effort the message of justification will not be relevant, because it will not respond to the needs of the men and women of our continent.

Furthermore, the biblical reading we have done of Paul has been conditioned by our Latin American eyes, our experience of God, and present pastoral exigencies. But even at that, the reading needs to be nuanced for a variety of reasons. One obvious one is that today there is no theological tension between Judaizers or Jewish Christians and converted pagans, or between "Gnostics" and Paul. Another is that our socioeconomic and political reality is different from that of Paul and his communities. Moreover, we carry with us not only Paul's own statements, but also the whole heritage of interpretations of this doctrine throughout the Christian tradition, and those interpretations also form a part of the deposit of faith of present-day believers.[2]

Both from the way Paul interpreted the message of the gospel and from the content of the message itself, however, we can see several points that must be central to any effort at theological reconstruction. They can be summarized under the following two headings: concerns in the life of the Christian communities as a precondition for the theological discourse, and foundational perspectives that are the wellsprings of all of Paul's affirmations concerning justification.

122

CONCERNS IN THE LIFE OF THE CHRISTIAN COMMUNITIES

In the first place, it is necessary to recall that in each letter Paul's theological argument related directly to the concrete life of the Christian community to which it was directed. That is to say, his theoretical reinterpretation of the law, of sin, of the justice of God, and of justification came after he had entered into dialogue with the primitive communities of faith, in the framework of their daily life in which conflicts, sufferings, worries, misunderstandings, joys, and hopes abounded on both the theological and the social level.

Similarly, Paul's own praxis as a disciple of Jesus led him to elaborate a theology of sin, justice, and grace. Taking into account this intersection of Paul's life experiences and his theological reflection is basic to any reinterpretation we might carry out in our present context. Working only from the abstract meaning of what Paul supposedly said about grace and justification, for example, could easily lead to disputes that have no concrete meaning, as has often happened in the history of thought.[3] On the other hand, the biblical characters who speak and to whom one speaks in a particular context give substance to the theological postulates.

Paul wrote to communities made up of people who were already believers, who knew Jesus Christ, and who intended to live a new life. They believed that they had been cleansed of their sins, sanctified, and justified or made just in the name of the Lord Jesus Christ and the Spirit of God (1 Cor. 6:11; 1:30). Paul's purpose was not primarily to present the gospel in a way that would cause people to turn from their sins and believe in Jesus: They had already been baptized (Rom. 6:3). It is necessary, therefore, to press on, and to recognize the wellsprings of his theological affirmations that can serve as keys for our reading of justification today.

WELLSPRINGS OF JUSTIFICATION BY FAITH IN PAUL

It is impossible to determine precisely the intentions or concerns of an author simply through his or her formal arguments, but clues in the text itself, the circumstances of the author's context, and the contribution of the present reader from his or her own perspective[4] can allow us to deduce those intentions. Four aspects seem foundational to Paul's development of the meaning of justification by faith.

The Inclusion of the Excluded in the People of God

Paul's emphasis on justification by faith and not by works of the law must be seen against the background of the burning theological issues

123

and tensions of that time. In some sectors of the Jewish Christian community, circumcision and the observance of other provisions of the Mosaic law were required of anyone who wanted to have access to the promises of God that had been given to Abraham and his descendants, or who wanted to belong to the people of God. Through his mission among Gentiles who were excluded by being outside the Jewish law, Paul affirmed that the law is incapable of justifying the human being before God. Instead, in the life of faith of Jesus Christ, God received by grace all human beings as God's own sons and daughters, and God both made just and declared just all people who have faith in the resurrection of the dead. By speaking of justification by faith, Paul affirmed all peoples as equals, on the same plane in their relationship with God. With this theological principle the division of the world's people into Jews and Gentiles was overcome, and the Christian faith made universal, so that all people might have the possibility of access to the promises made to Abraham.

One of Paul's intentions that generated his theological proposal of justification by faith and not by works of the law was to include the excluded in the divine project of salvation, under the same conditions that prevailed for people considered under Jewish tradition as the elect. As a theological argument supporting that intention, Paul established that all human beings are sinners, including those who have the law and those who sit in judgment over others. He proved similarly that the law does not justify or make just, and therefore all people alike need the grace of God in order to do justice before humankind and before God.

That is the framework of the specifically theological dispute that arose in the primitive Christian communities. But the logic that affirms the inclusion of the excluded on the basis of their justification by faith has ramifications beyond the religious realm. Even from the outset, the cultural dimension was present in the contrast between Jewish culture and the cultures of the Gentiles. Paul himself transcended the limits of specifically Jewish concerns, in order to deal also with the social and sexual dimensions of exclusion. He was thus led to affirm that in Christ there is neither master nor slave, neither female nor male (Gal. 3:28), thereby overcoming two other inequalities dividing human beings from one another. The reality of injustice converted into sin, which Paul describes in Romans 1 and 2 and which can be seen in its most specific cruelty in Romans 8:18-38, requires that the category of exclusion be amplified to include economic, political, and cultural dimensions as well.

The Absence of True Justice and Knowledge of God

In yet another realm, Paul's theological amplification of the theme of justification was expressed in a way that linked it to the daily life of all human beings who lived in the first century. Like those to whom he wrote, Paul himself felt the impact of the socioeconomic reality of inequality in the Roman Empire. In his theology of sin (*adikia* and *hamartia*) and of the justice of God and the action of justifying (*dikaiosynē theou* and *dikaioō*), which Paul developed in Romans 1–3, he did not mention the empire explicitly. He spoke of impieties and injustices of those human beings who imprison truth in injustice (1:18), and he maintained that there is no one capable of doing justice. But a study of the Roman situation from the perspective of the poor immediately makes the connection between the power of sin and the socioeconomic situation; between the justice of God and the justice of the empire; between the grace of God that grants God's justice as a gift (in the face of the practical impossibility for any human being to realize that justice by his or her own power) and the merit system of status, wealth, and power that undergirded the imperial law.

Paul seemed to see in the systems of the Roman Empire a structural, economic, political, and military power impossible to confront. Therefore those specific institutions acquired the dimensions of an overarching structure of sin *(hamartia)* that leads to death. Paul saw the institutions of the empire as a system that, under the guise of being the protector and pacifier of the provinces, hid in its own bosom the practice of injustice. For Paul this practice of injustice was equivalent to the absence or ignorance of God—in short, idolatry.

The absence of justice that is an absence of the true God led Paul to reflect theologically on the reign of sin since Adam. The Roman Empire was neither the first nor the only instance in which peoples suffered domination. Therefore, he concluded, there must be something deeper in human nature that both makes one responsible for injustices and ensnares one in them. In any given moment the injustices themselves acquire autonomy and turn themselves into structures of social relations marked by sin—structures that are uncontrollable and that enslave all human beings.

On the other hand, Paul could not find in his own day any expression of justice that had the seal of truth. The Jews thought that by fulfilling the law they were doing true justice, but Paul proved the opposite: Though they wanted to do the justice dictated by the law, the result was injustice (Rom. 2:21–23). The authorities even killed Jesus by following the law! Sin, then, was shown to be able to make use of the law itself.

The Revelation of the Justice of God to Benefit All

Paul wrote to communities made up of believers who had already been baptized, and who supposedly were already leading a new life. However, the context in which they lived was hostile to them: They were suffering hunger, oppression, and discrimination. That being the case, Paul interpreted the theme of the justice of God in opposition to the supposed justice—in fact the lack of justice—that tangibly affected those communities.

The term "justice of God" has a number of different connotations related to forensic justice, to the just way God has always acted in history, and to a justice that God hopes human beings will carry out. These various connotations all point to the difference between this justice of God and the other types of justice (both forensic and social) that the Christians of the first century experienced. The forensic justice they encountered was discriminatory, and what passed for social justice represented its own lie, namely injustice.

Since there was no objective or subjective possibility for an individual person to do justice in an unjust world dominated by sin, the proclamation of the justice of God came as great news. Paul simply reminded them of that justice, because it had already arrived with Jesus—in his life, death, and resurrection. Recalling that justice gave security and confidence to the Christian community. In addition, recalling God's justice opened the horizon of hope, because with the freely given justice of God, which makes a person just despite still being a sinner, the communities could take their stand, doing justice with valor, even though that meant going against the stream of the dominant society (2 Cor. 4:7-12).

Paul concluded that, given the precariousness of life and the impossibility for human beings to overcome what makes them at once the victims and the perpetrators of injustice, the justice of God empowers them truly to do justice. Jesus was the first such agent of justice, and through him all others have access to this empowering grace of God. Even those who victimize others can be empowered to do justice, if the victimizers are able to believe in the God who raises the dead (Rom. 4:24-25). This faith in the impossible (Rom. 4:19) strengthens the believer in her or his daily existence, struggles, and dangers (1 Cor. 15:31-32).

Clearly Paul's principal intention was neither to contrast divine and human initiative in the doing of justice, nor to contrast works and faith. Beginning from concrete reality, Paul considered it impossible for any creature to realize either justice or justification by his or her own merits. Paul spoke simply and realistically, and working from that base he posited a just and loving God who does not allow human beings to fall into their own traps or to cause others to fall to their death in turn.[5] According to Paul, God had to intervene in history to announce the news of the transformation of human beings into sisters and brothers, and into subjects who do justice, as a grace-filled consequence of the faith of Jesus Christ and the believers' own faith in the one who raises the dead.

The Divine Within the Human Being: Power to Confront the Unjust World

The Christian communities in Paul's day were insignificant from every point of view—socially, culturally, religiously, and militarily. Paul, however, assured the Christians of Rome that if God is with them, no one can be against them (Rom. 8:31). Nothing can separate them from the love of Christ—neither the sword, nor hunger, nor persecution, nor oppression (Rom. 8:35-36). Paul intended to give both security and confidence to the communities to which he wrote, reminding them of the revelation of the justice of God in history through the medium of Jesus Christ. But that was not simply the purpose or aim of God. What was important was God's effectiveness: that God's purpose would in fact be fulfilled in those who conducted themselves according to the Spirit (Rom. 8:4). In other words, God's justice would actually be done by those who believed that Jesus was resurrected, and whose own lives reproduced Christ's image (Rom. 8:29). The way of justice is the totality of Jesus' life of faith—the commitment in solidarity of his life, death, and resurrection. Paul used the verb *dikaioō*, "to justify," to express the gift of God in making the human being able to do justice.

The apostle appealed to the divine power within humankind, since when people receive the gift of justice by faith, divinity becomes part of them, for they "live in Christ" or "are in Christ." Consequently, their thoughts, attitudes, and actions take shape according to God's own logic. Paul could thus make the theological affirmation that such human beings are children of God, heirs of God, and heirs together with Christ. It appears to have been important for Paul that the baptized person recognize the strength of his or her own spirit and of the Spirit that unites itself with the believer, in order to bear witness that the believer has the power of God. The believer has this power because he or she is a free child of God (Rom. 8:15-16). When one is thus justified by God, one ceases to be a slave of the law and of sin. One becomes a son or daughter of God and reigns in history (Rom. 5:17).

CHAPTER SEVEN

JUSTIFICATION BY FAITH AND THE THREATENED LIFE OF THE POOR

LAW OF EXCLUSION, REIGN OF DEATH

In order to carry out a rereading of justification by faith from the perspective of Latin America, it is important to begin with the threatened life of the poor.[1] That threat against the poor has been provoked by a specific human project. That project is characterized by the drive to accumulate possessions, not by the goal of guaranteeing the basic necessities of life for the majority of the world's people. Oriented as it is toward guaranteeing freedom of choice and preference for a consumer society—the possibility of selecting one's favorite from among a variety of available products and brands—that project excludes in its very design a vast sector of human beings.[2] The life of the poor is vulnerable and permanently threatened until the logic of this project is reoriented toward providing instead for the basic vital necessities of all people.[3]

The poor, who are excluded from the dominant economic project because they do not have access to basic consumer goods, are not all alike. They have many faces, and their degree of marginalization and oppression varies by their class, color, ethnicity, and sex. However, despite these differences, poor people are united by the logic of exclusion. Their precarious life has a public face disfigured by misery and humiliation. In summary, they are dehumanized.

Justification has been correctly understood as a synonym of humanization.[4] However, generally that interpretation has addressed only the psychological dimension of the human being: feeling oneself free from guilt and recognizing oneself as a finite subject without the necessity of constantly being reassured before God, others, and oneself.[5] This interpretation is not sufficient in a divided world where the excluded are irrupting

129

into history.[6] There is a profound connection between the psychological dehumanization that leaves one with a craving for approval as a human being, and dehumanization that is corporal, cultural, and social—that is to say, where one can feel the scars of malnutrition and insignificance.[7]

Death lurks between hunger and insignificance. There the reign of sin is granted legitimacy by the law of exclusion. It is a reign of death, not because sin is dead, but because sin kills. Sin itself is very much alive, and its life maintains itself by absorbing the blood of the excluded. What is at stake is an idol—not something false or in some sense unreal, but something that truly exists, and that imposes itself as sovereign.[8] Killing is not its original intention, but since its justice is oriented toward giving life to only some people, the rest remain excluded. Their life is threatened and put at risk by the logic that sustains itself by exclusion. Anguish is added to the experience of hunger or to the threat to life. The same anguish that diminished the life of Luther because of his insecurity about his eternal salvation is translated today as the anguish that the poor experience in their concrete life, where they are threatened by hunger, repression, and insignificance.

This reign of sin has a logic oriented toward death, and to that end it drags along everything it encounters in its path. Every law that grows from roots in this reign is condemned to the attraction or pull of the logic of death, even when the law itself might be good or intended to support life. Furthermore, what Paul observed in the practice of his contemporaries was that even those who had a just and holy law were incapable of doing justice. The sinful reign itself remains unjustifiable and only brings upon itself the wrath of God. For in a definitive way the truth has been imprisoned in injustice, just as it was in the time of Paul, precisely because of its supposed goodness and piety.

Behind this reality one can read a theological parody linked to freely granted justification, but by its opposite pole: justification by merits. The system oriented by criteria of productivity and privilege proclaims salvation by means of the law of maximum profit (realized today in the privatization of the production of both goods and services). It is the law of merit. All those who want to be recognized by the world as worthy subjects, and thus to save themselves, must submit themselves to that law on its own terms. Since salvation is achieved by merits (social, economic, and cultural criteria of worthiness), many people remain outside and are lost. These are the "condemned of the earth." There is no pardon for them because the system knows neither the dimension of grace nor that of faith. Even the single proposal offered as a way out—that of a loan—leads also to death, because the payment of the debt is death.[9]

This necrophilic reign, though seeming to be eternal because of its ability to accommodate and readjust itself to new circumstances, carries in its bosom the seed of its own condemnation to complete destruction, not only that of the excluded. For in the long run, this reign amounts to death for everyone. Killing another human being and the world that surrounds him or her destroys one's own self as a human being as well.[10] Dehumanization is thus present not only in the poor and insignificant person, but also in the assassin and the powerful person. In the act of killing, every human quality is lost and replaced by irrationality. There is no place for affection, love, zest for life, or even the will to live. This logic thus condemns everyone to death—assassinated and assassins alike. All are condemned to nothingness, to eternal death. And if this sentence is carried out, God disappears from human history, because God is the God of the living.[11]

However, despite the power of this reign of sin, those who believe (as Paul did) that the grace of God abounds the more wherever sin abounds (Rom. 5:20) are aware of another logic empowered by the God of life. The sentence of that logic of grace turns into justice for all, and the justice of God is revealed in order that there might be life in abundance (John 10:10). Since that justice and abundant life are for everyone, they are not rewards offered selectively. On the contrary, God's justice reacts against privilege and preference. The preferential love of God for the poor expresses precisely God's opposition to all attitudes that marginalize others. God's effective love consists in there being no more poor people because poverty itself is abolished. By fulfilling the commandment to love one's neighbor, one seeks to overcome all discriminatory favoritism.

Through love for the excluded person, the logic of grace declares a kind of amnesty that rejects the death sentence both for the condemned and for the one who condemns to death. When condemnation is rejected and a sentence of life is proclaimed for all, condemnatory logic loses its value and disappears. This proclamation is a promise or affirmation that pertains to the "long time."[12] It is eschatological and thus valid also in the "short times" of history, for all who believe.

Therefore, prior to justification in the classical sense of the term (meaning forgiveness of sins and the exclusively forensic declaration of justice), there is a proposal that effects life for all people, which is justification in biblical terms, and a proclamation of the death of sin.[13] Justification leads to a process of life-giving, where the one who sustains life is the one who raises the dead and calls into being that which does not exist.[14] This is the promise to which the poor cling out of faithfulness to themselves (that is to say, to their condition as human beings), or, what amounts to the same thing, out of faithfulness to their Creator.[15] Created by the God of life, with the vocation to live as brothers and sisters[16] and to give life, they have the destiny of recovering their authentic humanity—their creation in the very image and likeness of the God of the living. They are representatives of a humanity that has been trampled by the other who exhibits a mutilated image of God. For, as Leonardo Boff says, the entire creation, including humankind, is "called by God in order to form with God a radical unity in the richness of diversities."[17] Those who are "conquered and humiliated" have a future, and the "conquerors and opportunists" find a meaning in life.[18]

THE RECOVERY OF THE IMAGE OF GOD

The first sign of life is the recovery of the image of God in humanity choked by sin, where death lies in ambush in hunger and insignificance.[19] It is a matter of feeling the pulse of God "in the depths of Hell," and of experiencing grace on the garbage dump.[20]

Human beings were created by God in the divine image and likeness in order to live together, to have and to give life. Whenever a person kills or is killed, the divine image is broken: There is dehumanization, and God is absent when the divine image has been broken. The task of recovering the vocation of life is paramount in a society that thoroughly denies that vocation because it is constructed not on the foundations of the God of life, but around an idol of human creation that now demands human sacrifices.[21] The unbeliever considers such a task to be absurd and scandalous. Even for the believer it is an enterprise that can be carried out only in the realm of the impossible: How indeed can one encounter the image of God in death?

The mere idea of the revelation of God's justice declared for all eternity is, by itself, insufficient to equip men and women to recover their authentic human image, which is the image of God. That justice must instead be revealed on the boundaries of human history,[22] and it must be revealed in the body. For just as injustice is characterized by mortal wounds, so also justification must show the marks of a fruitful and abundant life. The encounter between human beings and God (the divine-human encounter) is thus indispensable in the course of "measurable times."[23]

Though all human beings manifest a broken image of God (the victimizers as well as the victims), God chooses a meeting place so that God's image might be reproduced in every living being. God makes this choice not in order to exclude some people, but precisely in order to negate exclusion by including all people, beginning among those presently excluded. God's "preferential option" is to begin with the excluded who cry out to God in their abandonment—who know that they are excluded and who demand from the God of life the end of God's absence.

In the cry, "My God, why have you forsaken me?" or "how long?" or "why?" one can feel the pulse of the divine image in the human being. In the beating of the human heart it is clear that, though the divine image has been broken, it has not been completely destroyed. In that step of speaking *to* God and not *about* God, and of knowing that God hears, hope is born in life. The desire for life revealed in the cry of the oppressed is what discloses the image of the God who, before speaking, listens to the sufferings of God's people.[24] In knowing that they have been heard, and in entering into dialogue with the God who listens, the excluded recover their divine image that conveys the dignity of the human being, as a person and as a subject of history.

Faith in the possibility of life illuminates the divine image in the human being. This faith in the possibility of life holds on to faith in the solidarity of God that occurs in the manifestation of the human God. In the humanity of Jesus we encounter that solidarity of God.[25] The written revelation itself teaches that. There is a close relationship between Jesus and the excluded. The history of the excluded can be read in the ancient story of the life and death of Jesus on the cross.[26] This story, in turn, reveals to us in all its crudeness this present reign that usurps the position of God, displaces the Son, and breaks the divine image in the human being. The justice of God is revealed in the history of the concrete life of faith of Jesus of Nazareth who died and was raised, and that same life reveals the injustice of the reign of death, of sin, and of the law.

The source of this revelation of God's justice is in faith in the resurrection of the one condemned to death on the cross. That faith that reveals God's justice is not faith in death itself. If it were faith in death, there would be no difference between Jesus and all the innocent people crucified in his time, or even since the time of the prophets. Nor are we talking about faith in the resurrection by itself, for a number of religions in the Hellenistic world also had gods who were raised from the dead. Rather, revelation is found in believing that God raised precisely the excluded one who—even though he was just in God's eyes and in the eyes of the poor—was crucified.[27] Jesus Christ on the cross is thus the excluded person par excellence.[28] In the most critical moment, Jesus was abandoned by all, including by God and by his friends.[29] From the cross, Jesus cries out his abandonment, and there the excluded one bears the sufferings of God.

But there also God the Father shouts the verdict: justice and justification for all—a verdict diametrically opposed to the condemnation to death of the excluded. The verdict of justice for all—justification (Rom.

4:25)—is carried out in the event of the resurrection of Jesus, the excluded one. By Jesus' being resurrected after the cross, all people are made just. We are justified by the merits of Jesus Christ, realized in his practice that brought him to death. In contrast with Adam, it is Jesus' work of justice that obtains all justification (Rom. 5:18), and it is by his obedience to God's will for life that all are constituted as just (Rom. 5:19). Jesus is thus the first of many to be resurrected, and therefore also the first of many to be justified. In him the promise of the resurrection of the body is a promise made possible for everyone (1 Cor. 15:20-21).

The excluded—by being aware that their history coincides with that of this God-human who, despite having the dignity of a God, nevertheless cries out like them—recover confidence in themselves.[30] For, as Bonhoeffer says, "Only a God who suffers can save us."[31] The excluded recognize that they are not alone, that God is with them crying out in unison with them, as God was in the Son. There the power of faith in the one who conquers death on the cross begins to blossom. Being justified implies recovering by faith the image of God and the dignity of the human being created for life, and re-creating that life in justice. This is the experience of justification by faith, granted in the judgment of God in one's favor.

There is no room in such a moment of celebration for a debate about the opposition of faith and works! The experience of feeling oneself to be a worthy human being, a subject able to make decisions in history, capable not only of resisting but also of transforming the reality that kills, invokes only an experience of gratitude. Life is received as a gift that is worth defending, because there the totality of the human being is at stake.[32]

SOLIDARITY AS THE ROOT OF JUSTIFICATION

The roots of justification as the affirmation of dignity and justice are thus anchored in solidarity: God is in solidarity with humanity in Jesus Christ, the prototype of the excluded.[33] In this way, God summons all men and women on earth to the practice of brotherhood and sisterhood based on God's justice. It is thanks to the solidarity of God, manifested in Jesus Christ as the first among many, that the human being rediscovers his or her divine image as a being justified by God. It is by means of the practice of solidarity that justification becomes tangible.[34] "Christian praxis is not just the consequence of an interior *metanoia* but also the way in which that *metanoia* is turned into something *real*, as opposed to something merely felt or pondered in thought."[35] We interpret solidarity as a symbol of justification in two metaphors: the solidarity of friends in the fruitful encounter of the two *logoi* "God" and "human being," and the solidarity of sisters and brothers in the gift of relationship.

Solidarity of Friends, Fruitful Encounter in Justification

We have spoken of two types of discourse: the eschatological affirmation that justice has been revealed in Jesus Christ,[36] and the immediate cry of the excluded one: "My God, my God! Why have you forsaken me?" They are two types of discourse that proceed from different initial words (*logoi*) that must be joined in order to be fruitful. If they are not united in a common syntax, they will be words thrown into the wind, which will show no more than the impotence of a frustrated faith. The task in our present world is to enable the first *logos* to respond effectively to the cry of the second, and the second to recognize in God a companion in solidarity. In order for that encounter of the two *logoi* to take place, it is necessary to take into account the concrete realities of time and space.

The word of the excluded is a real cry, emerging from a body that has been disfigured, and from a spirit that has been distorted by insignificance. If to be fully human means to share with others the destiny of a common history, and to have access both to the substance that nourishes life and to the celebration of life as grace, only with great difficulty can human qualities be discerned in this second *logos,* the cry of the excluded.

The word of the revelation of the justice of God is also real, but not corporal. It is real because it can be believed and assumed in the specificity of human lives, and thereby generate that justice in human history (as indeed happened in Jesus Christ). The proclamation of the revelation of justice shows itself as "the dream that makes praxis effective."[37] But it is not corporal, because it is grace, a gift granted as communion and summons to the one who believes.[38] It is also not circumstantial, because it is a cry pronounced from eternity.[39] It is universal, and for that reason its truth only shows itself in circumstances and in that which is corporal.

The revelation of the justice of God and the cry of the person made destitute by exclusion are brought together in the time and space of Jesus Christ. From his childhood to the climactic moment of his death, there is a relationship of mutual solidarity between Jesus and the poor, but the passion is the climax of the common ground shared by the hidden God and the excluded human being.[40] In this climactic historical moment, in an image of God that is unrecognizable and shocking because of the effects of torture and insignificance, the two excluded *logoi* are joined by mutual love: love of the Son for the excluded and love of the excluded for the crucified one.[41] The marginalized person becomes aware of his or her image as excluded like God, and aware also of the love of that God, who is in solidarity with him or her. The life of the marginalized person is made fruitful by a love whose purpose is the quest for life for all, and the rejection of every logic of exclusion.

At stake is nothing less than the power of the faith (as it is expressed in the popular hymn) "of the poor person who believes in the poor person." In that mutual confidence we encounter within history itself the solidarity of God with the excluded, and from that beginning point, solidarity with all other people as well.[42] Whoever is capable of perceiving and believing that precisely in that shame-filled corner is where one encounters the deliberate and solidary presence of God, is capable of being a friend of God.[43] God calls that person "friend," just as God called Abraham "friend." Solidarity becomes another symbol of life, an image of God. It is the response to the cry of the excluded one—the first sign of life.

Solidarity Between Sisters and Brothers, Symbol of Justification

A paradigm of the solidarity of God through faith is the Trinity. That paradigm is seen not only in the perfect relationship of communion among Father, Son, and Holy Spirit, but (understood from the angle of justification) also in the work of the three divine manifestations in the very process of justification.[44] Paul himself points to the full participation of God in the event of justification. By taking on the weakness and precariousness of humanity in faithfulness to the Father, Jesus, the incarnate Son, becomes the brother of all. All those who have faith in the surrendered life of the Son are converted into his sisters and brothers. When they are converted into sisters and brothers of the Son, the Spirit is united with their spirits in order to pronounce the Word proper to the Son: Abba, Father (Rom. 8:15). All who pronounce that word make themselves sons and daughters of the one Father who adopts them by divine grace. By trusting in the same Father, all are transformed into sisters and brothers of one another. What comes into being is precisely that brotherhood and sisterhood which defends, shares, and celebrates life as the essence and vocation of the human being.[45]

With this new image every expression of egotistical individualism is destroyed. The human being in general is justified precisely in order to be reconciled with herself or himself, with the neighbor, with God, and with his or her own center. And the human being is justified in order to carry forward the ministry of reconciliation (2 Cor. 2:15-18). Solidarity among human beings is a symbol of the solidarity of God. Without it, there is no justification whatsoever. Now, authentic solidarity does not proceed from the works of a law that demands justice in order to achieve justification. If merits themselves are a requirement, there is no real solidarity of God.[46] Brotherhood and sisterhood—being able to be a sister or brother—is a gift that we receive in gracious relationship to the Son. Therefore we recognize that gift itself as made with "divine material," inseparable from the Holy Spirit. It is a project of life without end, eternal, but that still has to blossom. As González Faus recognizes, brotherhood or sisterhood is "the face" and "historical display" of our adoption by God.

> [Sisterhood or brotherhood] is not a *subsequent* precept, disconnected (or able to be disconnected) from adoption, but rather its realization and demonstration. It is what converts into a "new" thing the "old" commandment (1 John 2:7-8). And it is that which has made it possible for a person to cease having his or her own spirit (which is a spirit of master or servant) and to be transformed into having (or, better put, being able to be grasped by) the Spirit of God.[47]

Solidarity, then, is opposed to the law that requires merits or achievements. The latter marks a distance between the acting subject and the loving subject, and it runs the danger of suppressing the spontaneity of unconditional love. The work of grace (or of faith) is born of the free deliverance of the sons and daughters of God to their vocation of giving life, living, and celebrating life in gratitude. A good example of the justified person is in Matthew 25:31-46. There the poor are helped by grace, with no second thoughts—that is to say, without rationalizing that such action is in one's own self-interest, because God is present in them, and that one is therefore really serving God.[48] In fact, if an act is done for love of God, and not out of regard for the life of the poor, it is done according to law and not grace. Solidarity comes from grace and develops in grace.[49]

Therefore, one does not love the neighbor out of love for God, but out of love freely given for the neighbor. To love God is to love the neighbor without secondary motives. To act out of that love is to act with the same grace as that with which God received us. If solidarity is given "for the love of God" in an interested manner, one is following the logic of works of the law and not of grace. "Whoever believes one loves in an unmediated way an isolated God, and God alone, loves an idol, for one can only love God (1 John 4:20) on the horizon of 'that which can be seen,' and that is the brother or sister."[50] Finally, whoever acts out of love for God in order to accumulate merits negates the justification that is freely given, because that person continues to be under the regime of the law and not of grace.

THE COMMUNITARIAN CELEBRATION OF GRACE

It is true that to write about grace today is a challenge. In order to speak of the grace of God in Latin America, one must enter the world of the poor and excluded. It is difficult to speak from a distance. For the more one seeks grace, the more one encounters only dis-grace.[51] Words written by an objective pen tend only to sketch the thirsty skin of a body that begs for justice. The lips only read the wounds of insignificance and indignity in the subhuman condition of the poor and marginalized person. Therefore, to speak of grace here as the forgiveness of sins is an irony for the poor. One needs faith and courage in order to be able to look beyond the visible and the objective, and one needs imagination in order to write about the promise of life for all. Without this dimension, which is even a dimension of gratitude, theology totters and stumbles when it finally manages to discern the gravity of sin at this point in history, and the cynicism of its agents.[52] And the exhortation to love the neighbor ends up hanging by a thread or trembling in the resonance of an echo that repeats it a thousand times without there being anyone who can effectively give it substance. Despair takes over, and the ghost of a feeling that one is powerless to express hope.

But the fundamental thing is to recognize not the reality of exclusion or of anti-life, but the favorable time of salvation (Rom. 3:21; 2 Cor. 6:2).[53] This news is reason for a great joy and it is only effective and pleasing, despite the cost, when it is shared and communicated with those whose lives are threatened. Speaking of this propitious time of salvation, Paul uses a strong imperative to call people to the ministry of reconciliation between human beings, since without reconciliation, grace turns out to be in vain (2 Cor. 5:20; 6:1-3).

When those whose lives are threatened and those who have faith in the solidarity of God recognize this love that sustains their existence, they celebrate life as a gift—as grace. There is no way to do that in secret, privately. The excluded are many, and insofar as they recognize themselves both as the excluded and as those favored by the triune God, they tell one another the history of this solidarity of God, and they celebrate it.

All who recover their divine image give meaning to suffering or view it with objectivity. They discern the dimensions of life and death in their world, and they wager on the superabundance of grace in the face of the abundance of sin.[54] That is why they lodge their confidence in God and can, with the confidence God gives them, celebrate life in the midst of death. They can do so because they do not believe in the victory of death, but in the triumph of life for all, guaranteed by the resurrection (1 Cor. 15:55-58).

This collective memory of the passion and resurrection—the memory of God's solidarity with humankind—is celebrated both in the breaking of the bread and in everyday life. "Do this in memory of me" are words of Jesus that resonate as a perennial challenge and as an action of grace in the community. "Do this in memory of me" is more than the ritual that we call the "Lord's Supper." It is sharing the bread and wine in friendship[55] in the Christian community and in everyday life, and forgiving one another one's offenses. Julio de Santa Ana reminds us that it is an event of many meanings:

Communion is a reminder of liberation, it is a commitment to the Reign of God, it is an expression of a militant community, it is a mystery of the presence of Jesus Christ with all who believe, it is a motivation toward unity, it is food and power to remain strong in the struggle that the development of the mission of the people of God requires. . . . It is an intense feeling at the same time that it is an illumination of the mind. It is a motive for obedience to God and a summons to the exercise of hope.[56]

But communion also involves looking death in the face—the particular and real death of an innocent person, the one sent from God. Communion demands the recognition that the human being is capable of killing unjustly under the guise of legality. It is "to confess that we killed when we rejected life in its truth and reality."[57]

Only the celebration of life and justice as a gift for all can bring one into a communion of equals. At the communion table there is no place for the logic of exclusion. Therefore it is affirmed, rightly, that grace has a character that is intrinsically social and communitarian.[58] It is possible to celebrate the festival of communion even when one's life is in danger, because in justification, the place of sorrow and lament gives way to confidence in God as a friend with whom one lives in solidarity.

Furthermore, the community is never alone. In the midst of times of struggle and when life itself has to be defended, the community has the assurance that there is someone who keeps watch in the vital times of rest.[59] The dimension of grace allows the symbols of life—which at the end of time will be life in all its fullness—to be celebrated, feted, and enjoyed already now, in the historical meantime.

The communitarian celebration of grace includes life and the body. Justification is related to the affirmation of life, and life is related to the body. Human life is not lived without a body, nor is a body a human being without life. When life is affirmed, the body is affirmed. When the body is affirmed by grace, one experiences the desire to live, the desire to feel life, a zest for life. Then one believes in the resurrection of the body.[60] The resurrected body is the body of the community that proclaims life for all and keeps vigil so that all can have life and celebrate in communion with one another; and it is the body of the person who enjoys life in all its dimensions. That celebration is the *fiesta* of the oppressed.

According to the Scriptures, the community of those justified by faith is the body of Christ (1 Cor. 12:12-27). It is a body of bodies with life—a consequence of baptism (Rom. 6:3-4)—because it is founded on the resurrection. The living bodies are the ones that give life to the body that includes them. But it is the body of the entire community that keeps watch, defends, and proclaims the right to life of all as an inalienable gift from God. The reality of the Trinity is a challenge that is always present. It is a communion that invites people to live it and to experience it. By its very nature, the reality of the Trinity rejects every sort of exclusion.[61] Therefore, no one who is justified by faith[62] can accept any project of life that excludes the life of anyone, for that exclusion itself negates the purpose of the project, which itself is communitarian. The struggle for life ceases being a cursed burden like that of the first Adam in the sterile land (Gen. 3:17). Despite its difficulty, that struggle is marked by the hope of the resurrection of bodies. It can be celebrated beforehand, both privately and publicly.[63]

The present-day church is being challenged to reaffirm this experience of life and grace among its members. Similarly, it is being challenged to rediscover the surging pulse of God in those places where it least appears that God is breathing, in order to rescue those people whose lives are threatened, even when they do not form a part of the particular body that is the church. Those people, like all whose lives are threatened, are the principal recipients of the proclamation of the justice of God and of justification: life for all.[64]

CHAPTER EIGHT

JUSTIFICATION
AS THE AFFIRMATION OF
THE LIFE OF ALL

THE GIFT OF BEING SUBJECTS OF HISTORY

In light of the discussion thus far, it is possible to affirm that the act of justification by faith makes men or women subjects of their own history.[1] The power of justification consists in the following:

a) It makes human beings worthy persons, conscious of their right to life, their right over every law that kills, a right that is inviolable because it proceeds from the grace of God.
b) It allows one to discern sin and recognize the capacity of human beings to destroy and exclude their neighbors, acknowledging that every human being is a sinner: The justified person can never forget that he or she is a sinner.
c) It allows people to know that men and women are not alone in the defense of and struggle for life. The solidarity of the Triune God in justification has given them the security of God's company even though they are sinners.
d) It goes to the extreme of making the human being not only a friend, but also a part of the divine lineage through Jesus Christ. The poor then immediately recognize that they are human beings of dignity and worth, in that they recognize that they are part of that divine lineage.

The fact of the justified person's power as subject of his or her own history leads to an examination of that person's relationship to the law, faith, and the sovereignty of God.[2] That implies taking up again core issues we have already examined, adding new data, and, as a result, finding new richness in the meaning of justification.

141

THE POWER TO TRANSGRESS THE LAW:
THE FREEDOM OF GOD AND THE IDOLS THAT ENSLAVE

Prior to the experience of justification, the human being does not control his or her own life. In a world of inverted values, with a necrophilic orientation, the actions of some obey selfish interests that are generated by the logic that strives for the life only of some privileged beings. The poor are not excluded from this enslavement as both victims and accomplices, for they are equally slaves to the same logic that marginalizes them.[3] Their situation reflects a demonically evil paradox: Either they fight to the death in order to enter the same competition of the market but on a lesser scale, or else they rob and kill one another in order to be able to live, for life is the ultimate purpose of the will of God. In other words, God wants the human being to live, but in order to be able to live in a present-day society, a person must be an accomplice in sin.

In this situation the law is imposed as legitimator of that anti-life dimension that is called "sin." "Law" is used in the broad sense to refer to the logic of the entire socioeconomic and cultural system, which includes the laws of the market, judicial law, and the implicit and explicit norms of a way of life. Similarly, sin is understood as a social and historical fact, including the absence of brotherhood and sisterhood and of love in relationships between people, the breaking of friendship with God and with other human beings, and, consequently, inner division within the human being as well.[4] All who live within this logic turn into slaves. They do not have the ability to decide or to act on their decisions. The law has usurped its place because sin has taken command over the law, and consequently the law functions according to the standards of sin. Under these circumstances the human being is not able to pursue his or her own longings for life and liberation. Instead, what he or she does is to fulfill the requirements of the law. At this point it does not matter whether one does good or evil, because the result always leads to the knowledge of sin (Rom. 2:17-23; 3:20). The fruit of one's action will be legitimated or censured by a law that has been taken captive by sin. In this complete inversion of society, to fulfill the law is an act of sin, for sin is expressed in the law. Sin "acts through the law and uses the law. . . . Sin operates through the legal structure and its prevailing law, and not through the transgression of the law."[5]

Human beings, then, cease to be truly human because they have ceased to be free. Their right to decide was stolen by the law. Although the law is personified and praised, human beings are dehumanized by the power that kills, and that is hidden inside the law. It is not coincidental that in

142

limited democracies and dictatorships there is a constant elaboration of laws whose purpose is to "maintain order." In the face of that crushing reality, it is important to recognize that, with the eruption of the logic of life in Jesus Christ and verified in justification by faith and not by works of any law, the excluded recovered their ability to distinguish God's truth about themselves and about others. Together with this discovery they also became aware of their freedom as historical subjects, participants in the divine lineage,[6] by being children of God and brothers or sisters of Jesus Christ.

Moreover, the experience of justification by grace through faith in the one who raised the Son from the dead leads persons who are excluded to discover dimensions of both collective and personal life that are profoundly liberating.[7] They are freed not only from the stigma of insignificance with which they have always been evaluated by the society that excludes them, and which they have internalized by the power of the sin of discrimination, but they are freed as well from the fatal feeling of incapacity for deciding their own destiny as historical subjects. In that freedom, the excluded will recover confidence in themselves, self-affirmation, the loss of fear of deadly forces that diminish the human being and superimpose themselves in the uncertainty and despair that gnaw away at life. The poor are called to be "protagonists with God."[8]

At the same time, by discerning with the aid of the Spirit the gravity of sin and its agents that was brutally manifested in the crucified one, the excluded person recognizes the capacity of every human being, including himself or herself, for destroying the life of others. This recognition that one is a sinner, as well as that one has the right to be a subject of history, is profoundly liberating for the excluded person and for all victims of sin. It permits them to carry out constant, critical, self-evaluative reflection, and realistic projection of a meaningful future. Moreover, as Sobrino indicates, "The eradication of historical sin can be empowered by the recognition of one's own sin and by the acceptance of pardon."[9] On the other hand, becoming conscious of the fragility and power that are part of the human being makes satisfying and welcome rest possible.[10] All these dimensions must come together into expression in attitudes inherent in the subject who creates history, which is the task of every man and woman. The following fragment of a poetic discourse of Frei Betto summarizes the profound significance of the experience of justification of the forgiven sinner. The subject is the justified person who already lives in the new logic of faith that leads to life: his or her power, fragility, and will as subject, and the constant accompaniment of God as a mother.

God is a mother. Neither necessary, nor superfluous, self-giving, with no strings attached. Already in the endogenous dryness, he knew, with the third eye, that no alternative remained: divinity had oozed under his skin, twisted itself like a cobra around every one of his bones, flowed in his veins, transpiring through every one of his pores. That made him frighteningly free, which was transforming him into a rash sinner. Filled to the brim with love, he was traveling against the stream of the itinerary of the elect and was welcoming those who were feeling themselves condemned by heaven and earth. He embraced Christianity as a religion of sinners and not of saints. In it he learned the theophanous exercise of following Jesus. Finally he placed his confidence in this ultimate certainty: he could wallow in excrement, smear himself with mud, fall again shamefully, meriting the repudiation carried in every glance, tottering raggedly between precepts and conventionalities like a cat on a table of crystals and porcelains. For God, like those mulatto women of the marketplace—obese, eaten away by a hard life—who by the bounty of destiny encounter a man to love, would go to find him, shelter him, drag him unwillingly to the house and, protesting loudly, with their breasts in anguish and swelled with pain, would spend the night caring for him.[11]

Those who are called children of God, incorporated into the logic of faith that has as a criterion the life of all, are—we insist—the ones who wager on the superabundance of grace in contexts where sin and death abound (Rom. 5:20; 8:35-39). The law is not excluded from this orientation of faith, but rather can take it on and be reshaped by it (Rom. 7:12).[12] For every law that is oriented by this logic and that serves the needs of God's creatures, is established by God (Rom. 3:31). That confirmation of the law is not marked by its fulfillment or transgression in itself, but rather by its characteristic of supporting the basic necessities of life for every needy human being. That was Jesus' attitude toward the law: He transgressed it in the process of confirming its function (Matt. 12:9-13; Mark 2:23-28; 3:1-6; Luke 6:5-10; 13:10-17; John 5:1-18).

Faith in the one who raises the dead always has priority over the law. Faith has the power to glimpse beyond the known; it is "a permanent invitation . . . , a project for the human being insofar as it grants him or her a new vision of things, a new relation with other people, a new hope for the becoming of history."[13] The law, in exchange, because it operates only within given mechanisms,[14] cannot affect the essence of the mechanism that imprisons it, but instead is confused with it. Therefore, the person who is justified by faith has the power to transgress every law that is not at the service of the production and defense of the real life of all. That is why the life of the human being is above every law that wants to dominate him or her, making him or her into a slave.

SOVEREIGNTY AND TRUST IN GOD

To affirm that the God of life takes possession of the human being does not imply that the latter returns to being a slave—now a slave of God—with no space of one's own to be a subject. To say that God takes possession of the human being is probably a poor choice of words. In reality, the affirmation of God's claim over human beings is expressed doxologically, with the desire that, in the midst of this history that is so hard and so burdensome for the excluded, the just and liberating spirit of God might guide them—even in the face of a feeling of objective powerlessness—in order to oppose the power of the idols that enslave them. That desire is expressed in their complete trust and gratitude for the mercy of God. It is for this reason that every obstacle that is conquered is celebrated as the power of God in the human being.[15]

A god who demands the life of the faithful or makes them into slaves in exchange for justification is not the God who justifies by grace, or who calls "friend" the person who has faith in the resurrection of the dead. The God who justifies is not the father who gives birth to his children only in order to take their lives later. On the contrary, the God to whom the gospel bears witness deprives of authority and condemns to death everything that threatens the life of God's people, and every law that condemns the human being to slavery. The glory of the Father is in seeing God's sons and daughters mature in freedom and justice to the stature of God's Son, by faith—a capacity that is granted by the gift of justification.[16]

To speak, then, of the sovereignty of God in the life of free women and men is equivalent to saying that they have taken the true position that corresponds to them as human beings on the earth. Their position is not as beings inferior to God, but simply as God's creatures summoned to live worthily, to give life to all, to defend it, and to enjoy it in communion with others. The sovereignty of God coincides with the realization of the human being. The sovereignty of the idol coincides with dehumanization.[17]

The trust that exists between God and God's children is mutual. Curiously, theology has emphasized the absolute trust of human beings in God, but little has been said about the trust of God in God's own creatures, despite the many times God has been betrayed by them. On the one hand God has justified by faith, without taking into account past sins, because God trusts in God's creatures, God's own creation. On the other hand, all who receive the gift of justification recover confidence in themselves as subjects who create history, because God has liberated them from the slavery of the law, of sin, and of death. But their confidence in themselves is solid because they trust that in everything their task is sustained by

145

the Holy Spirit. And they place their trust in the God of life, because they recognize that human beings are sinners, that they have the potential to kill others and to destroy their environment. As Míguez Bonino observes, Christian faith facilitates mature praxis, because a Christian, declared and made a historical subject by grace, does not have a self-image to protect.

> [A Christian has no] need to justify himself or herself by the unobjection-able nature of his or her actions or orthodoxy; one does not need to give to one's achievements any value apart from their importance for the neighbor; one need not reclaim "correctness" for one's action. The Christian can offer his or her praxis to the fire of criticism, totally and without restriction, in confidence in free grace, and likewise can offer her or his life, totally and without restriction, in the hope of the resurrection.[18]

Mutual confidence is generated on the frontiers of faith.[19] The law, on the other hand, faithful to its intrinsic logic, remains confined by the limits of suspicion. Therefore, the justified person does not trust in the law, but rather is suspicious of the truth it claims to express. Because of its fragility and the lack of life and dynamism within it, the law can fall captive to sin and lies (Rom. 2:21-22; 7:7-13). Wooden obedience to any law signals the degree of slavery and submission of the one who fulfills it outside the system of faith. On the contrary, free and mature fulfillment of the law that is subjected to the service of the neighbor is based on the trust of the human being. That trust is lodged *in the believer himself or herself,* as a son or daughter of God and a brother or sister and follower of Jesus Christ; *in God,* as the one who gives life to all, for all eternity; and *in the Holy Spirit,* as a companion on the way, a defender and comforter who is bold in the face of the logic of the law.

We can affirm, then, that the justified person has been re-created by God to be the subject of a new history. By faith in the resurrection, he or she has the power and the right to transgress every law that kills or threatens the life of human beings.[20] Faith in the sovereignty of God over every other order gives the justified person the authority to transgress or not to fulfill any law that is turned against any human being, or against the environment.

There is no danger of misunderstanding or manipulating this God,[21] because the God who justifies all human beings, even when they are sinners, does so in order to be in solidarity with the poor and insignificant—with those excluded from history. That break from the traditional ways of conceiving of God's nature and way of acting annuls every attempt to reclaim one's own sovereignty in history through egotistical and exclusivistic interests. If humankind is ruler of history, they are that insofar as they are in the lineage of God. Their authority comes "from above," from the relationship with God in Jesus Christ. That "sovereignty in history" does not reflect a person's relationship to other men and women, nor to God from whom one receives the gift of being a historical subject. Instead it is an expression of humanity's freedom relative to the idolatrous mechanisms of domination that want to enslave people, taking away their right to decide the destinies of their own history. It is in this sense that the wise words of Luther, read from the perspective of those who opt and fight for the life of all, turn out to be highly pertinent: "A Christian is a perfectly free lord of all, subject to none. A Christian is a perfectly dutiful servant of all, subject to all."[22]

Thus, then, the revelation of the justice of God for all, actualized in justification, is sustained by the sovereignty of God over the whole creation. The sovereignty of the human being in history is legitimated by that sovereignty of God over the universe, because all things belong to God. We understand, then, that the sovereignty of God is not expressed over against God's creatures who live according to the logic of faith. Instead it is opposed to the idols of death that try to displace God, and to their agents who remain under the regime of the perverted law and promote it in order to impose themselves over the God of life and to dominate God's sons and daughters. Therefore it is important to emphasize the sovereignty of God in the face of other gods that are false precisely because they neither give life nor liberate those threatened with death.

It is clear that what is at stake is not a confrontation between two powers (God and the idol) who compete for supremacy. What is at stake in that "struggle of the gods" is the affirmation of the life of the human being, who can be the subject of his or her own destiny. The establishment of God's sovereignty in the midst of the world takes place precisely so that the sovereignty of individual human beings and of peoples might become a reality able to neutralize the idols that enslave men and women in order to dehumanize them. In this sense, it is the sovereignty of the oppressed person that God defends, because, in God's own sovereign free will, God has granted that sovereignty to people as a free gift in justifying them by faith.[23]

In summary, it is not God who enslaves, but the idols, for they are the ones who steal life and every human capacity for decision. The sovereignty of the true God is reaffirmed not over against the realization of the human being, but over against the idols who kill. Faith that God is sovereign conveys power to the human being to transgress every law that threatens the life of human beings—especially the life of the most despised—and that harms the integrity of the creation.

FAITH AS THE WAY OF JUSTIFICATION

The Power of Faith in the Impossible

The attitude of faith is the key that allows Paul to include all the excluded people of all periods of history. Thus, Abraham, who did not have the privilege of the Mosaic law to teach him the ways of justice, was made just by faith (Gal. 3:6; Rom. 4:9-12). Paul does not proclaim that everyone has access to the privilege of the law in order to allow those who have been excluded from it to enjoy that same privilege. In other words, Paul's gospel does not authorize the law for all, in order that all might be made just by its works. That would be one way to include the excluded, and many (such as the Jewish Christians and in particular the Judaizers) had just such an expansion of the privilege of the law in mind. Instead, for Paul it is the way of faith that leads to the new life God gives, and that enables one to receive it. The way of the law—any law whatsoever—is unable to accomplish that task.

"The just will live by faith." For the oppressed, the core importance of that sentence is neither in faith nor in the one who is just in himself or herself. Rather, the accent is on the result: the possibility of life. One's faith is what guarantees that possibility. If the law would guarantee life for all when its justice was fulfilled, it would have the same value as faith. However, in a context of objective cynicism,[24] of inverted meaning in which the truth is presented as a lie and the lie as truth (Rom. 1:18), laws turn out to be ineffective because they legitimate lies. They enable the person who is not just, or the thing that is not just, to seem to *be* just, and in so doing, they legitimate death itself.[25]

The law, then, is unable to generate justification. Faith is the only human attitude that is possible in the face of the justifying action of God. But this faith, in order to be effective, has to ground itself in a solid hope, in something that not only believes itself to be true, but that *is* true. In the grave situation of the "objectively cynical" world, where death attacks in the guise of legality, what is needed is not only a faith that affirms the hidden presence of God in solidarity with the excluded. Equally necessary is a faith that is convinced that there is a power that can overcome the powers that deny life. Faith again becomes hope for the impossible, but that does not mean false hope. In biblical terms, such a hope is equivalent to believing in the resurrection of the dead, or in the God who raises the dead.[26] On the plane of what is possible, such a hope is equivalent to being convinced that the world of death can be transformed. The basis of that certainty is that in the revelation of the justice of God, the right of all people to live with dignity as human beings and as subjects of their history on this earth has been made manifest, despite the power of the forces that tend to abandon the majority to death. The active expression of such a hope would be equivalent to affirming that justice can be done in order to transform this world where death abounds,[27] despite the laws or even by transgressing them, because God, in God's grace, has made and declared us to be just by the faith of Jesus Christ, and we believe that for God nothing is impossible,[28] for God raised Jesus from the dead as the first among many.

Now, faith in what is not feasible in history—the resurrection of the dead—needs convincing assurances ahead of time, if it is to be a faith of deep conviction.[29] In the case of the resurrection, that faith is grounded in the recognition of a saving eschatological event already anticipated in the past, which would continue to be effective in the present as the guarantee of a promise. The resurrection is clearly not the final act of God, nor the destination toward which God has been moving. For God is an active God, and the resurrection describes God's persistent activity, which through the negation of pain, frees history for the future.[30]

Two sources help to ground this stance of faith. The first and central one—source of sources, which nourishes faith in the impossible—is the christological event. The fact that "those who believe" are justified by "the faith of Jesus Christ" (Rom. 3:22) points toward two dimensions of faith. The first symbolizes the totality of the life of faith of the Son of Nazareth, patient and long-suffering, who did not falter even when he faced death on the cross. This faith-trust-obedience of the Son made possible the justification that is freely granted to all, with no strings attached (Rom. 5:19). Therefore we affirm that we are justified through the merits of Jesus Christ. The other dimension of faith is faith in the one who raises the dead (Rom. 4:24-25), who gives life to "that which is not" (Rom. 4:17). The faith that God raised Jesus of Nazareth after his death on a cross is the faith that verifies justification, liberation, and the gift of life. For we believe that Jesus' resurrection was not unique, but rather that Jesus is the first among many (1 Cor. 15:20-23). This same conviction of the heart also leads to justice (Rom. 10:9). As Míguez Bonino observes, "The resurrection of Jesus *is* in itself (and not only 'means' or 'causes') our resurrection, our justification, the defeat of the powers, the power of their death, the general resurrection, the active presence of Christ."[31] This faith in the hope of fullness of life leads to the conclusion that it is worthwhile to live, to defend life, and to struggle for it. Therefore faith is not in vain (1 Cor. 15:14), because we believe in the power of the God who conquers death.

But we must not forget that we begin from a painful reality that keeps the cross always in focus, but that at the same time projects itself actively toward a future full of hope: in the words of Alves, "In theological language: the resurrection is the child of the cross."[32] Similarly, Sobrino insists that whenever we speak of the resurrection, we must ask ourselves who has been resurrected.

> Jesus' resurrection is not only a symbol of God's omnipotence, then—as if God had decided arbitrarily and without any connection with Jesus' life and lot to show how powerful he was. Rather Jesus' resurrection is presented as God's response to the unjust, criminal action of human beings. Hence God's action in response is understood in conjunction with the human activity that provokes this response: the murder of the Just One. Pictured in this way, the resurrection of Jesus shows *in directo* the triumph of justice over injustice. It is the triumph not simply of God's omnipotence, but also of God's justice, although in order to manifest that justice God posits an act of power. Jesus' resurrection is thus transformed into good news, whose central content is that once and for all justice has triumphed over injustice, the victim over the executioner.[33]

The other source that supports faith even in the resurrection of the dead is faith in what has been accomplished in history, before and since the time of Jesus of Nazareth.[34] The justice of God is recognized in those who have believed in the God who creates life or raises the dead (Rom. 4:17, 24). Paul gives us the example of Abraham, a character known for his faith (Genesis 15). In fact, we can see that because of his faith Abraham did not kill his son (Genesis 22), even when the logic that prevailed in his day supported the sacrifice of the firstborn child. According to Hinkelammert, the faith of Abraham, or what was new in his obedience to the voice of God (or of an angel), was not that he obeyed the logic of going out to sacrifice his firstborn son, as was the custom. Such obedience would in no way have been original. The valiant faith of Abraham can be seen instead in the second part of the account when, in radical contradiction to his culture, he decided to respect the voice that said, "Do not kill your son."[35] Abraham was justified by faith because he did not kill his son—because he trusted in that voice of God heard outside the law, which invited him to follow another logic, that of *not* sacrificing. In order to save his son, he transgressed that law which demanded that one kill one's firstborn child. Similarly, in Romans 4:19 Abraham is presented as believing the impossible when he believes that despite physical "laws," he will have children in his old age.

In addition to examples like that of Abraham from before the time of Jesus, there are also present-day examples of faith in the resurrection. They are the testimonies of Christians, followers of Jesus, who struggle daily for life and on behalf of life. Many of them are martyrs who believe not in death but in the resurrection. Through faith in the resurrection, they are able to surrender their lives for the lives of many.[36] Their struggle is guaranteed by faith in the resurrection of the body, not in an abstract resurrection, removed from history.[37] The Pauline term "resurrection of the body" offers continuity and discontinuity with our history. According to Míguez Bonino, it is in the resurrection of the body that this paradox reaches its fullness.

> The first concept allows Paul to underline the continuity at the same time, in that the reconcilable identity between both is affirmed at the same time as the transformation of our present historical life. Such transformation is not a disfiguring or a denaturalization of our bodily life, but rather its completion, its fulfillment, the elimination of corruptibility and weakness. Far from losing itself, only in the resurrection does bodily life achieve its true form, its full meaning: communion, love, praise. The resurrection—far from involving the rescue of a spiritual element of human life that is purified from the bodily experience and bodily identity that is achieved through the process of growth—is the total redemption of humankind. It effects the true and unlimited realization of a bodily life purified from self-deceit and from the search for oneself (the flesh) and perfected in transparent (glorious) unity of purpose and experience (spiritual) and full communion with God.[38]

Thus, faith is grounded not only in the certainty that the Triune God is a faithful companion in the sufferings of the poor and excluded. It is grounded also in the power of God. God is the all-powerful one who raises the dead. For that same reason, the believer can confess with courage that Jesus is Lord, and not only the one crucified and excluded by the rulers of his time (Rom. 10:9). The affirmations of Jesus as the excluded one of history and as Lord of history express parallel and yet contrasting truths. The first affirmation is based on the cynical reality of the exclusion of the many people with whom Jesus is in solidarity. The second is based on the negation of that exclusion under a new project of life in which those who suffer with Christ are also glorified with Christ (Rom. 8:17). But the lordship of Jesus, like the sovereignty of God, is proclaimed in order to liberate those who are slaves to other masters, not in order to enslave Jesus' followers. Jesus Christ is the elder brother and heir together with the excluded (Rom. 8:17). They call themselves servants of Jesus only to the extent that they reject the role of being masters who enslave their neighbors.

In summary, Míguez Bonino concludes that faith in the resurrection of the dead is far from being "an egotistical grasping of one's own life, nor is it a compensation for the sufferings of this life, nor is it a projection of unrealized dreams."

[Eschatological faith is] the confident affirmation of the triumph of the love of God and of God's solidarity with humankind. It is the testimony of the permanent responsibility of humankind for the creation, and the testimony of humankind's participation in love, which is the ultimate justification of every struggle against evil, destruction, and death.[39]

The Following of Christ: Substance of the Faith That Justifies

The resurrection *reconfirms* the validity of the ministry of Jesus, his struggle for life so that all might have life (John 10:10). We see that without faith in the resurrection, faith is in vain. Now, to have faith in the resurrection without having that faith operate in love for the life of all turns out to be equally vain (James 2:15-26). For the substance of faith is neither believing in the cross, nor believing in the resurrection, nor even believing ecstatically in both. The substance of the free gift of faith is believing that he, the crucified one through whom we are justified, is the first of many raised from the dead, and that therefore it is worth continuing in the life of faith that Jesus lived.

The struggle for the defense of physical life gives consistency to faith; it forms a central part of following Christ (discipleship). "The following of Jesus is the *totality* of the Christian life. And precisely in its quality as following, and not pure imitation, it is the *process* of achieving the realization of the Christian life."[40] Thus, the death of Christ reveals the quality of the life of faith that God received, in order to make us just by a free gift, and it reveals also the power of the injustice that kills. The resurrection reveals the judgment of God in favor of life, and it strengthens and guarantees the hope of faith. But following the life and commitment of Jesus gives substance to faith. In other words, the dimensions of faith, hope, and love are intertwined, but it is love that gives consistency to the other two dimensions (1 Corinthians 13).

In other words, the Christian courage of one's own resurrection lives on the courage to overcome the historical scandal of injustice. The hope that is necessary in order to believe in Jesus' resurrection as the blessed future of one's own person passes by way of the practice of the historical love that gives life here and now to those who are dying in history.[41]

The gift of justification that leads to life is granted to everyone,[42] but that gift that is granted through Jesus Christ is received and made visible when one follows Jesus and, in so doing, struggles with the authority of a child of God on behalf of the life of those who are threatened. Faith is thus operative and effective because it is realized in love (Gal. 5:6). One is justified by grace in order to be able to do the true works of justice that are also accomplished by grace. Those works are manifested as unconditional and disinterested love and charity for the neighbor, freely given · with no strings attached.[43] That grace-filled work of justice is the divine image in the human being acting through faith. According to Sobrino,

> Those who defend the life of the poor with mercy, with truth and propheticism, with solidarity and responsibility, with surrender and hope, are re-creating, in historical fashion, the very mercy and tenderness of God, God's own truth and love, God's surrender to the very end on the cross of Jesus.[44]

The work of faith is not a product of the law, a work that has value in itself, independently of whoever performs it and of the neighbor whom it serves. For it is not "a work marketed in order to buy 'justification,'" says Míguez Bonino. "The work of faith . . . is not objectivized, but is the believer acting out of love."[45]

In times of severe repression the work of faith sometimes leads to death and to the sacrifice of one's own life. That has happened in the past, and it continues to happen.[46] However, since the faith of the justified person is grounded in the God who raises the dead, he or she knows that death is not the final word of God. Even death does not diminish hope. A person who has been justified trusts in the Triune God as one who is in solidarity with those who suffer and as a God who is powerful. Faith in what is impossible for human beings but possible for God is the source of a mystery that gives power (Rom. 8:37), as can be seen in the myriad testimonies by and about our present-day martyrs in Latin America. The Helsinki Document expresses that point in the following way:

> It is an encouragement for all of us to know that there have always been men who have lived their lives in conformity to Christ and who in the conflict with the evil powers of the world have even submitted to death in the power of the resurrection. Through the resurrection of Christ the cross has become a sign of victory for all who have given their lives as a testimony to Christ and his coming.[47]

The action and accompaniment of the Spirit, not only in its function of enlivening and comforting, but also as one who calls to conscience and consciousness, make possible that "obedience of faith" of the person who has been justified by grace.[48] Without that presence of the Spirit in solidarity with humankind, the risk of unfaithfulness would be continuous and discouraging. For no subject, even one who has recovered the divine image and been transformed into a new man and woman by justification, is exempt from sin. This sort of reading of justification as affirmation of

153

life demands that one always stay alert to the possibility of one's own sin, just as one is always alert to receive the forgiveness of God. The affirmation that in Christ we are made in the lineage of God, with the power to transgress laws that enslave human beings, must be accompanied by its parallel truth, namely, that every human being is also a sinner.[49] Such an approach would avoid any attempt to justify human sacrifices, by claiming that one has divine authority against those who offend God. In other words, this avoids the danger that one will be metamorphosed into the child of an idol.[50]

On the other hand, as Sobrino indicates, the concrete realization of love "is beset with errors and sins," and "when it is expressed in certain stages of the revolutionary struggle, many negative, historically inevitable, by-products appear."[51] Thus, the accompaniment of the Spirit is indispensable. Like an intimate companion in the following of Christ, the Spirit has the function of showing us Christian militancy through paths of honesty and humility. At the same time, the Spirit works to strengthen us and remind us of the dignity of the sons and daughters of God (Rom. 8:16) in the hardest moments of the struggle for life. The Holy Spirit will defend us and comfort us whenever we are accused or harassed by the forces of death.

CHAPTER NINE

OBSERVATIONS ON THE MEANING OF THE SACRIFICE OF CHRIST, JUDGMENT, AND FORGIVENESS

INTRODUCTION

The approach we have taken to justification as the affirmation of life has led us to reformulate the traditional connection of that doctrine to the redemptive work of Jesus centered solely on his death as a salvific sacrifice necessary for the expiation of human sin. Our key for reading Paul's writings on justification has been neither the cultic nor the legal one, for though Paul used them, they are not central to his thought. Instead, our emphasis has been on the resurrection, which Paul considered vital in justification, and which puts the cultic-legal focus to one side.[1]

The route we have chosen obviously excludes the theory of penal satisfaction, which claims that it was necessary for God to make a bloody sacrifice of God's own Son in order to satisfy divine justice and to obtain forgiveness of sins. That sacrifice would have been understood as the redemptive work necessary to satisfy the debt that humankind incurred for having offended God through sin.[2] In fact, today many efforts have been expended to disconnect that theory, which has usually been elaborated in abstraction, from the historical facts about Jesus' death.[3]

A reading of justification as the affirmation of life also transcends this sacrificial interpretation. If in Romans justification has its roots in the freely given solidarity of the Triune God with the excluded people of history, God cannot at the same time demand the spilling of blood of the excluded par excellence as a condition for reconciling the world with God. Such a theory is wholly contradictory to a liberating God, the God of life, who reclaims justice for the innocents and life for all.

However, it is appropriate to reexamine several dimensions of the sacrifice of Jesus Christ, the judgment of God, and forgiveness, since classically they have been related to justification. For example, the reading of sacrifice proposed by François Varone proves to be in keeping with our reading of justification.[4] He affirms that access, communion, and fullness are fundamental aspects of sacrifice in the Bible. As a ritual, sacrifice is a symbolic act through which the people can approach God in order to encounter in communion with God their own fullness. The letter to the Hebrews presents the sacrifice of Jesus Christ in this sense. According to Varone, the whole life of Jesus is perceived as an access to God in the framework of the sacrifice given "once for all."[5]

According to Hebrews the four constitutive elements of that sacrifice are: (1) *existence*—to do the will of the Father; (2) *death*—the result of practice (the veil is torn);[6] (3) *access to perfection*—access, communion, and perfection in arriving at the Father: God makes Christ perfect, savior, Great High Priest; and (4) *the proclamation of faith*—Jesus is the precursor. Our reading of justification with an economic and political key can include all four of these dimensions.

However, our interest in this final chapter is not to reread justification from the cultic-legal plane. Rather, we are interested in examining in detail certain aspects of sacrifice, judgment, and forgiveness, with the same interpretative key used earlier to read the doctrine of justification. Although much of what we address here has already been explored in the foregoing pages, we have not explained the liberating meaning that these three themes might have if they are seen from the perspective of the excluded.

THE LIFE, DEATH, AND RESURRECTION OF JESUS CHRIST AS THE END OF HUMAN SACRIFICES AND OF THE LAW THAT KILLS

The paschal faith sees in the death and resurrection of Jesus the end of the ritual sacrifices required by the Mosaic law for the forgiveness of sins. With this event not only the sacrifices themselves were deauthorized, but so also was the law that demanded them and the focus on the Temple with its sacerdotal system that mediated the granting of forgiveness.[7] If that is the case, the meaning of paschal faith lies in:

1) Limiting the authority of the politico-religious powers with a hegemonic claim to mediate between God and human beings. By being presented as the sufficient, once-for-all sacrifice (Heb. 7:27), Jesus Christ breaks the process of exclusion. All people have access to God because God has received humankind in Jesus Christ.

2) This apparently endless vicious circle of sin-expiation-forgiveness, sin-expiation-forgiveness, which does not change in any fundamental way the situation of human beings in the concrete dimensions of life, is finally overcome. This fundamental change comes about through justification by grace through faith, empowered by life in the Spirit. With Jesus the reign of God—or, in Pauline terms, the revelation of the justice of God—was inaugurated.[8] Because of God's love of the excluded, God's justice justifies all people, transforming them into new beings oriented toward life, without taking into account their past sins. The aim of the human being is not to wait for the day of the Great Expiation, but to be transformed into a son or daughter of God and to live like the Son, according to the Son, and with the Son, "reproducing his image" (Rom. 8:29).

The first interpreters of the life, death, and resurrection of Jesus used traditional Jewish sacrificial language in order to proclaim the end of the ritual practice of the priests of the Temple. It is not meaningful in our present context to speak of redemption using the language of sacrifice, propitiation, or the blood of Christ that was appropriate to the Jewish ritual schema.[9] The redemption of Jesus Christ cannot be reduced to his death. His redemptive work appears already in the incarnation. All of his life is salvific, including his death and resurrection.[10] Current Christologies from Latin America and from other latitudes emphasize this broader understanding of the redemptive work of Christ.

But it is a fact that the use of sacrificial ritual language has been internalized by many believers because of the emphasis on it in the tradition. What constitutes a serious problem today is the use of this sacrificial language by the dominant economy. Hugo Assmann and Franz Hinkelammert show how the sacrificial theological discourse runs parallel to the purposes of the neoliberal economic system. The traditional concept of death as necessary for the salvation of all translates the economic claim that people need to accept sacrifices, in the hope that at some future time they will manage to obtain the goods and services necessary for life.[11] If the inequitable economic system has used sacrificial theological language to accomplish its goals, there is something perverse or ambiguous in that language.[12] It is therefore crucial to take up again the theme of sacrifice in order to reread it from another angle.

It would betray the intention of Paul to affirm that the event of the crucifixion of Christ by itself—in abstraction from his life—was necessary for justification, salvation, or forgiveness. All of Jesus' life forms a part of the redemption.

> Our theology of the cross must be historical. Rather than viewing the cross as some arbitrary design on God's part, we must see it as the outcome of God's primordial option: the incarnation. The cross is the outcome of an incarnation situated in a world of sin that is revealed to be a power working against the God of Jesus.[13]

As Assmann affirms, the death of Jesus is not necessary in order to accomplish a particular purpose, but rather is the inevitable result of a specific cause.[14] The cause is Jesus' freely given love for human beings that is expressed in his history, to the extreme of giving his life for them. It is his courageous practice that leads to his death. Because of his faithfulness in fulfilling the will of the Father on behalf of God's creatures, they kill Jesus on the cross. The Father, faithful to the identity of a merciful and liberating God, confirms the ministry of the Son, redeeming the Son from death through the resurrection. Even though that death was not necessary in order to effect redemption, it turned out to be *inevitable* in the actual course of events.

The resurrection, on the other hand, was *necessary* in order to conquer death and to give life to its victims. The resurrection, however, was not inevitable, if God had not been revealed as the God of life. The resurrection was necessary for the confirmation of the practice of Jesus that leads to life, and for the justification of all those who believe in the God who raises people from the dead. The resurrection was necessary in order to show that it is worth following in the steps of the resurrected one, when the gift of the Spirit is received, for the Spirit is the actualized and dynamic presence of Christ crucified and risen. The meaningful presence of the Spirit in the event of justification also breaks the fixation on an ahistorical understanding of Christ's sacrifice.

Relative to expiation, José Comblin affirms that to expiate sin does not mean to suffer a punishment, but, on the contrary, to perform a protective gesture that suppresses the danger of sin, and that removes the evil of sin from this world. Therefore the one who expiates is God; the human being is the beneficiary. He continues, "In the sacrifice of Jesus there is no punishment. His death was not a necessary condition in order for God to forgive. God accepts his death because God was disposed to forgive."[15]

What is fundamental about the sacrifice of Christ is that the work of Jesus on the cross not only unmasked the injustice of human sacrifices of all times, but it also declared the end of such sacrifices.[16] Christ's resurrection severed at the roots any legitimacy that might be attributed to them. Julio de Santa Ana indicates that when we try to understand the meaning of sacrifice in the New Testament, we find ourselves facing a reality different from the sacrifices that the idols of the market demand:

In the first place, it is Godself, incarnate in Jesus Christ, who is sacrificed. God does not require that others be sacrificed. The God of life, the one who opts for the poor in order to make them heirs of God's Reign, does not present Godself as a terrible father, a castrating authority. That God is a God who loves and who for that very reason does not require from human beings more than they can give. Jesus definitively abolished sacrifices. That leads us to a second affirmation: through the generous offering of Godself in favor of the cause of the poor, it is possible to say that there is no reason for more sacrifices. The abundant life that Jesus claimed to bring for human beings (John 10:10) does not require new expiations, new holocausts, new immolations.[17]

An economic system that demands the sacrifice of innocent people in order to be able to function well is intolerable. Theologically, according to the justice of God, in justification human beings have been transformed in order to live in dignity and to struggle for the life of others, and not in order for the system to live at their expense. For when the system continues to live at the expense of innocent people, it acquires the characteristics of an idol that demands sacrifices of human lives in order to be able to maintain itself.

The *necessary* sacrifices fall under the reign of the law, of sin, and of death. It is in this realm that the wrath of God is revealed, for that wrath is "against the impieties and injustices of the human beings who imprison the truth in injustice" (Rom. 1:18). All of that which (or everyone who) would speak of the necessity of human sacrifices negates the resurrection of Jesus and thereby also justification by grace. That is to say, such a person or thing denies the true God, who raises the dead, and despises the death of Christ on the cross.

THE JUDGMENT OF GOD IN FAVOR OF INNOCENT VICTIMS

It is important now to take up again the issue of judgment as a whole in its forensic expression, but read within the same interpretative framework and using the same interpretative key. We have observed that the laws that have been held captive by the logic of sin lead to the condemnation of the excluded. Since these laws have been elaborated in order to effect and to legitimate a way of life that is exclusive, the marginalized are not able to fulfill these laws, and thus are condemned to death. For example, by not having the power to participate in the law of supply and demand, one is condemned to hunger and insignificance, which leads to death. By transgressing the law of national security, one can be condemned to death openly. And by submitting to the mercy of the law of rising expectations, one is condemned to the requirement of infinite sacrifice. The sentence is always the same: death.

Now, this mechanism and its "legislators" are not exempt from the death sentence either. On the one hand, the destruction by human beings themselves of the life of the environment in which they live is in itself an anti-human act, and it is turned against everyone and everything. On the other hand, just as the blood of the condemned claims justice from the giver of life, God condemns to death the assassin, because "the wages of sin is death" (Rom. 6:23).

However, the judgment of God is revealed against every condemnation (Rom. 8:31-37). It is revealed not only against the sentence of a system that kills, but also against a just sentence by the same God, such as the death sentence for homicide. Through the cry of the excluded ("My God, why have you forsaken me?"), and by the condemnation to death of all, the effective judgment of the living God is pronounced—the God who is known as the one who does justice for those who are destitute and helpless.

This divine judgment occurs in history, for the law that kills does so historically, that is to say, in the body and in the soul, by hunger and insignificance. The sentence of God's judgment unfolds in three parts: the right to life for all, condemnation to death for every logic that kills, and ransom of the law that is oriented by the Spirit who leads to affirmation—eternal enjoyment of concrete life. The pardon of the sinner is implicit in this process of re-creation and reorientation toward life.

Since divine judgment is both historical and eternal, it is real in "the short time" of history. Its effectiveness lies in the fact that it justifies human beings or makes them just, in order that they might do justice, and so that through that justice, all might live. The historical practice of this divine justice (granted with the gift of justification) signals the effectiveness of the judgment of God.

The guarantee of this judgment is eternal because it was written with blood in the very being of God in God's assassinated Son.[18] It is Jesus who recapitulates the history of the spilled blood of innocents and martyrs both before and after the death on the cross. As an advocate, he cries out his abandonment by God and at the same time—as an excluded person himself—proves the innocence of those condemned by the perverted justice of the powers that sit in judgment.

But this time, in contrast to times past, God was not guided by the standards of the just law—death for the assassin, life for the poor person. God's judgment, through love for the excluded, was carried out on the foundation of grace: unmerited grace for all, new life based in justice. The sentence "death for the assassin" and "life for the poor person" is a just law, merited, but limited even for the poor themselves, because of their condemnation to the infinite repetition of their oppression. Therefore the African theologian and political leader Canaan Banana, son of a continent both exploited and discriminated against, affirms: "Distasteful as it might be to victims of oppression, the oppressor has to be liberated along with the oppressed."[19]

The privileged historical moment when judgment was pronounced was in the death and resurrection of Jesus.[20] The Jewish and Roman authorities judged and condemned to death the excluded man from Nazareth. That was the human judgment incarnate in that time: to condemn to death the innocent for going against the logic that excludes. But God also judged and pronounced sentence in the resurrection: life for the excluded person and an end to the death of innocents. The resurrection is the judgment of God,[21] in opposition to the condemnation of the powers that kill. By restoring him to life, God declared Jesus Christ, the condemned person par excellence, to be just.

The sentences of God the Judge are carried out in interhuman history: On the third day God raised Jesus as the first of many, and Jesus talked and ate with the disciples, who became witnesses of Christ's glory. Thus, in this judgment that has many meanings, God declared innocent all who have been condemned and excluded. God accomplished that through the redemptive work of Jesus Christ, in which God pronounced a judgment of life for all people. At the same time, God did not condemn the guilty to God's wrath, because in this new moment, God did not take into account anyone's sins. The historical expression of God's judgment (life for all) in the resurrection is justification by faith in the one who raises the dead: God's creatures can now do justice, because they have the possibility of receiving the Spirit that leads to life.

The way of the justified person is faith. This is understood as *faith* in the resurrection. It is also *trust* in the eternal solidarity and power of the Triune God with those who are excluded, so that they, in turn, will not fall into the temptation to marginalize others. Finally, this faith includes the *availability* of the human spirit to receive the Spirit of Jesus as an inseparable companion in the practice of and search for the vocation of the free son or daughter of the God who does justice.

In other words, the judgment of God is the resurrection, but the epiphany of the resurrection appears in the new humanity. As Bonhoeffer said:

> The risen Christ bears the new humanity within Himself, the final glorious "yes" which God addresses to the new man. It is true that mankind is still liv-

ing the old life, but it is already beyond the old. It still lives in a world of death, but it is already beyond death. It still lives in a world of sin, but it is already beyond sin. The night is not yet over, but already the dawn is breaking.[22]

LIBERATING FORGIVENESS

We have said little about the dimension of forgiveness in the event of justification, because we have concentrated our attention on the experience of justification of the excluded person. In fact, the experience of such a person is oriented more toward the freely given solidarity of God that increases his or her human dignity as a daughter or son of God, giving him or her the power to change the world. The praises of God as omnipotent and as the one who forgives, or as a faithful friend in the struggle for life, emerge from gratitude for God's justice revealed in Jesus Christ. Unfortunately, the oppressor who is a sinner arrives at the awareness of sin only with difficulty. Paradoxically, it is the poor who maintain it, whether by traditional piety or by a new liberating piety.[23]

But it is evident that forgiveness is also present in and is even a consequence of justification. We understand pardon in the work of Jesus Christ in the following way: In order to give abundant life to all human beings, Jesus acted above the law when it was a matter of favoring the excluded. The Jewish and Roman authorities did not pardon the transgressions of Jesus, and they condemned him. Acting in concert with the law of their time, they killed him. In judging by God's own justice the actions of both the crucified innocent and the crucifiers, God decided to raise the innocent one from the dead and to justify human beings, transforming them into doers of justice. By judging in this way, God pardoned the crucifiers and condemned to death the logic that leads to human sacrifices. All people are saved by God's grace. The centrality of justification is thus the affirmation of concrete life against the logic that kills. We have observed several times that this logic that condemns to death does not arise from nothing. Human beings are responsible, through self-centered desires for self-enrichment or through insulating themselves against solidarity. And there is no person who is exempt from this human weakness: In sin also, human beings are connected as sisters and brothers (Rom. 5:12-14; 7:14-24).

Moreover, it is appropriate to speak of justification by grace because in the process of justification of the creature, God not only grants it freely, with no strings attached, but God also does not take into account the sins previously committed (Rom. 3:25). God's desire is more to save or to liberate than to forgive. God transforms God's creatures because it is God's will that they should live with dignity their own history in communion and solidarity with God and with one another. Therefore, according to Bonhoeffer, "This forgiveness within history can come only when the wound of guilt is healed, when violence has become justice, lawlessness has become order, and war has become peace."[24] According to Gustavo Gutiérrez, to recognize one's own sin implies also the will to restore broken friendship and leads to asking for forgiveness and reconciliation. The capacity for forgiveness itself creates community.[25]

Two truths run parallel in the human being: He or she is a son or daughter of God, created in God's image, and he or she is at the same time a being capable of killing a brother or sister. Both truths must be taken with the same seriousness as is faith in the one who raises the dead. It is the event of justification by faith that, through the Spirit, makes possible the acceptance of both truths. On the one hand, it makes its members arms of the justice that leads to life (Rom. 6:13) because it frees them from enslavement to the law, to sin, and to death (Rom. 8:2). On the other hand, it reminds them of the freely granted forgiveness of sins that happened in re-creation. It is in this sense that forgiveness is liberating and generates liberation.

According to Sobrino, remembering the forgiveness of sins leads the human being to recognize the truth that he or she is also a sinner. Conversely, to recognize oneself as a sinner leads one to recall the forgiveness of sins.

> The forgiven one brings to liberation the memory of the sinfulness, real and always possible, of those who orient their lives toward a liberating practice. This memory is not, once again, masochistic: it is a salvific memory, just as is the "dangerous memory" of Jesus. For, even though it is demanding, that memory brings us back to truth, and to integrity with what is real.[26]

Thus, then, these realities of sin and forgiveness are dynamically correlative in the one who is justified by faith, and they constitute an unavoidable dimension in the spirituality of those who struggle for the defense of the life of all. The attitude of recognition of sin and of liberating forgiveness permits the justified one to accomplish the practice of justice with honesty, humility, simplicity, gratitude, and faithfulness to the liberating work of Jesus Christ.

The justified person does not seek to kill those who crucified Jesus, because in the proclamation of life for all, God has forgiven them. The justified person has the capacity for forgiving with the same grace as that with which God has forgiven him or her.[27] Thus, as Sobrino affirms, if the poor are the ones offended, the possibility of others' sharing in the for-giveness they have received from God will have to be mediated by them. The honest human being who recognizes his or her own sin in the pres-ence of those who are excluded will feel freed from guilt when he or she has been forgiven by God through them. The importance of recognizing in the poor those who can forgive is that one's own sin against them can be acknowledged. It is in this sense that "the availability to be accepted-forgiven is also one of the structural elements in the task of historically eradicating sin from the world."[28] However, the justified person cannot forgive the condemnatory logic of the system that excludes. Instead, on the contrary, the justified person continually struggles against that logic. The system that excludes comes under the wrath of God, and God has condemned that system to death.

CHAPTER TEN

JUSTIFICATION BY FAITH: GOOD NEWS TO THE EXCLUDED

In the preceding chapters we have developed a rereading of justification by faith from a context of oppression, marginalization, and struggle. Hunger and insignificance were the realities with which we began to examine the doctrine of justification by faith today. The key of exclusion allowed us to arrive at an understanding of justification not only as realized, but also as appealing to conscience: All people, not only a few, have the right to live with dignity as subjects, because life is a gift of God.

We departed from the traditional approach of focusing the interpretation of justification on the death of Jesus on the cross. We granted to the resurrection (as the "daughter of the cross") a central place in the same justifying act of God. This allowed us to underline the dynamic inherent in justification, and to hear justification by faith as good news for the excluded. The excluded are not simply human beings who stand forgiven before God, and who are thus empowered to do justice. They are also worthy historical subjects re-created for life, with the power to transform their history that has tended to marginalize the majority of the people. They are persons whose sins are not counted against them, because the will of God in Jesus Christ was precisely to liberate all people for life.

Finally, we identified several recent interpretations of the sacrifice of Christ, judgment, and forgiveness. We concluded that, from Paul's perspective, the death of Jesus was not a necessary condition for justification. The resurrection, on the contrary, *was* necessary in order to conquer death and give life to those who have been sacrificed. God's commitment to life for all people does not allow for additional human sacrifices. The judgment of God has been pronounced against every instance in which innocent people are condemned to death. In this view of God's will for humankind, every logic that demands human sacrifices is unpardonable.

Pardon or acceptance by God in justification occurs precisely in order to heal the wounds that sin has produced, and where there is no healing there is no justification.

We concluded that, by declaring human beings to be just and making them just, justification by faith (understood as the historical action of God that makes concrete the revelation of God's justice) is good news for the thousands of excluded people of history. There are several reasons behind that conclusion:

—By considering the solidarity of God as the root of justification, the excluded person is aware that God is present in solidarity in Jesus Christ, the excluded person par excellence, and also in all others who are excluded. This fact allows the excluded person to be aware that he or she bears the image of God. Heard by God in the figure of the resurrected Jesus Christ, the excluded person recovers his or her dignity as a daughter or son of one who is the same Father of all. And these sisters and brothers celebrate in community together the gift of life that is granted by grace. Exclusion is condemned because all have freely received the right to a life of dignity.

—Insofar as it is by faith and not by law that one is justified, the excluded person becomes aware of being a historical subject and not an object, either of the law or of a system that subjects her or him to marginalization. By being justified by faith in the one who raises the dead and brings to life that which does not exist, the excluded person is incorporated with power into a new logic. That new logic is the logic of faith whose criterion is the life that Jesus Christ brought, a life both dignified and free, that is granted to others. Faith in the resurrection of the body as the fulfillment of life on earth gives power to struggle and defend the life of all people.

—Incorporated into the new logic of the Spirit, whoever has this faith forgets neither his or her past as a victim excluded by sin, nor the possibility that he or she too subjects others to exclusion. Such persons know that they have been accepted by God purely by the merciful solidarity of God, not because they are just. The death of the crucified one reminds them always of the cruelty of sin that kills with the full sanction of the law. When the solidarity of the Triune God—as friend and as brother or sister—is received by faith, this presence of God through the Spirit turns into a permanent critical appeal to conscience in the paths of justice.

ABBREVIATIONS

AB	*Anchor Bible*
BZ	*Biblische Zeitschrift*
CBQ	*Catholic Biblical Quarterly*
CT	*Cuadernos de teología*
DEI	*Departamento Ecuménico de Investigaciones*
ER	*Ecumenical Review*
EstT	*Estudos teologicos*
ETR	*Etudes théologiques et religieuses*
EvT	*Evangelische Theologie*
IRM	*International Review of Mission*
LCL	*Loeb Classical Library*
NTS	*New Testament Studies*
RB	*Revue biblique*
REB	*Revista eclesiastica brasileira*
RevistB	*Revista bíblica*
RIBLA	*Revista de interpretación bíblica latinoamericana*
RLT	*Revista latinoamericana de teología*
RTP	*Revue de théologie et de philosophie*
ScEs	*Science et esprit*
SeBiLA	*Seminario Bíblico Latinoamericano*
TDNT	G. Kittel and G. Friedrich (eds.), *Theological Dictionary of the New Testament* (10 vols.)
TV	*Teología y vida*
VP	*Vida y pensamiento*
WW	*Word and World*
ZNW	*Zeitschrift für die neutestamentliche Wissenschaft*
ZTK	*Zeitschrift für Theologie und Kirche*

NOTES

INTRODUCTION

1. See, e.g., *Liberating Grace*, trans. John Drury (Maryknoll, N.Y.: Orbis Books, 1979), by the Brazilian theologian Leonardo Boff; and two books by the Peruvian theologian Gustavo Gutiérrez: *We Drink from Our Own Wells: The Spiritual Journey of a People*, trans. Matthew J. O'Connell (Maryknoll, N.Y.: Orbis Books, 1984) and *On Job: God-talk and the Suffering of the Innocent*, trans. Matthew J. O'Connell (Maryknoll, N.Y.: Orbis Books, 1987).

2. The Spanish Jesuit theologian José Ignacio González Faus devotes a large section of parts 3 and 4 of his book, *Proyecto de hermano: Vision creyente del hombre* (Santander: Sal Terrae, 1987), to the topic of justification.

3. See the discussion of liberation theology and the poor in the essays of G. Gutiérrez, L. Boff, I. Ellacuria, and J. Sobrino, in Julio Lois, *Teología de la liberación: Opción por los pobres* (San José: DEI, 1989).

4. I believe with Victorio Araya that sin is everything in us and in society that negates the will of God. Sin that is structural, social, and objective is the manifestation of sin that transcends the individual arena and becomes concrete in objective historical dimensions, with their structures, agents, and mechanisms: Thus, e.g., racism, militarism, infant mortality, and the foreign debt represent an embodiment of sin that contradicts the salvific plan of God. See Victorio Araya, *God of the Poor: The Mystery of God in Latin American Liberation Theology*, trans. Robert R. Barr (Maryknoll, N.Y.: Orbis Books, 1987), pp. 73, 104-6.

5. Raymond Fung, "Good News to the Poor—A Case for a Missionary Movement," in *Your Kingdom Come: Mission Perspectives* (Geneva: World Council of Churches, 1980), pp. 84-85 (Report on the World Conference on Mission and Evangelism, Melbourne, Australia, May 12-25, 1980).

6. The Spanish word *insignificancia* is difficult to translate. It refers to the negative assessment of poor and marginalized people by those more powerful. That assessment is internalized as a sense of one's own unimportance according to the world's categories. The criteria underlying it are sociopolitical or economic, and not the existentialist *ennui* or sense of the meaninglessness of life. In this translation, the cognate "insignificance" will be used to render that term (translator's note).

7. The phrase "right to life" in the Latin American context refers to the fundamental human right of all people to the physical and social necessities for sustaining a dignified life. The phrase should not be heard as meaning the same as it does in the legal and political struggle taking place in the United States over reproductive choice (translator's note).

8. Although of course the Bible has always been fundamental for Protestants, today it has

become a different book for many because of the new hermeneutical key of the poor. Since Vatican II, Catholics too have welcomed it as a central book, particularly in the ecclesial base communities. The rereading of the Bible is a continuing labor in academic circles as well as on the popular level. Consider, e.g., such recent events as the new collection of biblical commentaries on a popular level published jointly by Roman Catholic, Methodist, and Lutheran presses; the formation of the network of biblical scholars from all of Latin America; and the seemingly infinite number of journals, pamphlets, and small documents of biblical interpretation produced across the continent.

1. PERSPECTIVES ON JUSTIFICATION BY FAITH FROM LATIN AMERICA

1. This process in the theological task of beginning with the reality of oppression-liberation and of the experience of God in concrete life has been, from the beginning, picked up again and reformulated as a distinctive foundation of Latin American theology of liberation, and a constitutive part of its method. Gustavo Gutiérrez (*A Theology of Liberation: History, Politics, and Salvation*, trans. Caridad Inda and John Eagleson [Maryknoll, N.Y.: Orbis Books, 1973], p. 13) refers to this when he speaks of theology as "critical reflection on Christian praxis in the light of the Word." See also Juan José Tamayo-Acosta, *Para comprender la teología de la liberación* (Estella, Navarra: Verbo Divino, 1989).

2. On this first point we begin with oral tradition and experience (testimonies, evangelizing sermons, group discussions, informal discussions, family devotions, and study times). As far as we know, there is no specific bibliography that is the foundation for such use. However, in many of the more formal studies cited below, one can see the authors' concerns to overcome the individualism, dualism, subjectivism, and passivity of many Protestant Christians.

3. The popular Spanish translation of the Bible prepared by the United Bible Societies, with the title *Dios habla hoy*, has influenced that understanding by its usual translation of words with the root *dikaio-* as "free(d) from guilt," or "accepted by God" (Rom. 1:17; 2:13; 3:21-22, 30; 4:3; 5:1). See Victorio Araya, "Justificación y práctica de la justicia," *VP* 6 (1986): 19.

4. What is curious is that the traditional emphasis on the forensic aspect of justification is almost never mentioned. That may be due to the abstraction and sophistication of the argument as it is usually developed, and therefore its perceived alienation from the Latin American situation.

5. The same thing happens with theology of liberation. Criticisms, questions, and fears in the face of that theology are often the motives behind the old dispute over faith and works. See, e.g., Gottfried Brakemeier, "Justification by Grace and Liberation Theology: A Comparison," *ER* 40 (1988); and Vítor Westhelle, "O desencuentro entre a teología luterana e a teología da libertação," *EstT* 26 (1986). But the concerns transcend confessional boundaries. One of the questions directed to Gutiérrez during the defense of his thesis in the University of Lyon was about the relation between the theology of liberation and justification by faith. See Gutiérrez, "Lyon: debate de la tesis de Gustavo Gutiérrez," *Páginas* (1985), p. 15.

6. That is especially dangerous in times of crisis, when ambiguity comes to resemble a lie. See Eduardo Galeano, *Voces de nuestros tiempos* (San José, Costa Rica: EDUCA, 1983), p. 9.

7. The consequences of structural sin are reflected in the drama of the Third World, which constitutes 75 percent of the world's population, but which disposes of 6.5 percent of the world's income. It produces 80 percent of the raw materials, but only consumes 7 percent of the world's production. "There are 250 million people living in *barrios* of huts, 250 million children who lack schools, 300 million permanently unemployed, 550 million people who are illiterate, 700 million suffer serious malnutrition, 800 million have a daily income of about thirty cents (US), 1.2 billion have no access to water or sanitation. The debt of the countries of the Third World is $300,000,000,000. The average daily income per inhabitant is eighteen times less than in the developed countries. At the end of the 1980s, the per capita GNP of the least developed countries was projected to be $219; for those in process of development, $931; and for the developed countries, $11,832" (Ezequiel Ander-Egg, *El holocausto*

del hambre [Buenos Aires: Humanitas, 1982], p. 30). In the particular case of Latin America, infant mortality averages 67 per thousand; a million children die each year from hunger and malnutrition ("El estado mundial de la infancia" [New York: UNICEF, 1982]). In 1990, the number of unemployed will have increased by 35 million ("La crisis en América Latina, su evaluación y perspectiva" [Santiago: Economic Commission for Latin America (ECLA), 1985], p. 84). As for the repression of the "popular sectors" of the population, the picture is clear in the reports of the international organizations supporting human rights, or even in most newspapers.

8. Jon Sobrino, "Pecado personal, perdón y liberación," *RLT* 5 (1988): 17.

9. Tomás Hanks, "El testimonio evangélico a los pobres y oprimidos," *VP* 4 (1984): 4.

10. Concerning the absolution of Argentinian soldiers who were involved in the violation of human rights—a burning problem since the fall of the dictatorship—it is necessary to reexamine the political interpretation of the Christian faith, and its limitations, in light of the concepts of reconciliation and forgiveness. See Enrique Vijver, "¿Reconciliación y perdón una posibilidad política?" *CT* 8 (1987).

11. Theologians of liberation both Protestant and Catholic are careful to make clear this principle of the Christian faith. See, e.g., Gustavo Gutiérrez, *We Drink from Our Own Wells: The Spiritual Journey of a People*, trans. Matthew J. O'Connell (Maryknoll, N.Y.: Orbis Books, 1984), pp. 109-12.

12. This misunderstanding is not new, but was already present in the times of Paul (Rom. 3:7-8) and, much later, John Wesley, where the polemic appeared in his essay "On Christian Perfection": "Once more, beware of Solifidianism, crying nothing but 'Believe, believe!' and condemning those as ignorant or legal who speak in a more scriptural way" (Thomas S. Kepler, ed., *Christian Perfection as Believed and Taught by John Wesley* [Cleveland: World Publishing, 1954], p. 119).

13. José Míguez Bonino, "Justificación, santificación y plenitud," in *La tradición protestante en la teología latinoamericana*, José Duque, ed. (San José, Costa Rica: DEI, 1983), p. 251. His concern is to affirm a synergism that does not threaten the priority of grace, and he finds that synergism in covenant theology (ibid., p. 252).

14. Juan Luis Segundo, *Liberation of Theology*, trans. John Drury (Maryknoll, N.Y.: Orbis Books, 1976), pp. 133-38.

15. Gutiérrez (*The Power of the Poor in History: Selected Writings*, trans. Robert R. Barr [Maryknoll, N.Y.: Orbis Books, 1983], pp. 192-93) notes that in recent years Latin America has become characterized by a growing awareness of a society that is radically different.

16. This explains why current readings of the theme in Europe again address the danger of human self-affirmation as a historical subject. See Eberhard Jüngel, "*Homo humanus*. La signification de la distinction réformatrice entre la personne et ses oeuvres pour la façon dont l'homme moderne se conprend lui-même," *RTP* 119 (1987): 33-50; and José Ignacio González Faus, "Los pobres como lugar teológico," in Xavier Alegre et al., *El secuestro de la verdad: Los hombres secuestran la verdad con su injusticia (Rom 1, 18)* (Santander: Sal Terrae, 1986), p. 138.

17. Míguez Bonino, "La justicia del cristiano," in *Lutero ayer y hoy* (Buenos Aires: Aurora, 1984), p. 53.

18. Jürgen Moltmann (*The Way of Jesus Christ: Christology in Messianic Dimensions*, trans. Margaret Kohl [San Francisco: HarperCollins, 1990], p. 189) proposes at least six components of the process of justification: forgiveness of sins, liberation from the power of sin, reconciliation, new life in the service of justice, the inheritance of a new creation, and participating passionately in the new just world of God, with all the risks that that implies. We are thus not alone in our search for new meanings of the doctrine of justification in the face of those that deny the human being. That search has raised concerns particularly among Lutherans, whose concerns are recorded in the document *Justification Today* (*Lutheran World*, Supplement to No. 1, 1965), which came out of the meeting of the Lutheran World Federation in Helsinki in 1963. See also the work of the Swiss theologian Denis Müller ("Annihilation de l'homme ou justification par la foi?" *ETR* 51 [1976]: 495-500), who acknowledges both this uneasiness and the imperative of a reexamination of the doctrine of justification.

19. Ernst Käsemann, *Commentary on Romans*, trans. and ed. Geoffrey W. Bromiley (Grand Rapids: William B. Eerdmans Publishing Co., 1980), p. 98.

20. Míguez Bonino analyzes these problems, and the searches for perspective taking place in Protestant churches, in his article, "Visión del cambio social y sus tareas desde las iglesias cristianas no-católicas," *Fe cristiana y cambio social en América Latina* (Barcelona: Sígueme, 1973), pp. 179-202.

21. Karl Barth (*Church Dogmatics* 4/1, trans. Geoffrey W. Bromiley [Edinburgh: T. & T. Clark, 1956]) understands reconciliation as the central work of God between creation and fulfillment, and within this central work he interprets justification as part of reconciliation.

22. In situations of oppression and liberation, reconciliation is a double-edged theme. On the one hand, the conflictive setting itself requires that we rework that theme historically. (See José Comblin, "O tema da reconciliação e teologia na América Latina," *REB* 46 [1986]: 272-314.) On the other hand, there is always the risk that the official call to general reconciliation will fail to take into account the need to redress obvious injustices.

23. *The Kairos Document: Challenge to the Church—A Theological Comment on the Political Crisis in South Africa* (Stony Point, N.Y.: Theology in Global Context Program, Occasional Bulletin #1, 1985), p. 9.

24. We will deal with those—mostly coming from Protestant traditions—that explicitly speak of justification by faith. We have included José Porfirio Miranda's *Marx and the Bible: A Critique of the Philosophy of Oppression*, trans. John Eagleson (Maryknoll, N.Y.: Orbis Books, 1974) because, even though the author's central focus is not on justification by faith, his study on the justice of God, particularly in the Old Testament, has influenced the rereadings of justification that are discussed.

25. Walter Altmann, *Luther and Liberation: A Latin American Perspective*, trans. Mary M. Solberg (Minneapolis: Fortress Press, 1992), p. 41.

26. Roberto Hoeferkamp, "La viabilidad de Lutero hoy," *VP* 6 (1986): 12.

27. Araya, "Justificación y práctica," p. 17.

28. Leonardo Boff, a Catholic theologian, does a similar thing with the interpretation of the concept of justification in the Council of Trent. Prior to translating the language of the decree, he explains, "Instead of using the term 'justification' (a key word in the theology of Paul and the Council), I shall use the term 'liberation.' It is the same reality, but now elaborated in terms of its dynamic, historical dimensions" (*Liberating Grace*, trans. John Drury [Maryknoll, N.Y.: Orbis Books, 1987], pp. 151-52; see also pp. 152-55).

29. I do not believe that the reaction of Jorge Pixley ("El evangelio paulino de la justificación por la fe: conversaciones con José Porfirio Miranda," *Diakonia tou logou* [special issue of *RevistB*, 1979]) to Miranda's *Marx and the Bible* was written in the spirit of reopening old confessional disputes. Rather, it is a dialogue between exegetes about the concept of justice in Paul. It is also obvious that the articles of the Lutheran theologians Brakemeier, Hoeferkamp, and Westhelle (cited earlier), which compare the new theology coming out of Latin America with the classical reading of justification, were not written to discredit any theology, but precisely to deepen the reading of the doctrine by the new perspectives, and to enrich the theology of liberation. Leonardo Boff ("Lutero, entre la reforma y la liberación," *RLT* 1 [1984]: 97-98) believes that, even in the face of the individualism of Latin American Protestantism, which "feels itself to be mute and impotent in the face of structures of injustice," one can address the liberation of the poor by picking up again some important aspects of the tradition. He notes, "This articulation must be constructed beginning from some intuitions of Luther, and especially from the frankly liberating spirit within the church." Finally, in an address presented to a meeting of Lutheran theologians from Latin America and the United States held in Mexico in 1985, entitled "¿Está la justicia enraizada en el Nuevo Testamento?" (*RevistB* 48 [1986]: 15), Ricardo Pietrantonio said: "I believe that in the exegetical area the ancient Catholic-Protestant theological polemic is far from the present horizon, even though we can assume that belonging to a particular tradition does influence the exegete. . . . One finds Catholics speaking like Protestants, and *vice versa*. The reason for that can be found in the search for answers in the face of extreme situations of injustice, both local and international."

30. Araya, "Justificación y práctica," p. 31.

31. See Altmann, *Luther and Liberation*, pp. 27-41.

32. Míguez Bonino, "The Biblical Roots of Justice," *WW* 7 (1987): 12-21, and "La justicia del cristiano," *Lutero ayer y hoy*, pp. 35-53; Emilio Castro, "Gerechtigkeit—Gottes Handeln, menschliches Tun," lecture delivered to the Landessynode der Evangelischen Landeskirchen in Baden, Germany, April 1988; Pietrantonio, "¿Está la justicia enraizada en el Nuevo Testamento?" pp. 89-119; Héctor Laporta, "La Revelación de la justicia de Dios en Pablo" (unpublished thesis; San José, Costa Rica: Seminario Bíblico Latinoamericano, 1984); Pablo Leggett, "El triunfo de la justicia en Pablo," *Lectura teológica del tiempo latinoamericano* (ed. Carmelo Alvarez; San José, Costa Rica: SEBILA, 1979), pp. 19-26; Néstor Míguez, "Testimonio de la justicia y la renovación de la justicia," *CT* 8 (1987): 197-212; Tercio Machado, "Justificación y justicia," in *La tradición protestante en la teología* (ed. José Duque; San José, Costa Rica: DEI, 1983), pp. 237-42. See also the special issue of *VP* (vol. 6, no. 1 [1986]) on justification and justice, which includes the following articles: Victorio Araya, "Justificación y práctica de la justicia," pp. 17-25; Irene Foulkes, "Justificación y justicia en parábola: Un sermón sobre Mt. 18.23-24," pp. 39-42; and Plutarco Bonilla, "Justificación y justicia en el testimonio de Isaías," pp. 57-58.

33. See Hanks, "El testimonio evangélico."

34. Rubem A. Alves, *A Theology of Human Hope* (Washington, D.C.: Corpus Publications, 1969), pp. 134-58; Sílvio Meincke, "Justificação por graça e fé: um novo espaço para a vida," *EstT* 23 (1983): 205-30.

35. Miranda (*Marx and the Bible*, pp. 109-99) has identified a basis in Latin America for a new interpretation of the justice of God in the Bible, even though his view of justification and sin in Paul has been called into question as reductionistic and utopian because he reads those concepts as referring to social justice. (See Jorge Pixley, "El evangelio paulino de la justificación.") Other studies that refer to the Old Testament are: Laporta, "La Revelación," pp. 31-34; Bonilla, "Justificación y justicia," pp. 57-58, who concludes that our justification implies the demand of justice; Machado, "Justificación y justicia," pp. 38-42, who looks at God as creator and sustainer, and thus sees the Israelite cult as connected to justice; N. Míguez, "Testimonio de la justicia," pp. 198-204; and Pietrantonio, "¿Está la justicia enraizada en el Nuevo Testamento?" pp. 89-119.

36. Miranda, *Marx and the Bible*, pp. 109-37; Míguez Bonino, "The Biblical Roots," p. 13; Laporta, "La Revelación," pp. 31-34.

37. Miranda, *Marx and the Bible*, pp. 44-53; Leggett, "El triunfo," pp. 24-25; Severino Croatto, "Conocimiento y salvación en Romanos 1.18–3.20," *RevistB* 41 (1975): 48.

38. Miranda, *Marx and the Bible*, pp. 35-76; Leggett, "El triunfo," pp. 22-25; Croatto, "Conocimiento," pp. 44-55.

39. Miranda, *Marx and the Bible*, p. 170.

40. Ibid., p. 181.

41. Ibid., p. 182. The law condemned Jesus. Miranda understands by "justification of the ungodly" God's justification of Jesus the "outlaw" (not the sinner) (p. 189). "In some way when God raised up the outlawed Jesus, he was justifying the impious one, him whom the whole of the law and human civilization crucified for being impious. This is the justice of the law: It crucified the only man 'who knew no sin' (2 Cor. 5:21)." In a similar vein, Miranda observes (p. 192), "By raising him from the dead, God showed that the one whom the law and the civilization controlled by the law condemned as impious was indeed just."

42. Pixley ("El evangelio," p. 53) criticizes him for the absolute rejection of the law.

43. Miranda, *Marx and the Bible*, p. 241.

44. Leggett, "El triunfo," p. 24.

45. N. Míguez, "Testimonio de la justicia," p. 296.

46. Ibid., pp. 206-9.

47. Pietrantonio, "¿Está la justicia enraizada en el Nuevo Testamento?" p. 11.

48. Ibid., pp. 12-24. I have called attention to this last point of Pietrantonio because, from a different perspective, it will be one of the keys to the reading that will form the basis for this essay in theological reconstruction of the doctrine of justification.

49. Foulkes ("El Reino de Dios y Pablo" *VP* 1 [1983]: 15) notes the following points in common between the two messages: the origin of everything in the divine will and initiative

concerning human beings; the divine purpose that both individual persons and the larger society do what is "good"—that is, live lives marked by love and justice; the obstacle to the realization of that purpose in the concrete practice of evil (injustice and sin), both by individuals and in the structures of the society; the judgment they incur because of those actions, from which the only way out is forgiveness and rehabilitation through repentance, clinging to Jesus, and rectifying any wrongs committed; the concrete and deadly confrontation between those who practice injustice and sin, and those who incarnate the values represented in the life and work of Jesus and his followers; the new community made possible by following Jesus and abandoning the values that deny life; and the nature of the limited present and limitless future of the new reality brought by Jesus.

50. Foulkes, "Justificación y justicia," p. 38. See also pp. 39-42.

51. Castro, "Gerechtigkeit," p. 10.

52. Mortimer Arias, "Mission and Liberation," *IRM* 73 (1984): 46.

53. J. Severino Croatto, *Exodus: A Hermeneutics of Freedom*, trans. Salvator Attanasio (Maryknoll, N.Y.: Orbis Books, 1981), pp. 67-82.

54. Ibid., p. 80. Paul reads language found in Exodus (such as *lutroō*, "deliver" or "redeem"; *eleutheria*, "freedom"; *sōzō*, "save"; and *hilastērion*, "propitiation") from a christological perspective.

55. Segundo, *El hombre de hoy ante Jesús de Nazaret. Sinópticos y Pablo*, 3 vols. (Madrid: Cristiandad, 1982), 2/1, pp. 278-563.

56. Ibid., p. 378.

57. See Altmann, *Luther and Liberation;* Bonino, "Justificación, santificación"; Westhelle, "O desencuentro"; Brakemeier, "Justification by Grace"; and the various authors whose essays are included in *Lutero ayer y hoy.*

58. Westhelle, "O desencuentro," pp. 48-49.

59. Ibid., p. 49.

60. This problem can be seen clearly in "Statement of a Consultation. Justification and Justice: A Meeting of Lutheran Theologians of the Americas," *WW* 7 (1987): 78-79.

61. Míguez Bonino, "Justificación, santificación," p. 253.

62. In "La justicia del cristiano" (p. 52), he gives three examples: (1) The relegating of the second justice to a secondary position, optional and dispensable because of the "external" and "alien" character of the first justice: "Since the first is the one that saves, any emphasis on the second seems enthusiastic, a justice of works"; (2) the making absolute of the distinction between the private and the public person, reducing Christian life to the private realm, and leaving the public realm to its own devices; (3) the "de-christologization" of the second justice, as if the "form of Christ" were irrelevant for public life.

63. Ibid., p. 52.

64. Míguez Bonino, "The Biblical Roots," p. 12.

65. Ibid., pp. 15-16.

66. Altmann, *Confrontación y liberación*, pp. 56-57. Concerning the anti-ecclesial dimension, Segundo observes (*El dogma que libera* [Santander: Sal Terrae, 1989], p. 306) that what divided Catholics and Protestants was not the doctrine of justification, but the protest against the absolutions being granted by the Catholic Church. However, there seems to us to be a connection between the doctrine and an oppressive structure (whether ecclesiastical or not), as Altmann intuits. Hanks ("El testimónio evangelico," p. 11) notes further that we Protestants often forget that justification by faith alone does not constitute support for the status quo. On the contrary, it is a radical and revolutionary theology.

67. Hanks, "El testimonio evangélico," p. 11.

68. Alves, *A Theology of Human Hope*, pp. 134-58.

69. Ibid., p. 142. Humanistic messianism refers to the praxis of justice without incorporating God or the transcendent dimension in any form.

70. Ibid.

71. Ibid.

72. Ibid., p. 144.

73. Ibid., p. 157.

74. Meincke, "Justificaçâo por graça e fé," p. 229.

2. CHALLENGES FROM LATIN AMERICA TO JUSTIFICATION BY FAITH

1. The poor are the privileged theological locus. See Gustavo Gutiérrez, *The Power of the Poor in History: Selected Writings*, trans. Robert R. Barr (Maryknoll, N.Y.: Orbis Books, 1983), esp. pp. 16-22, 131-43, 199-214, 218-21; Leonardo Boff, *Do lugar do pobre* (Petrópolis: Vozes, 1984); José Ignacio González Faus, "Los pobres como lugar teológico," in Xavier Alegre et al., *El secuestro de la verdad: Los hombres secuestran la verdad con su injusticia (Rom 1, 18)* (Santander: Sal Terrae, 1982).

2. The entire system is captive to a logic of the accumulation of capital that completely contradicts the principle that the primary purpose of all goods and services and products of human labor should be their equitable availability to all. See *Aliados en la esperanza. Elementos para un análisis de la coyuntura latinoamericana* (Bogotá: Latin American Network of the Commission for the Churches' Participation in Development [CCPD], 1989). In Latin America, Franz Hinkelammert, Hugo Assmann, Raúl Vidales, Julio de Santa Ana, and Enrique Dussel have studied most extensively the situation of exclusion generated by the present economic system and the ideology that legitimates it. See Hinkelammert, *Crítica a la razon utópica* (San José, Costa Rica: DEI, 1984), pp. 53-93, *Democracia y totalitarismo* (San José, Costa Rica: DEI, 1987), pp. 133-228, and *La fe de Abraham y el edipo occidental* (San José, Costa Rica: DEI, 1989), pp. 65-101; Assmann, *Tecnología y necessidades básicas* (San José, Costa Rica: DEI, 1981); Assmann and Hinkelammert, *A idolatria do mercado. Ensaio sobre economia e teologia* (Petrópolis: Vozes, 1989); Dussel, *Etica comunitaria* (Buenos Aires: Paulinas, 1986). See also the work of Ulrich Duchrow, *Global Economy: A Confessional Issue for the Churches?* (Geneva: WCC, 1987).

3. For an analysis of the nature and depth of the present crisis in Latin America, see *La crisis de América Latina: su evaluación y perspectivas* (Santiago: Economic Commission for Latin America [ECLA], vol. 4 [1985]); José Duque, "La misión del protestantismo en la coyuntura actual latinoamericana" (unpublished research in process).

4. *Aliados en la esperanza*, p. 16.

5. On the effects of liberalism, see the special issue of *Le monde diplomatique* devoted to that theme, with the title *Le libèralisme contre les libertés* (1988).

6. Chile is often pointed to as an example of a country that, under Pinochet, opened its doors to a free market economy. The result has been an increase in poverty equal to the relative growth in the economy. Brazil is the other most dramatic case. In the period of the "Brazilian miracle," the mortality rate increased in one of the neighborhoods of the richest city of the country. According to Eduardo Galeano (*Open Veins of Latin America: Five Centuries of the Pillage of a Continent*, trans. Cedric Belfrage [New York: Monthly Review Press, 1973], p. 304), in systems that are organized backward, when the economy grows, so does social injustice! These two countries show us the other face of progress, which, by being attached to a system whose primary interest is profit, produces simultaneously and inevitably the deaths of thousands of innocent persons. This situation prevails generally throughout Latin America and the Caribbean, with the exception of Cuba. According to statistics gathered by the International Labor Organization in Geneva (1976), in Latin America there are more than 110,000,000 persons in conditions of abject poverty, of whom 60,000,000 are indigent. Incomes that are less than the average minimum cost of food, according to ECLA statistics, reach 42 percent in Brazil, 43 percent in Colombia, 49 percent in Honduras, 31 percent in Mexico, and 45 percent in Peru. The goal of devising a new international economic order is found among economists of the First World as well as those of the Third World. See Jon Tinbergen, *Reshaping the International Order* (New York: E. P. Dutton & Co., 1976); R. H. Green, ed., *The International Financial System: An Ecumenical Critique* (Geneva: CCPD, 1985).

7. Bernard Kucinski and Sue Branford, *The Debt Squads: The U.S., the Banks, and Latin America* (Atlantic Highlands, N.J.: Zed Books, 1988); Luis Vitale, *Historia de la deuda externa latinoamericana y entretelones del endeudamiento argentino* (Buenos Aires: Sudamericana/Planeta, 1986); Hinkelammert, *La deuda externa en América Latina. El automatismo de la deuda* (San José, Costa Rica: DEI, 1988). See also the book published in 1989 in Río de Janeiro by the Ecumenical Center for Documentation and Research (CEDI), *Dívida externa e igrejas. Uma visão ecumenica*, which includes seven articles by various economists and theologians and eight

pronouncements from churches and ecumenical agencies concerning the debt. See also Peter Körner et al., *IMF and the Debt Crisis* (London: Paul Knight, 1986). The disasters wrought by the debt are of concern to many Christians, including from latitudes outside the Third World. A large gathering to examine that issue was held in Berlin in August of 1988, on the occasion of the meeting of the World Bank and the International Monetary Fund. For a report on that conference, see Lynne Jones, ed., *Debt: Resource Material* (Geneva: CCPD, 1988).

8. Hinkelammert, "El Dios mortal, lucifer y la bestia," *Capitalismo, violencia y anti-vida. La opresión de las mayorías y la domesticación de los dioses*, ed. Saúl Trinidad and Elsa Tamez (San José, Costa Rica: DEI, 1978), pp. 199-313; de Santa Ana, "Costo social e sacrificio aôs idolos," *Dívida externa e igrejas*, pp. 73-91; Assmann and Hinkelammert, *A idolatria do mercado*, chap. 4.

9. On the origins and manifestations of the doctrine of national security, see José Comblin, *El poder militar en América Latina* (Salamanca: Sígueme, 1978). As an illustration of concrete analysis, see Gustavo Gallón Giraldo, "La república de las armas. Relaciones entre Fuerzas Armadas y Estado en Colombia 1960–1980," *Controversia* (1983), nos. 109-10.

10. Galeano (*Open Veins*, pp. 300-307) chronicles the abusive labor practices followed by institutionalized governmental repression and terror that are common throughout the region, and that are the equivalent of human blood offered on the altars of productivity.

11. Javier Gorostiaga, *Geopolítica de la crisis regional. Hipótesis de trabajo sobre el marco estratégico de la alternativa regional para Centroamérica y el Caribe* (Managua: IIES, 1983).

12. Hinkelammert, *Democracia*, pp. 151-53, emphasis added.

13. Ibid., p. 154.

14. Leopoldo Zea, *Filosofía americana como filosofía sin más* (Mexico City: Siglo XXI, 1969), pp. 9-31.

15. In his book *Ariel* (trans. Margaret Sayers Pedén [Austin, Tex.: University of Texas, 1988], pp. 70-71), which was written in 1900, José Enrique Rodó (1871–1950) already criticized this attitude that is so common in Latin America when confronted with countries like the United States. He called the attitude *"USA-mania."* This attitude includes the desire to imitate the culture and values believed to be superior and more prestigious. The resulting vision of an America that has been "de-Latinized" and re-created in the image and likeness of the archetype of the North, he said, haunts the dreams of many who are concerned with the future of Latin America.

16. Enrique D. Dussel, *Philosophy of Liberation*, trans. Aquilina Martínez and Christine Morkovsky (Maryknoll, N.Y.: Orbis Books, 1985). For a more complete study along this line, see Roque Zimmermann, *América Latina o nâo-ser. Uma abordagem filosófica a partir de Enrique Dussel* (Petrópolis: Vozes, 1987).

17. Zea, *Filosofía*, p. 19.

18. Gutiérrez, *Power of the Poor in History*, p. 137.

19. Raúl Vidales, *Utopía y liberación: el amenecer del indio* (San José, Costa Rica: DEI, 1989), p. 44.

20. James H. Cone, *A Black Theology of Liberation* (Philadelphia and New York: J. B. Lippincott, 1970), pp. 34-35.

21. Vidales, *Utopía y liberación*, p. 44.

22. There have been conferences in Latin America of and about native peoples (in Ecuador, Peru, Bolivia, Mexico, Guatemala, and Brazil), blacks (several times in Brazil and in Costa Rica), and women (in Mexico, Peru, Argentina, Brazil, and other countries). Movements of women have proliferated, including Mujeres por la Vida (Argentina), Madres de Desaparecidos (El Salvador), Madres de la Plaza de Mayo (Argentina), Asociación de Mujeres "Luisa Amanda Espinoza" (Nicaragua), and Mujeres Pro-Vivienda (Mexico). Women's struggles have sought their own rights, as well as the right to better conditions of life for all people.

23. Language that is more elliptical and allusive than analytical begins to point toward the different experiences of the races. *Indigenous peoples* long for their past, live from their "deep times"—their vital roots—with lights from the past seeking to project those roots toward an obscure future. The present, denied by them and by Latin American society, is dragged along by Western society. They struggle simply for the right to exist as indigenous peoples with their own culture and *logos*—both word and logic. Their present life has been threatened for 500 years. Discriminated against among their brothers and sisters because of their

ethnicity and their own civilization, they are seen as foreigners in their own land. *Blacks,* stigmatized for their entire lifetime because of their color and their slave history, tell the saddest story of this Latin American "plural subject." By imposing on themselves a past that is shrouded in shadow, they are denied ahead of time both the present and the future. Of all the poor they are the most despised because of their color. Because of their color, they must demonstrate superior merit in order to be recognized as human beings. Seen as strangers in a land alien to their culture and *logos,* their very skin is like a book that tells aloud of a forced and shameful past, whose deep roots extend to Africa. *Mestizos,* neither indigenous nor white, are a union of two histories that reject each other. They bear the features of indigenous peoples and the desires of white people, or the profiles of white people and the longings of indigenous peoples. They are rejected by indigenous peoples and whites alike. They consider themselves and are considered superior to indigenous peoples, and inferior to whites—a blending of cultures, an undefined *logos.* The Mestizo, a person divided, knower of two different *logoi,* is incapable of creating his or her own self or of resisting an imported one.

3. PAUL AND HIS CONTEXT

1. The author applies the method of genetic structuralism to literature. For his analysis of literary production, see Lucien Goldmann, *Pour une sociologie du roman* (Paris: Galimard, 1965), pp. 338-48.

2. As J. E. Crouch says, "To argue that Christian slaves who understood their call to freedom had only 'a superficial understanding of the Gospel' is to minimize the impact of this language in a world where slavery was a commonly accepted institution" (*The Origin and Intention of the Colossian Haustafel* [FRLANT 109; Göttingen: Vandenhoeck & Ruprecht, 1972], p. 127; quoted in Elisabeth Schüssler Fiorenza, *In Memory of Her: A Feminist Theological Reconstruction of Christian Origins* [New York: Crossroad, 1983], p. 209).

3. Joachim Jeremias, "Der Schlüssel zur Theologie des Apostels Paulus," *Calwer Hefte* 115 (1971): 20.

4. This attempt to present Paul as a concrete being and not an ahistorical theologian is not new. Gunther Bornkamm, among others, presents Paul as a man who refracts his theology through his concrete and circumstantial reality (*Paul,* trans. D. M. G. Stalker [New York: Harper & Row, 1971], pp. xxii-xxiv). Roland Hock portrays Paul as an artisan and tentmaker (*The Social Context of Paul's Ministry* [Philadelphia: Fortress Press, 1980]).

5. This continues in the evangelical and prophetic tradition (Luise Schottroff and Wolfgang Stegemann, *Jesus the Hope of the Poor,* trans. Matthew J. O'Connell [Maryknoll, N.Y.: Orbis Books, 1981]). Paul sides with the poor members of the Christian community in Corinth, whose social composition led to conflicts. This situation that appears from the very beginning of the letter, and that indicates a crisis in the community, cannot be reduced to a theological polemic or mere partisan squabbling. As Gerd Theissen notes (*The Social Setting of Pauline Christianity: Essays on Corinth,* trans. and ed. John H. Schütz [Philadelphia: Fortress Press, 1982], pp. 69-73), in 1 Corinthians 1:26-27 there is a clear sociological sense in which one can observe the social stratification of this community composed principally of members of the lower classes. However, one must recognize that there are contradictions or inconsistencies in some parts of the apostle's letters, especially with respect to women and slaves. In the particular case of women, Paul reflects neither the theological tradition of equality found in the primitive missionary movement (Gal. 3:28), nor the fact of the preeminence of women in his communities, nor the effective practice of his female colleagues in the missionary enterprise. Therefore, although in practice there was an acceptance and respect for women's work (Rom. 16:1-16), one encounters also several pronouncements harmful to them (1 Cor. 14:34-35), which were picked up again and reinforced by Paul's followers (Eph. 5:21-24). Such attitudes seem to contradict his theological proposal concerning the justice of God and justification by faith.

6. This saying shows the zeal of the Romans to maintain the divisions of status. It appears in the letter from Pliny the Younger to Tiro, when he advises him concerning conduct in the administration. He concludes: "However, I cannot forbear adding a caution to my praise, and recommending you to conduct yourself in such a manner as to preserve the proper distinctions of rank and dignity, which, if once confounded, and all thrown up on a level, nothing can be more unequal than that kind of equality" (*The Letters of Caius Plinius Caecilius Secundus*, trans. William Melmoth; rev. F. C. T. Bosanquet [London: George Bell and Sons, 1878], p. 300).

7. Schüssler Fiorenza, *In Memory of Her*, p. 263; see also p. 183.

8. Joseph Holzner, *Paul of Tarsus*, trans. Frederic Eickhoff (St. Louis: B. Herder, 1944), pp. 2-10. The discussion is extensive, and there is no consensus among scholars. Some have seen in the theology of Paul a large influence of Hellenism. Others affirm that the theology emerges especially from rabbinic Judaism, and still others see in Paul a theologian who is unique, and who separated himself almost completely from Palestinian Judaism. It seems that this disagreement is not rooted in the content or structure of the concepts, but rather in the fact that, be they of Hellenism or of Judaism, they acquire dynamism, meaning, and novelty because of the concrete socioeconomic life of that epoch.

9. *Dio Chrysostom*, LCL, 5 vols., trans. J. W. Cohoon and H. Lamar Crosby (Cambridge: Harvard University, 1961), pp. 344-45, 350-53, 356-59.

10. Martin Dibelius and Werner G. Kümmel, *Paul* (Philadelphia: Westminster Press, 1953), pp. 15-19; Bornkamm, *Paul*, pp. 9-10.

11. It is difficult to acquire reliable data concerning the Jewish population, but it was clearly fairly large. In fact, shortly before the fall of Jerusalem in 70 c.e. the Jewish population was close to seven million, of whom only about a third lived in Palestine. That information is taken principally from the work of the Syrian chronicler Barhebraeus, who wrote in the thirteenth century. André Paul, *Le monde des juifs à l'heure de Jésus: Histoire politique* (Paris: Desclée, 1981), pp. 99-100; C. Saulnier, *Histoire d'Israël: De la conquête d'Alexandre à la destruction du temple* (Paris: Cerf, 1985), p. 287.

12. Bornkamm, *Paul*, p. 5.

13. Hermann Strathmann, *"polis, ktl."* TDNT, vol. 6, p. 527.

14. Saulnier, *Histoire d'Israël*, p. 291.

15. Paul, *Le monde*, p. 110.

16. Ibid., pp. 110-11.

17. With Vespasian this contribution passed into the Roman treasury under the name *fiscus judaicus*. See Josephus, *J.W.* 7.218 (*Josephus*, LCL, 8 vols.; trans. H. St. J. Thackeray [New York: G. P. Putnam's Sons, 1928], vol. 3 (*The Jewish War, Books 4-7*), pp. 566-69).

18. According to Saulnier (*Histoire d'Israël*, p. 191), 75 percent of the inscriptions in the Jewish catacombs in Rome are in Greek, 20 percent in Latin, and 1 percent in Hebrew or Aramaic.

19. Joachim Jeremias, *Jerusalem in the Time of Jesus: An Investigation into Economic and Social Conditions During the New Testament Period*, trans. F. H. and C. H. Cave (Philadelphia: Fortress Press, 1969), pp. 266-67.

20. Jacques Dupont, "La conversion de Paul," *Foi et Salut selon Saint Paul* (Rome: Pontifical Biblical Institute, 1970), p. 75.

21. Against the thesis of a radical separation between Hellenism and rabbinic Judaism in the first century, W. D. Davies (*Paul and Rabbinic Judaism: Some Rabbinic Elements in Pauline Theology* [Philadelphia: Fortress Press, 1980], pp. 322-24, xxvi) opts to see in the theology of Paul the central concepts of Judaism—Torah, obedience, and community—seen from the perspective of Christ. According to Ulrich Wilckens (*Rechtfertigung als Freiheit* [Neukirchen: Neukirchener Verlag des Erziehungsvereins, 1974], p. 7), no other theologian of the early church thought and acted from as deep within the Jewish tradition as did Paul. He was a Jew and, at the same time, an irreconcilable enemy of Judaizing tendencies within Christianity.

22. E. P. Sanders, "Jesus, Paul, and Judaism," in *Aufstieg und Niedergang der Römischen Welt: Principat*, vol. 2.25.1, Wolfgang Haase, ed. (Berlin: Walter de Gruyter, 1982), pp. 434-35.

23. E. P. Sanders, *Paul and Palestinian Judaism* (London: SCM Press, 1977), p. 552.

24. E. P. Sanders, *Paul, the Law, and the Jewish People* (Philadelphia: Fortress Press, 1983),

p. 208. Sanders also notes ("Jesus, Paul, and Judaism," p. 449), "The importance of Paul in the history of Christianity is above all that he pushed inclusiveness to its logical extreme. . . . Paul insisted that the Gentiles were also to be included and he was the apostle to the Gentiles. The inclusion of the Gentiles, however, required not just the extension of the covenantal promises of salvation, but their redefinition. 'The children of Abraham' are those who are 'in Christ Jesus,' and those alone."

25. Krister Stendahl, *Paul Among Jews and Gentiles* (Philadelphia: Fortress Press, 1977), p. 2. Stendahl's intuitions with respect to the meaning of the Pauline message seem well grounded. However, if one relates the socioeconomic situation with the theological proposal of Paul concerning justification, that would become more meaningful than Stendahl realizes. He considers that justification by faith is not as central for Paul as the tradition suggests.

26. Adolf Deissmann, *Paul: A Study in Social and Religious History*, trans. William E. Wilson (New York: Harper & Row, 1957), p. 51.

27. There is considerable debate whether Paul was really a Roman citizen, as Luke affirms in the book of Acts. If he was, he would have enjoyed a position of considerable privilege. However, a close examination of his letters and of the contemporary context leads Wolfgang Stegemann to conclude that that seems unlikely ("War der Apostel ein römischer Bürger?," *ZNW* 78 [1987]: 220-29). See also Klaus Wengst, *Pax Romana and the Peace of Jesus Christ* (London: SCM Press, 1989), p. 77.

28. Derek Tidball, *An Introduction to the Sociology of the New Testament* (Exeter: Paternoster, 1983), p. 94; E. A. Judge, *The Social Patterns of the Christian Groups in the First Century* (London: Tyndale, 1960), p. 39.

29. Hock, *The Social Context*, pp. 24, 34. It is thus that the lives of Kerdon (Herodas, *Mimes* 6.63), Philiscus (*Teles: the Cynic Teacher* 4 B), Micyllus (Lucian, *The Dream, or the Cock [Gallus]* 2), and others serve as points of reference. Micyllus the cobbler is an example of an artisan who had few advantages. He arose each day at dawn, and the little that he earned barely allowed him to go to the baths and to buy a modest dinner. His profits allowed him to buy only a used clock. Usually he is described as going hungry, ill-clad, and suffering from the cold. See Herodas, *The Mimes and Fragments*, trans. and ed. Walter Headlam and Alfred Dillwyn Knox (Cambridge: Cambridge University, 1966), pp. 278-79; *Teles: the Cynic Teacher*, ed. and trans. Edward O'Neal (Missoula, Mont.: Scholars Press, 1977), pp. 48-53; *Lucian* (LCL, 8 vols.; trans. A. M. Harmon [Cambridge: Harvard University, 1968], vol. 2, pp. 172-239).

30. Hock, *The Social Context*, p. 35. According to Traugott Holtz (*Der erste Brief an die Thessalonicher* [Zurich: Benziger Verlag, 1986], p. 86), the phrase "work day and night" is an idiomatic expression. In any event, that phrase illustrates Paul's experience of arduous manual labor at the same time that he was proclaiming the gospel.

31. Hock, *The Social Context*, p. 36.

32. Thomas Wiedemann, *Greek and Roman Slavery* (London: Croom Helm, 1981), p. 8. See also M. I. Finley, *The Ancient Economy* (London: Hogarth, 1985), p. 60.

33. The workshop could also have been situated in a private house called an *insula*. The *insula* was a type of apartment house, common in the large cities of the Roman Empire, in which there were shops opening onto the street. Abraham Malherbe, *Paul and the Thessalonians* (Philadelphia: Fortress Press, 1987), p. 17.

34. Simon is described as someone who discussed philosophy in his workshop with the Cynic Antestenes or with Socrates, Pericles, and others (Hock, *The Social Context*, p. 39).

35. Being freeborn allowed him at least to have access to direct relationships with persons of higher social classes, be they officials of the government or influential people. He was well able to take advantage of this opportunity as an independent artisan, for it was often denied to his companions because they were slaves or freed slaves.

36. Whatever one concludes about Paul's membership in the middle or lower classes on the basis of his way of earning a living, it is still important to recall that in the Pauline communities there were people who were quite wealthy, especially among the leaders. (Deissmann, *Paul: A Study*, p. 57; Theissen, *The Social Setting*, pp. 72-73).

37. Peter Lampe, "Paulus—Zeltmacher," *BZ* 2 (1987): 258ff. In reality, it cannot be known with certainty whether Paul made tents from fabric or leather. The proposal of Lampe is that Paul made tents out of fabric, and especially linen, for the production of which Tarsus was

famous. Hock (*The Social Context*, p. 24) is inclined to think he worked in leather. Tents of leather were used by Roman soldiers as well as by civilians. If Paul worked in leather, surely he did so for private clients, since the imperial household included slaves who were artisans, and who would carry out their craft on a larger scale.

38. Wayne A. Meeks (*The First Urban Christians: The Social World of the Apostle Paul* [New Haven: Yale University, 1983], p. 73) identifies status inconsistency as a characteristic of the members of the Pauline communities. His study reflects especially an elevation in the status of various members of lower-class origins (slaves or freed slaves), who for a variety of reasons acquired a degree of wealth, but who because of their origins never could attain to truly elevated status, and hence who suffered this ambiguity.

39. Theissen (*The Social Setting*, pp. 27-67) concludes that Paul's attitude would have been one of the points raised by his opponents in Corinth, who would have seen the acceptance of support from the community as the norm. Paul defended his posture and prided himself on his self-sufficiency. Theissen contrasts the pattern of itinerant charismatics to that of Paul the community organizer. Hock (*The Social Context*, pp. 50-65) moves the discussion into the surrounding Greco-Roman society, and the question of the support of philosophers. For the philosophers the alternatives were to charge for their teaching, to accept the hospitality of rich and powerful people's households, to beg for alms, or to work. Paul's self-sufficiency mirrored the last, while the itinerant charismatics reflected the first two. Whatever may have been the reason is not that important, but the fact is that Paul continued work as an artisan, and that connected him to the world of artisans and business people of all races and religions.

40. Gerd Lüdemann, *Early Christianity According to the Traditions in Acts: A Commentary*, trans. John Bowden (Minneapolis: Fortress Press, 1989), p. 249.

41. Bathieu Beltrán Villegas, "Una visión de la gracia: la justificación en Romanos," *TV* 28 (1987): 277-305.

42. See the discussion in Peter Stuhlmacher, *Gottes Gerechtigkeit bei Paulus* (Göttingen: Vandenhoeck & Ruprecht, 1965).

43. Niels Hyldahl, *Die Paulinische Chronologie* (Leiden: E. J. Brill, 1986), p. 50; Peter Stuhlmacher, *Der Brief an Philemon* (Zurich: Benziger/Neukirchener Verlag, 1981), p. 21.

44. Pierre Ducrey (*Traitement des prisonniers de guerre dans la Grèce antique* [Paris: E. de Boccard, 1968], pp. 338ff.) has studied the treatment of prisoners of war in ancient Greece. Concerning their treatment in Roman times he notes only that it was even more repressive.

45. Theodor Mömmsen, *Römisches Strafrecht* (Graz: Akademische Druck und Verlaganstalt, 1955), p. 305.

46. Peter Garnsey, *Social Status and Legal Privilege in the Roman Empire* (Oxford: Clarendon, 1970), p. 277.

47. Ibid., pp. 99-100, 103-52.

48. Ibid., pp. 277-78. If Paul counted on Roman citizenship to protect him, it appears not to have helped the three times he was whipped under the provisions of Roman law (*tris erabisthen*), according to 2 Corinthians 11:25, unless he kept that privilege hidden.

49. Mömmsen, *Römisches Strafrecht*, pp. 304-5.

50. Lüdemann, *Early Christianity*, p. 249. The *lex Iulia* forbade the taking of money from prisoners. Felix acted on the margin of the law.

51. The term *dietia* used in Acts 24:27 corresponds to the technical legal term *biennium*. According to Hans Conzelmann (*Acts of the Apostles*, trans. James Limburg, A. Thomas Kraebel, and Donald Juel; ed. Eldon Jay Epp with Christopher R. Matthews [Philadelphia: Fortress Press, 1987], p. 201), the two years refer to the time Paul spent in prison, and not to Felix's term of office in Jerusalem, as some conclude.

52. For Paul, both divine and human law are overturned by human ungodliness and injustice. Karl Kertelge observes (*The Epistle to the Romans*, trans. Francis McDonagh [New York: Herder & Herder, 1972], p. 24) that ungodliness is equivalent to injustice, since in abandoning God people overturn both divine and human laws, because human law has its deepest foundation in God. The result is a world turned upside down, in which law is perverted and truth is suppressed, including the truth about God and about people's life in society and in communities.

53. For a study of the fallacy of the "peace and security" of the Roman Empire, see Klaus Wengst, *Pax Romana and the Peace of Jesus Christ*, trans. John Bowden (Philadelphia: Fortress Press, 1987), pp. 9-26; Néstor Míguez, "No como los otros que no tienen esperanza. Ideología y estrategia del cristianismo paulino en la gentilidad. Lectura socio-política de la primera carta de Pablo a los tesalonicenses," unpublished doctoral thesis (Buenos Aires: ISEDET, 1989), pp. 625-31. Míguez considers the use of *pax* with a complement such as "concord" or "security" to reflect the propaganda of the Roman Empire and conformed likewise to the program of the principate. Coins, which according to Míguez are a form of ideological communication, exhibit the attributes of peace, security, concord, and fortune as goddesses who accompany and crown the imperial undertakings. One example of the use of the words "peace" and "security" is found in the discourse of the general Cerialis, who is charged with pacifying a revolt in Gaul (Tacitus, *Hist.* 2.4.74-75; *Tacitus: The Histories*, LCL, 4 vols., trans. Clifford H. Moore [Cambridge: Harvard University, 1956], vol. 1, pp. 164-67).

54. Garnsey, *Social Status*, pp. 234-76.

55. These roads were used especially by military troops, members of the imperial administration, and officials of the government such as those responsible for the mail. They were also used by merchants, poets, philosophers, or itinerant missionaries. The sea lanes, controlled exclusively by the army, linked the most important cities of the Mediterranean and facilitated the exchange of such products as olives, wine, fabrics, porcelain, and glass. Exotic luxury goods desired by the aristocracy arrived from distant lands in the east thanks to this means of transportation. See Firmin O'Sullivan, *The Egnatian Way* (Harrisburg, Pa.: Stackpole Books, 1972). Concerning naval power, see Chester G. Stam, *The Influence of Sea Power on Ancient History* (Oxford: Oxford University, 1989), pp. 67-81; Fik Meijer, *A History of Seafaring in the Classical World* (London: Croom Helm, 1986), pp. 167-235.

56. Virgil, *Aeneid* 1.257-96 (*Virgil*, LCL, 2 vols.; trans. H. Rushton Fairclough [Cambridge: Harvard University, 1978], vol. 1, pp. 258-61); Aelius Aristides, "Oration XXVI: Regarding Rome" (*Complete Works*, 2 vols., trans. Charles A. Behr [Leiden: E. J. Brill, 1981], vol. 2, pp. 73-97); Horace, *Odes* 4.4.5 (*The Odes, Epodes and Carmen Saeculare*, ed. Clifford Herschel Moore [New York: American Book Co., 1902], pp. 343-54.

57. Michel Clévenot (*Les hommes de la fraternité*, 9 vols. [Paris: Fernand Nathan, 1981] vol. 1, p. 1) begins his book with these words: "There is Rome. Very distant: about 350 miles by the Flaminia road. Here is Ravenna, ancient Etruscan city on the shore of the Adriatic, now the second port of the imperial navy. There is the Emperor Augustus, his sister, his generals, his poets. Here is a workshop for naval construction—a very modest lean-to where three artisans work. There is the great history, that of Rome, of the Empire, of Roman art and Latin literature. Here is a lowly tracing on a funeral monument, a simple carved rock, paid for dearly by insignificant people in order not to fall completely into oblivion." The poor suffered greatly in Rome. The stark and shameful economic contrasts gnawed away at the life of the metropolis, whose poor people also had to cope with a high cost of living. Catherine Salles, *Les basfonds de l'Antiquité* (Paris: Robert Laffont, 1982), pp. 179-85.

58. See the list of items of income in gold, silver, and gems (200–157 B.C.E.) analyzed by Tenny Frank, *An Economic Survey of Ancient Rome*, 2 vols. (New York: Octagon Books, 1975), vol. 2, pp. 126-41. Concerning the prisoners of war after the defeat of the Jewish resistance in 70 C.E., Josephus writes that 96,000 Jews were sold as slaves (*Jewish War* 6.414-20). And that was in a time of relative tranquility, when the famous wars of conquest had nearly been concluded. However, the wars did not cease entirely, but continued at a lower intensity, and slave-prisoners continued to arrive in the markets throughout the region. K. R. Bradley, "On the Roman Slave Supply and Slavebreeding," *Classical Slavery*, ed. M. I. Finley (London: Frank Cass, 1987), p. 49.

59. Peter Garnsey and Richard Saller, *The Roman Empire* (London: Duckworth, 1987), p. 97.

60. M. I. Finley, *The Ancient Economy* (London: Hogarth, 1985), p. 91.

61. G. Salvioli, *Le capitalisme dans le monde antique* (New York: Arno, 1979), p. 84. Concerning land and immigration, see Keith Hopkins, *Conquerors and Slaves: Sociological Studies in Roman History* (Cambridge: Cambridge University, 1978), pp. 56-74.

62. The owners of land in the provinces were not only the rich people of a particular province, but frequently they were members of the Roman elite of the order of senators or

equestrians. Garnsey and Saller, *The Roman Empire*, p. 65; A. H. M. Jones, *The Roman Economy: Studies in Ancient Economy and Administrative History* (Oxford: Basil Blackwell, 1974), p. 125.

63. Michael Ivanovitch Rostovtzeff, *Social and Economic History of the Roman Empire*, 2 vols. (Oxford: Clarendon, 1957), vol. 1, p. 93.

64. G. E. M. de Ste. Croix, *The Class Struggle in the Ancient Greek World: From the Archaic Age to the Arab Conquests* (Ithaca, N.Y.: Cornell University, 1981), pp. 203-6.

65. Ibid., p. 261.

66. Ibid., p. 242. The difference between Italy and the Greek areas in the east with respect to the change from large-scale economic production based on slavery to a peasant form of production is that in the latter areas the peasants already constituted an important factor in the economy.

67. Ibid., p. 228. It appears that with Augustus a standard system of taxation was established in the provinces (see also Jones, *The Roman Economy*, pp. 164-66). That attenuated the frequent greed of the Roman elite under the Republic.

68. S. I. Kavaliov, *Historia de Roma* (Buenos Aires: Futuro, 1964), vol. 1, p. 331. If the Roman aristocracy despised usurious activity, as has been said, it was because they defined usury as the small loan. A usurer was someone who oppressed poor people. The usurious activity of the patricians was called financial dealing, and large loans were made to cities, vassal kings, and provinces, whose interest could be higher.

69. Salvioli, *Le capitalisme*, p. 55. Industry was not greatly developed as a source of wealth at that time. Since the economy was built on a domestic or familial base, each household attempted to produce what was needed for its own consumption. There was little of the division of labor necessary for manufacturing. The rich bought only imported luxury goods, since otherwise they had facilities in their own households to produce what they needed. Thus they provided no stimulation to the development of industry. Even though cities were centers of consumption, there were not many who had the capacity to buy manufactured goods. The large cities were full of domestic slaves, poor freed slaves, and the dispossessed. Such poor people who did not participate in the system of production also were unable to buy anything.

70. Meeks, *The First Urban Christians*, p. 12; Wengst, *Pax Romana*, pp. 26-30; Rostovtzeff, *Social and Economic History*, vol. 1, p. 358; vol. 2, p. 692. Thus the revolt in Palestine in 66 C.E., e.g., was directed not only against Rome, but also against the usurers, landowners, and local government officials (see P. A. Brunt, "The Romanization of the Local Ruling Classes in the Roman Empire," *Assimilation et résistance à la culture greco-romaine dans le monde ancien*, ed. D. M. Pippidi [Paris: Belles Lettres, 1976], pp. 161-70). The extension of Roman citizenship to the provincial aristocracies was in exchange for their submission and for the consolidation of loyalty to the empire. In the time of Trajan, the rich of Galatia and Bithynia had to quarter the Roman army for several days while they passed through the area, because the cities were unable to withstand the economic burden entailed.

71. Although the local leaders were allied with imperial politics for their own benefit, sometimes they were wary of it. Tacitus (*Agric.* 21.2) commented that the Bretons, in his experience, called "civilization" what in fact contributed to their own slavery, referring to the baths, theaters, and games (*Tacitus: Dialogus, Agricola, Germania*, LCL, trans. Maurice Hutton [Cambridge: Harvard University, 1958], pp. 206-7).

72. Rostovtzeff, *Social and Economic History*, vol. 1, p. 346; Meeks, *The First Urban Christians*, p. 14.

73. Frank, *An Economic Survey*, vol. 4, pp. 809-12.

74. Géza Alföldy, *The Social History of Rome*, trans. David Braund and Frank Pollock (Totowa, N.J.: Barnes & Noble, 1985), p. 106; Ramsay MacMullen, *Roman Social Relations 50 B.C. to A.D. 284* (New Haven, Conn.: Yale University, 1974), pp. 88-92.

75. *The Letters of Caius Plinius Caecilius Secundus*, pp. 93-94. Those orders existed already in the time of the Republic. Augustus reinstated them and defined them more clearly. (Garnsey and Saller, *The Roman Empire*, p. 112; Garnsey, *Social Status*, pp. 234-59.)

76. Most of these were veterans of the various wars who had also accumulated sufficient wealth to be part of the upper classes in the provinces. In an agreement with the elite of the provinces, they were given responsibility for the administration, judiciary, and law and order, while the elite consolidated their local power (Alföldy, *Social History*, pp. 165-66).

77. Garnsey and Saller, *The Roman Empire*, p. 124. The position of an order like that of the senate or the equestrians was hereditary, but when noble families died out the positions were left for other rich people who, along with their wealth, had accumulated the prestige necessary for such an office.

78. Note the vocabulary of privilege in Garnsey, *Social Status*, pp. 221-23. The social mobility that was possible according to the law (from slave to freed slave, e.g., or to full citizenship) amounted to nothing compared with the privileges of the rich nobles who belonged to the orders.

79. Juan Iglesias, *Derecho Romano: Instituciones de derecho privado* (Barcelona: Ariel, 1962), pp. 108-11. One could become a slave by birth, by being captured in a war, as penalty for a crime, or simply by disposition of the law.

80. José Arias Ramos, *Derecho Romano* (Madrid: Rev. de derecho privado, 1960), vol. 1, pp. 62-63.

81. Suetonius (69–126?) describes the response of Claudius to such a situation ("The Deified Claudius," *The Twelve Caesars* 25). A number of slaves who were either sick or exhausted had been abandoned by their masters on the Island of Aesculapius in the Tiber, in order to avoid having to provide proper medical attention for them. Claudius granted them their freedom and ordered that none who recovered would revert to the former master. He decreed also that any owner who killed a slave who was sick in order to avoid paying for medical care would be guilty of homicide (*Suetonius*, LCL, 2 vols., trans. J. C. Rolfe [Cambridge: Harvard University, 1950], vol. 2, pp. 48-53).

82. There was, e.g., the tradition that a slave cruelly mistreated could take refuge in front of a statue of Caesar, in order that the abuser might have mercy on the slave, but many were frustrated in those hopes (Hopkins, *Conquerors and Slaves*, p. 223).

83. Alföldy, *Social History*, pp. 140-41. It bears repeating that slavery and poverty did not always go together, nor did rank and status. If the slave was from the imperial household or even belonged to a rich citizen, he or she could ascend the social ladder. The empire used them as administrators or merchants, which allowed more than one to accumulate wealth and rise in status over other slaves from the city, freed slaves, or even freeborn persons. But of course that experience was limited and selectively enjoyed.

84. Concerning honor and shame in relation to the system of slavery, see Bruce J. Malina, *The New Testament World: Insights from Cultural Anthropology* (Atlanta: John Knox Press, 1981), pp. 25-50.

85. Wiedemann, *Greek and Roman Slavery*, p. 7.

86. *Philo*, LCL, 11 vols., trans. F. H. Colson (Cambridge: Harvard University, 1950), vol. 7, pp. 574-77.

87. From the perspective of the donors, benefactions were the principal means by which individuals or families achieved honor. As for the recipients, donations of wheat, e.g., were guaranteed only to a small part of the free poor population *(plebs frumentaria)* of Rome, and even for them they were insufficient. (Rostovtzeff, *Social and Economic History*, vol. 1, p. 145; Richard P. Saller, *Personal Patronage Under the Early Empire* [Cambridge: Cambridge University, 1982], p. 126; Peter Garnsey, *Famine and Food Supply in the Greco-Roman World* [New York: Cambridge University, 1988], pp. 221-23.)

88. Jane F. Gardner, *Women in Roman Law and Society* (London: Croom Helm, 1986).

89. Catherine Salles, "Diversité de la situation des femmes dans l'empire romain aux 1er et 2e siècles," *Foi et Vie* 88 (1989): 47.

4. JUSTIFICATION BY FAITH IN PAUL'S LETTERS PRIOR TO ROMANS

1. "This is the reason why in this, the greatest of his letters, Paul says so much about himself, about his conversion and call, his life and work, the gospel which he proclaimed and the battles he had to fight, and also about his theology. Romans not only tells us the questions and experiences which made Paul a Christian, the servant of Christ, and the apostle to the

Gentiles. It also shows how he worked at his ideas and their effects upon himself" (Günther Bornkamm, *Paul*, trans. D. M. G. Stalker [New York: Harper & Row, 1971], p. 96). Beyond Romans, this study deals with the authentic letters of Paul (except Philemon), which are, according to scholarly consensus, in chronological order: 1 Thessalonians, 1 Corinthians, Galatians, Philippians (a composite of several letters), 2 Corinthians (also a composite), Philemon, and Romans. The earlier letters help to ground Paul's work in a specific historical setting. By his own admission, Paul did not know personally the Christian communities in Rome (Rom. 1:10, 12). For that reason it is important to draw on the parallel realities manifest in the other letters to corroborate and contextualize Paul's theological reflection found in the first eleven chapters of Romans.

2. In this letter there is no polemic against Judaizers. If the problem was already under discussion, for the Thessalonians the discussion of whether justification was by works of the law or by faith had no relevance. What can be seen in the letter is the conflict of both Jews and pagans against Christians, both Jewish and Gentile. Paul's attitude toward the Jews here is negative, in contrast to that expressed in Romans 9–11.

3. John Wacher, *The Roman Empire* (London: J. M. Dent & Sons, 1987), p. 201.

4. That is the conclusion reached by Néstor Míguez after his careful analysis of the social composition of the community of Thessalonica ("No como los otros que no tienen esperanza. Ideología y estrategia del cristianismo paulino en la gentilidad. Lectura socio-política de la primera carta de Pablo a los tesalonicenses," unpublished doctoral thesis [Buenos Aires: ISEDET, 1989], pp. 356-411, esp. p. 408). According to Robert Jewett (*The Thessalonian Correspondence* [Philadelphia: Fortress Press, 1986], p. 122), given that the sources of wealth were distributed in an unequal manner in the Roman administration, many Christians of Thessalonica were witnesses of the economic greed of others, but they participated in it only marginally.

5. Traugott Holtz, *Der Erste Brief an die Thessalonicher* (Zürich: Benziger, 1986), p. 102.

6. Ronald Russell, "The Idle in 2 Thess. 3:6-12," *NTS* 34 (1988): 112.

7. There is a difference between Paul's conclusion and Luke's about who and what events instigated the persecution, but that difference does not negate the evidence that for the Romans any manifestation that might endanger their politics aimed at maintaining the public order was intolerable.

8. According to Winifried Elliger, the cults of Dionysus and of the Cabiri were especially strong (*Paulus in Griechenland: Philippi, Thessaloniki, Athen, Korinth* [Stuttgart: Katholisches Bibelwerk, 1978], pp. 95-99).

9. Daniel Patte, *Paul's Faith and the Power of the Gospel: A Structural Introduction to the Pauline Letters* (Philadelphia: Fortress Press, 1983), p. 136. He continues (p. 137) in a more daring way to conclude from the structure of 1 Thessalonians that for Paul "it is *not* because of what happened to Jesus, nor because of what Jesus did, that the Thessalonians are in the right relationship with God. Rather, it is because of what happened in their own experience." Clearly in this letter the author is not speaking of the death of Jesus for our sins as that which establishes our relationship with God.

10. Ibid., pp. 145-47.

11. Paul has imitated that, and therefore the Thessalonians imitate him and Christ (1:6).

12. In 1:10 Paul contrasts the living and true God with the inertia and falsehood of the idols. According to Néstor Míguez ("No como los otros," pp. 265-69), the words "Pax Romana et Securitas" appeared in various forms on the coins of the period, on monuments, and in speeches. The subjects uttering the phrase "peace and security" in 1 Thess. 5:3 are the Romans. The origin of the phrase is not biblical, for *shalom* is a term complete in itself and does not need a complement. Nor is the origin Greek, for to supplement *eirēnē* with another term is not in accord with Greek usage. On the contrary, "The use of Pax with some complement like 'concord' or 'security' characterized Roman propaganda." It was the Romans who trusted in the immutability of their "peace and security."

13. Perhaps Paul had in mind Jer. 10:25, where the prophet asks that God's wrath fall on those who disown and devour Jacob. In Romans he took up again the theme of the knowledge of God in relation to idolatrous, impure, and unjust practice, and God's judgment of condemnation (Rom. 1:18-32).

14. Those are the ones who constitute the new creature or creation in Christ. Faith, love, and hope make up their mode of existence. See Raymond F. Collins, *Studies on the First Letter to the Thessalonians* (Leuven: University Press, 1984), p. 228.

15. Wacher, *The Roman Empire*, pp. 208-9.

16. See Jerome Murphy-O'Connor, *St. Paul's Corinth: Texts and Archaeology*, Good News Studies 6 (Wilmington, Del.: Michael Glazier, 1983), pp. 14-17. The Isthmian Games were one of the four great pan-Hellenic festivals (the others being the Olympic Games and those of Delphos and Nemos). They were begun in the sixth century B.C.E. and were celebrated each spring. After the Roman invasion in 146 B.C.E., the games were moved to the outskirts of the city, but Corinth again became their site between 7 B.C.E. and 3 C.E. The games brought substantial income to the city from the many visitors. According to Murphy-O'Connor, Paul could not ignore them since he was probably in Corinth during their celebration in the spring of 49 and 51 C.E.

17. Alciphron, "Letters of Parasites," n. 24, 3, 60, *The Letters of Alciphron, Aelian, and Philostratus*, LCL, trans. Allen Rogers Benner and Francis H. Forbes (Cambridge: Harvard University, 1962), pp. 208-11 (cited in Murphy-O'Connor, *St. Paul's Corinth*, pp. 119-20).

18. Murphy-O'Connor (*St. Paul's Corinth*, pp. 120-21) suggests that the purpose of Alciphron (whose work he dates from near the end of the second century C.E.) was to disparage the city of Corinth. Christophe Senft (*La première épître de Saint Paul aux Corinthiens* [Neuchâtel: Delachaux & Niestlé, 1979], p. 16) notes that in Corinth were many slaves and other laborers who worked for the benefit of the wealthy classes.

19. Murphy-O'Connor, *St. Paul's Corinth*, pp. 142-44.

20. Normally such dinners were connected with religious rituals, including offerings of meat sacrificed to idols, which troubled the consciences of many Christians, as Paul noted in 1 Cor. 10:14-22.

21. The phrase "those of" *(hypo tōn)* refers to people associated with the household of another (in this case, Chloe). They might be slaves, employees, or members of the family who would be under the control of that head of the household. See Friedrich Lang, *Die Briefe an die Korinther* (Zürich: Vandenhoeck & Ruprecht, 1986), pp. 20-21.

22. In 1 Cor. 1:26, "wise" refers to educated people or to those skilled in a profession—the "intellectuals." The "powerful" are people with a high position in the government or in pagan religious establishments, slave owners, and military officials. The "nobles" are freeborn people, generally with Roman citizenship and descendants of noble families. In contrast to all these groups are people from the base, from lower social classes. See William F. Orr and James Arthur Walther, *I Corinthians*, AB 32 (Garden City, N.Y.: Doubleday, 1976), pp. 160-61.

23. This was not an unusual attitude in that society, which accorded great importance to social prestige, such as the activities taken on by the nobles and the rich of the city in order to receive praise. Such activities included sponsorship of games, construction of public buildings and areas, and distributions of food. The idea that one should not seek the praise of human beings but rather that of God is found also in 1 Thess. 2:4. It is God who "examines the hearts," rewards God's servants, and grants authority to them, and not the jurists or rulers of the city (Collins, *Studies*, p. 207).

24. The quotation is of Jer. 9:22-23, in which knowledge of God is related to the practice of justice. Jeremiah asks that the wise person not be praised for that person's wisdom, but for knowing God, because "I am Yhwh, who does mercy, right, and justice on the earth because that is my pleasure" (Jer. 9:23, author's trans.).

25. Even though Paul was using a metaphor, he had in fact been subjected to several human courtroom proceedings, facing charges of which he considered himself innocent. Perhaps that was why he put down such proceedings so vehemently.

26. Almost all commentators hasten to explain that no moral or ethical meaning is intended in the label "unbeliever," but only a synonym of "non-Christian." They also state that rejection of courts outside the community is a characteristic of Jewish tradition. However, a person who has suffered unjustly the experience of imprisonment has his or her own reasons for rejecting the courts and considering them unjust.

27. The use of the phrase "Realm of God" is directly related to the teachings of Jesus, of which this was one of the principal themes. Paul seldom uses it, perhaps because, as Orr and

Walther conclude (*I Corinthians*, p. 195), "The political rule in the Roman Empire, where Paul's churches were located, suggested to him the advisability of using other more or less interchangeable terminology."

28. Ibid., p. 197.

29. The same connection is made in 2 Cor. 4:7–5:10. According to Murphy-O'Connor ("Faith and Resurrection in 2 Cor. 4:13-14," *RB* 95 [1988]: 543-50), in 2 Cor. 4:10 Paul had in mind the world to which his existential proclamation was directed. For Paul, faith refers to sufferings (chaps. 7-12), and resurrection touches the existential plane more than the eschatological one.

30. Some think that the phrase "fought with wild animals" is meant literally. Maurice Carrez (*La première épître aux Corinthiens* [Paris: Cerf, 1987], p. 29) indicates that in 53 C.E. the authority of the procurators had been strengthened and extended, and such practices as the staging of spectacles in the amphitheater, often including battles between human beings and wild beasts, were encouraged. Paul, then, might well have experienced them. The apostle, however, did not mention this torture in 2 Corinthians 11-13. Others think that the meaning is metaphorical (Senft, *La première épître de Saint Paul aux Corinthiens*, p. 203). In any event, what is certain is that Paul alludes to a real and serious danger to people's lives. See Hans Conzelmann, *1 Corinthians*, Hermeneia, trans. Paul W. Leitch (Philadelphia: Fortress Press, 1975), p. 203.

31. Death is swallowed up in victory in the end of time (1 Cor. 15:54), when Christ will have destroyed every principality, dominion, and power, will have put every enemy under Christ's own feet (including the ultimate enemy, death itself), and will hand over the Realm to God (15:24-27). With no explanation, Paul declared that the sting of death is sin, and the power of sin, the Law (15:56). He concluded by exhorting them to stand firm, unmoved, and continuing in the work of the Lord, for that work is not in vain (15:58). Death here refers to "a power that causes human beings to die and reigns over all humanity. Only its definitive destruction will mark the transformation of the world into a new world" (Carrez, *La première épître aux Corinthiens*, p. 119).

32. Paul clarified certain misunderstood theological concepts, such as freedom and spiritual experience. According to Conzelmann (*1 Corinthians*, p. 13), such terms came to refer to a speculative principle that separated them from the world. It was precisely to emphasize the historical character of faith that Paul developed his theology of the cross in relation to weakness, and the resurrection of the dead in relation to the hope for which one must struggle.

33. Scholars debate about the location of the churches of Galatia and also about the date of the letter. See the discussion in Hans-Dieter Betz, *Galatians*, Hermeneia (Philadelphia: Fortress Press, 1979), p. 5.

34. Michael Ivanovitch Rostovtzeff, *Social and Economic History of the Roman Empire*, 2 vols. (Oxford: Clarendon, 1957), vol. 2, pp. 652-53.

35. Ibid., pp. 358, 696.

36. Joel Allaz et al., *Chrétiens en conflit: L'Épître de Paul aux Galates* (Geneva: Labor et Fides, 1987), p. 9. Dephos, however, was the most famous slave market of that period.

37. Betz, *Galatians*, pp. 2-3.

38. Ibid., p. 3.

39. Ibid., p. 2; see also Rostovtzeff, vol. 1, p. 193; vol. 2, p. 627.

40. Patte observes that under the influence of many of those religions, believers would be led to see their society and their individual lives as bound to conform to the cosmic order governed by the principalities and powers. Their very destinies would be determined by those same powers (*Paul's Faith*, p. 53).

41. Betz, *Galatians*, p. 29.

42. Betz (ibid., p. 9) suggests that the reason for the success among the Galatians of the opponents of Paul's gospel may have been the practical problem of the lack of norms for everyday life. Life according to the Spirit through Christ did not solve their concrete daily problems.

43. Here theological elements are introduced that Paul would discuss again and develop more fully in Romans: faith, justification, adoption, the new creation, the promise, grace, and love, in contrast to the law that enslaves, idolatry (4:8), the desires of the flesh (5:16),

and the resurrection of Jesus from the dead (1:1). All these elements, in addition to the theme of sin and the example of Abraham, are present when Paul speaks of justification. Interestingly, in the letter to the Galatians, Paul granted little space to the sort of explicit discussion of the concept of sin presented in Romans. In Galatians the law is identified as the enslaving agent.

44. E. P. Sanders, "Jesus, Paul, and Judaism," in *Aufstieg und Niedergand der Römischen Welt: Principat*, vol. 2.25.1, Wolfgang Haase, ed. (Berlin: Walter de Gruyter, 1982), p. 431. Betz's opinion is similar (*Galatians*, p. 6): One ought not to use Paul's position against his adversaries as the sole basis for defining the opponents. One must take into account the rhetorical origin and function of his language, as well as Paul's bent to caricature and sarcasm. Sanders (p. 429) affirms the same about the attitude of Jesus before the law. It is definitely a question of inclusion: Jesus wanted to prepare Israel for the coming age. To do that, he situated his own mission above the law of Moses, spoke of the future destruction of the Temple, and included in the coming reign those who had generally been left outside.

45. Sanders, "Jesus, Paul, and Judaism," p. 431.

46. According to J. Severino Croatto (*Exodus: A Hermeneutics of Freedom*, trans. Salvator Attanasio [Maryknoll, N.Y.: Orbis Books, 1981], pp. 69-70), the law loses its function as a way to salvation by an inversion of values: "The values of the Law are inverted the moment it moves out of the orbit of life and, consequently, humankind." He gives three reasons: (1) The law points to exteriority, to what comes from outside a person, and not to follow it results in punishment; (2) it is uncreative in that it is limited to what is already said and to my "justice," whereas the demand of love is infinite; and (3) the law becomes *gnōsis*: I am just because I fulfill the law that I know, so that the Pharisee is saved because he knows the law, but an ignorant person is condemned.

47. There is a connection between slavery to the law and slavery to the elements of the world of cosmic religion. Patte, *Paul's Faith*, p. 54; Sanders, "Jesus, Paul, and Judaism," p. 433.

48. Betz, *Galatians*, p. 33.

49. 2 Cor. 3:12-18. Circumcision, as a visible mark in the flesh, excludes women, whereas faith shows no favoritism.

50. Dennis R. MacDonald, *There Is No Male and Female* (Philadelphia: Fortress Press, 1987), p. 126.

51. It is not a matter of annulling the law (5:14), but of breaking the law's power to exclude. To live in Christ does not prevent one from following a law oriented by the logic of the Spirit. What is rejected is whatever enslaves human beings. In Romans Paul affirmed that the law is upheld by faith (3:31).

52. Macedonia served as a base for the penetration of Roman troops toward the Danube (Fanoula Papazoglou, *Les villes de Macédoine à l'époque romaine* [Athens: École Française d'Athènes, 1988], p. 1).

53. It is not clear from which prison the letter was written. Some suggest Rome or Caesarea, however, because of the frequency of the visits of members of the church at Philippi and the rapidity of communication that allowed Paul to exchange several letters with them over a short period of time. An even closer place such as Ephesus seems the most likely. See José Comblin, *Epistóla aôs Filipenses* (Petrópolis: Vozes, 1985), p. 14; Niels Hyldahl, *Die Paulinische Chronologie* (Leiden: Brill, 1986), p. 50 (though this author dates Philippians earlier than 1 Corinthians).

54. Norman Perrin and Dennis Duling, *The New Testament: An Introduction*, 2nd ed. (New York: Harcourt Brace Jovanovich, 1982), pp. 173-74. A and B were written from Ephesus and C from either Ephesus or Troas.

55. That implied announcing that Christ is Lord in a time when the Roman emperor was assuming centralized power, glory, and divinity. It also implied defending his gospel and enduring affronts and condemnations by some members of the churches.

56. It is important to note that none of Paul's letters speaks as insistently of joy as does Philippians. Imprisoned and oppressed by economic need, by opponents who insisted on distorting the gospel with the preaching of circumcision (3:2), and even by the serious illness of Epaphroditus, who was at the point of death (2:27, 30), Paul exhorted his addressees to rejoice (2:2, 17, 18; 3:1; 4:4). Speaking of his own death, he juxtaposed joy as a power that

overcomes that reality. He asked that they rejoice and rejoice with him in the hypothetical case that his blood were spilled, for it would be for him like "a libation over the sacrifice and the offering of your faith" (2:17). Paul saw his martyrdom proleptically as a testimony to the already evident faith of the Philippians, who lived to present the word of life in the midst of a "crooked and perverse generation" (2:14-15).

57. It is an intercessory prayer, similar to an exhortation. According to Jean-François Collange (*L'Épître de Saint Paul aux Philippiens* [Neuchâtel: Delachaux & Niestlé, 1973], pp. 48-50), from the formal point of view, three propositions are developed, each ending with a complement introduced by *eis*. He prays for love, purity, and blamelessness, and to produce a "harvest" of justice. The intercession is crowned by a concluding doxology.

58. The words *epignōsis*, *aisthēsis*, and *dokimazō* underline the type of love for which Paul prayed. The prefix *epi-* has the force of something added, meaning an advanced, developed knowledge of truth, with clearer reference to practical knowledge. This knowledge orients toward Christian love in its means, objectives, circumstances, and ways. *Aisthēsis* is the faculty of discernment of the spirit in situations that arise from experience. It is more specific than *epignōsis*. It is an intelligent and discriminating love, against an uncontrolled impulse. *Dokimazō* means to test or examine something in order to know if it is good or bad (such as one would do to gold coins), and if it passes the test, it is accepted. See Marvin Vincent, *Epistles to the Philippians and to Philemon* (Edinburgh: T. & T. Clark, 1897), pp. 11-13.

59. These texts, like those that speak of a last judgment, present problems for those who see salvation and justification as synonymous. Karl P. Donfried ("Justification and Last Judgment," *ZNW* 67 [1976]: 104) distinguishes between them. For him justification is a past event that has implications through sanctification, while salvation is a future event already anticipated and partially experienced in justification and sanctification, and clearly depending on them. Salvation is the natural and hoped for result of sanctification.

60. Alphonse Maillot (*Aux Philippiens d'aujourd'hui* [Geneva: Labor et Fides, 1974], p. 81) opts for the latter, concluding that salvation is the work of Christ set forth in 2:2-11.

61. The text has been used as the basis for theological disputes concerning the human being's role in achieving salvation, as opposed to the absolute initiative of God (2:13). According to Maillot (*Aux Philippiens*, pp. 82-83), it is correct neither to make absolute one of the two affirmations of Paul, nor to combine them in a kind of synergism. Rather, he urges that the two truths be affirmed as true, recognizing that it is of little consequence that our powers of logic prove inadequate to resolve the matter: One should not confuse salvation with logic, or Jesus Christ with the theory of conjunctions.

62. Collange, *L'Épître de Saint Paul aux Philippiens*, p. 109.

63. Walther Schmithals, "Die Irrlehrer des Philipperbriefes," *ZTK* 54 (1957): 331. However, 3:19 can also be interpreted as referring to observance of the dietary laws.

64. The use of the word *politeuma* here is significant. Citizenship related to freedom, to the sharing of privileges, which in that period could be enjoyed by only a very small group of people.

65. Note the parallels between this theological discourse and that of 1 Cor. 1:1-29. Paul's addressees in the two letters were different: Whereas in Philippians they appear to have been converted Jews, in 1 Corinthians most were converted pagans. The former boasted in circumcision and the observance of the law, and the latter in their own wisdom. Justification by faith and not by one's own merits was present directly or indirectly in both contexts.

66. The verb in the future tense evokes the final judgment, and the passive form corresponds to a Hebraism that characterizes the action of God. To be found in Christ is the same as being justified. (Collange, *L'Épître de Saint Paul aux Philippiens*, p. 115).

67. According to Sanders ("Jesus, Paul, and Judaism," p. 448), this concept of participation represents the deepest and most original expression of Paul's thought.

68. According to the hypothesis of Perrin and Duling (*The New Testament*, pp. 181-82), it is possible to delineate five letters: (A) 2:14–6:13 and 7:2-4 are part of a letter Paul wrote to defend himself against his opponents who carried letters of recommendation; (B) 10:1–13:13 belongs to the so-called tearful letter that Paul wrote after having been attacked and humiliated by his opponents in Corinth. In this letter Paul contrasted the power that is born in the weakness and suffering in which he lived by the power of God, to the posture of

those who saw their strength as residing in their mighty deeds (signs and miracles) and who prided themselves on their Jewish tradition; (C) 1:1–2:13 and 7:5-16 are part of a letter in which he made his apology—the letter of reconciliation. Titus, sent by Paul, personally delivered the letter to the Corinthians and explained the situation, for Paul wrote the letter pleased with the renewal of relations; (D) 8:1-24 is a letter of recommendation for Titus so that he could organize the collection; (E) 9:1-15 is part of a letter concerning the collection for the poor of Jerusalem. It appears that the fragment found in 6:14–7:1 (according to Bornkamm [*Paul*, p. 246] possibly a fragment from Qumran) is not from Paul.

69. Maurice Carrez, *La deuxième épître de Saint Paul aux Corinthiens* (Geneva: Labor et Fides, 1986), p. 29.

70. He conceives of the experience of that power as including even the fragility of his ailing body. Paul is aware of this reality, for he has heard God (2 Cor. 12:9). The apostle believes he has been called to experience grace as a power that is fulfilled, in its fullness, in weakness. See Daniel Marguerat, "2 Corinthiens 10–13: Paul et l'experience de Dieu," *ETR* 63 (1988).

71. C. K. Barrett, *The Second Epistle to the Corinthians* (London: Adam & Charles Black, 1976), p. 173.

72. Carrez, *La deuxième épître de Saint Paul aux Corinthiens*, p. 152.

73. The exhortation in 5:20 is pronounced not only with words. Rather, in all of his correspondence with the Corinthians, it is clear that all of Paul's life gave him authority as a minister of the justice of God to exhort them to be reconciled.

74. Bornkamm, *Paul*, pp. 169-70.

75. In 1 Thess., he did not deal with that theme directly, but one can see the practice of the communities as a way of manifesting the life of persons who have been justified.

5. JUSTIFICATION BY FAITH IN ROMANS

1. Klaus Wengst, *Pax Romana and the Peace of Jesus Christ*, trans. John Bowden (Philadelphia: Fortress Press, 1987), pp. 7-54; Néstor Míguez, "No como los otros que no tienen esperanza. Ideología y estrategia del cristianismo paulino en la gentilidad. Lectura socio-política de la primera carta de Pablo a los tesalonicenses," unpublished doctoral thesis (Buenos Aires: ISEDET, 1989), pp. 624-32, 262-67.

2. According to Helen Jefferson Loanne (*Industry and Commerce of the City of Rome: 50 B.C.–200 A.D.* [New York: Arno Press, 1979], p. 11), any research into the economy of the city of Rome has to focus on exports, for Rome itself produced little.

3. G. Salvioli, *Le capitalisme dans le monde antique* (New York: Arno Press, 1979), p. 84.

4. André Paul, *Le monde des Juifs à l'heure de Jésus: Histoire politique* (Paris: Desclée, 1981), pp. 144-45.

5. The famines occurred for a variety of reasons: natural causes (in the years 5-7, 51, and 62); both civil and foreign wars (62); as a result of speculation, negligence, or specific legislation (39-41 and 68); problems of transportation (39-41); massive fires (64). See Catherine Virlouvet, *Famines et émeutes à Rome des origines de la République à la mort de Néron* (Rome: École Française, 1985), p. 22.

6. Catherine Salles, *Les bas fond de l'antiquité* (Paris: Robert Laffont, 1982), p. 180.

7. Ibid., p. 182. In his *Satires* 3 (*The Satires of Juvenal, Persius, Sulpicia, and Lucius*, trans. Lewis Evans [London: Bell and Daldy, 1872], pp. 26-27), Juvenal wrote as follows: "Whether you attempt to say a word or retire in silence, is all one; they beat you just the same, and then, in a passion, force you to give bail to answer for the assault. This is a poor man's liberty! When thrashed he humbly begs, and pummelled with fisty-cuffs supplicates, to be allowed to quit the spot with a few teeth left in his head. Nor is this yet all that you have to fear, for there will not be wanting one to rob you, when all the houses are shut up, and all the fastenings of the shops chained, are fixed and silent."

8. Peter Lampe, *Die stadtrömischen Christen in den ersten beiden Jahrhunderten* (Tübingen: JCB Mohr-Paul Siebeck, 1987), pp. 46-52. There are indications (short of certain proof) of the

presence of Christians in Aventinus and Campus Martinus, wealthy neighborhoods with a much smaller percentage of poor people than in Trastevere and the Appian Way and Porta Capena.

9. Ibid., pp. 36-43, 52.

10. In contrast, in the neighborhoods of Avantinus and Campus Martinus the communities would have been able to meet in one of the apartment houses *(insula)* common in the area.

11. A look at people's relationship to the tax structure provides a guide for assessing their class identity. According to Lampe *(Die stadtrömischen Christen,* pp. 63-64), the bulk of the community was of the *peregrini* class, because according to Rom. 13:6 they paid taxes *(forous)* from which those of the citizen class were exempt (with the rich paying taxes principally on inheritances). Paul also assumed (Rom. 13:7) that some would be paying customs duties *(telos),* which would indicate that some Christians were involved in commerce.

12. The position taken in this study is that the letter was sent to Rome in its present form, including chap. 16, which is sometimes judged to be part of another letter sent to Ephesus. See Raymond E. Brown and John P. Meier, *Antioch and Rome* (New York: Paulist, 1983), pp. 106-9.

13. Peter Stuhlmacher, "Der Abfassungszweck des Römerbriefes," *ZNW* 77 (1986): 180.

14. Brown's thesis is that Roman Christianity originated in Jerusalem, and even that it associated Jews and Gentiles with such Jerusalem leaders as Peter and James. Both the Jews and the Gentile converts were more conservative than Paul with respect to Judaism. Brown and Meier *(Antioch and Rome,* pp. 1-9) conclude that it is inappropriate to speak of Jewish Christianity and Gentile Christianity, but rather that one is dealing with various types of Christianity in which those backgrounds are blended in varying proportions. They suggest that there are at least four varieties of Christians in the NT: (1) Jewish Christians and Gentile converts who demand the observance of the whole law, including circumcision; (2) Jewish Christians and Gentile converts who do not impose circumcision, but who require of Gentiles the observance of some Jewish laws (Peter and James and many of the Jerusalem Christians belong to this group); (3) Jewish Christians and Gentile converts who require neither circumcision nor the observance of the dietary laws (Paul and Barnabas belong to this group); and (4) Jewish Christians and Gentile converts who neither require circumcision or the observance of dietary laws, nor accord to the Jewish cult or festivals any permanent significance. This last group was even more radical than Paul (see John 2:19-21; 4:29; Mark 2:22).

15. Ibid., pp. 111-22.

16. The motivation for the letter has been a theme greatly discussed by scholars, especially relative to the theological disputes between Paul and his opponents. Some suggest that he wrote principally because of pressure from the Jerusalem Christians, to whom he was trying indirectly to explain his theological thinking in a more systematic and coherent form. It has also been suggested that representatives of that same group had arrived in Rome, or perhaps had returned there after having been expelled by the edict of Claudius (Acts 18:2; see Stuhlmacher, "Der Abfassungszweck des Römerbriefes," pp. 82-191). There is some truth in each of these possibilities, but the motivation for the letter cannot be reduced to this polemic of ideas, for that would limit the theme of justification to the conflict between Paul and the conservative Jewish Christians. On the contrary, this message of Paul for his contemporaries was born in a concrete reality that is much more vast: the life of the people with whom he shared his life and his own experience as an artisan, a Jew, and a prisoner. It is true that in his letters Paul spoke most directly about justification when he was faced with Judaizers who were imposing requirements of circumcision or the observance of dietary laws (Galatians and Phil. 3:2-3). However, even in those cases the logic of his theological posture led him to affirm the equality of Jews and Gentiles with respect not only to salvation, but also to privileges of ethnicity, class, or gender (Gal. 3:28). On the other hand, there are cases when Paul did speak of justice or justification when there were no Judaizing opponents. In 1 Cor. 1, e.g., that message is directed toward those who were boasting in their wisdom and their knowledge, humiliating in that way persons who were humble, ignorant, and without power. Similarly, there were those who, despite having been justified, were following the life-style common to their society, which discriminated against the poor (1 Cor. 6:1-11).

17. Pierre Bonnard ("La justice de Dieu et l'histoire," *Anamnesis: Recherches sur le Nouveau*

Testament [Geneva: Cahiers de la Revue de théologie et de philosophie, 1980], p. 170) affirms the importance of the relationship between the justice of God and history. He maintains that what dominates in Romans is a justice that appears on the world stage at the heart of a global conception of history and of the nations. Unfortunately he does not interpret his thesis in relation to the socioeconomic circumstances of the first century, which is precisely what this study seeks to restore, so that the message does not remain floating on the level of ideas, and can have a greater impact on the practice of Christians. The study by José Porfirio Miranda (*Marx and the Bible: A Critique of the Philosophy of Oppression,* trans. John Eagleson [Maryknoll, N.Y.: Orbis Books, 1974]) has offered significant help with this task.

18. Stuhlmacher, "Der Abfassungszweck des Römerbriefes," p. 78.

19. Ulrich Wilckens, *Der Brief an die Römer* (Zurich: Benziger Neukirchener, 1987), p. 82. Although it is a fixed formula, Paul's deliberate choice of it confirms that he had in mind the environment of Greco-Roman society. According to C. K. Barrett ("I Am Not Ashamed of the Gospel," *Foi et Salut selon Saint Paul* [Paris: Institut Biblique Pontifical, 1970], p. 20), the circumstances of the letter provide evidence that Paul intended to take the proclamation of Christian authority into the very center of the empire.

20. Ernst Käsemann ("'The Righteousness of God' in Paul," *New Testament Questions of Today,* trans. W. J. Montague [Philadelphia: Fortress Press, 1969], pp. 172-74) interprets grace as power—God's self-giving in the gift of justice. He emphasizes the aspect of re-creation in the event of justification and the absence of a separation between justification and sanctification in Paul's theological construction.

21. Miranda, *Marx and the Bible,* p. 89.

22. All human beings, and not just Gentiles, are included in this reference. See Franz Leenhardt, *The Epistle to the Romans: A Commentary,* trans. Harold Knight (Cleveland, Ohio: World Publishing Co., 1961), p. 59. The presence of the word *adikia* prevents interpreting *asebeia* in a cultic sense as meaning irreligious or immoral. See Ernst Käsemann, *Commentary on Romans,* trans. Geoffrey W. Bromiley (Grand Rapids, William B. Eerdmans Publishing Co., 1980), p. 38.

23. C. E. B. Cranfield, *The Epistle of the Romans* (Edinburgh: T. & T. Clark, 1975), p. 110.

24. According to Käsemann (*Commentary on Romans,* p. 47), ethical perversion is the result of the wrath of God and not the reason for it. It signifies the abandonment of the world to chaos. Juan Luis Segundo (*El hombre de hoy ante Jesús de Nazaret: Sinópticos y Pablo* [Madrid: Cristiandad, 1982], vol. 2, p. 321) substitutes for the sequence idolatry-punishment-dehumanization the following: "desire for injustice, deceptive justifying arguments, creation of a subhuman idol that justifies injustice, and finally the fall into subhuman relationships between people." That is the way truth is made captive to injustice.

25. At issue is the indignation of God against injustice, cruelty, and corruption. (Cranfield, *Epistle of the Romans,* p. 109).

26. According to Leenhardt (*Epistle to the Romans,* p. 61), truth should not be understood here as having an absolute sense. See also C. K. Barrett, *A Commentary on the Epistle to the Romans* (London: Adam & Charles Black, 1962), p. 35.

27. It is important to name separately "those who judge" and "the Jews," following the lead of J. Severino Croatto ("Conocimiento y salvación," *RevistB* 41 [1979]: 39-55). See also Philippe Rolland, *Épître aux Romains: Texte grec structuré* (Rome: Pontifical Biblical Institute, 1980), pp. 15-16; Héctor Laporta, *La revelación de la justicia de Dios en Pablo* (San José, Costa Rica: Seminario Bíblico Latinoamericano, 1984), p. 13.

28. As Xavier Alegre ("Los ídolos que deshumanizan al hombre," *El secuestro de la verdad* [Santander: Sal Terrae, 1986], p. 35) has put it, a bad theology entails a bad ethic, and a bad ethic implies and conditions a bad theology.

29. According to Bonnard ("La justice de Dieu," p. 139), in Paul *nous* is a term borrowed from the Greco-Roman context, but its nuance was transformed by the contact with Jewish and Christian traditions. Paul calls on the intellect valued by the Greeks to counterbalance the millenarian and spiritualist pieties that were threatening the churches. In the particular case of Romans 1 and 3, intellect is part of the human condition that is alienated from the Creator, the revealed law, and the gospel itself. "The exercise and renewal of the intellect are indispensable for the Christian."

191

30. Cranfield, *Epistle of the Romans*, p. 117; Käsemann, *Commentary on Romans*, p. 44; Alegre, "Los ídolos," p. 36; Segundo, *El hombre de hoy*, p. 320.

31. Note, e.g., the mention of snakes, unclean animals. The military emperor was accumulating for himself absolute power. That power was legitimated in the consciousness of the masses through an ideology with religious overtones. Caesar is the God one must worship for the good of the empire (see Míguez, "No como los otros," pp. 269-72 and 294-96). An inscription on a marble stone broken into five pieces can still be deciphered. It reads, "The emperor, Caesar, son of God, the God Augustus, of all land and sea, is the one who keeps watch." Adolf Deissmann (*Light from the Ancient East*, trans. Lionel R. M. Strachan [New York: George H. Doran, 1927], p. 347) indicates that *epoptes* was an honorary title used in Judaism and early Christianity as a predicate of God.

32. Gustavo Gutiérrez, *We Drink from Our Own Wells: The Spiritual Journey of a People*, trans. Matthew J. O'Connell (Maryknoll, N.Y.: Orbis Books, 1984), p. 59.

33. The sense here is that God has permitted such a fate (Cranfield, *Epistle of the Romans*, p. 121) or abandoned people to it (Alphonse Maillot, *L'épître aux Romains* [Geneva: Labor et Fides, 1984], p. 67). It is not a punishment directly from God, but rather the consequence of not recognizing God. "Men were free to refuse God, but they were not free to remove the consequences of this refusal" (Leenhardt, *Epistle to the Romans*, p. 66).

34. Rom. 1:26-27 has been a text traditionally used against homosexual persons by a homophobic society. According to George R. Edwards (*Gay/Lesbian Liberation: A Biblical Perspective* [New York: Pilgrim Press, 1984], pp. 89-90, 99), in Rom. 1:18-32 Paul uses a tradition (which includes the three elements of idolatry, adultery, and homosexuality) that reflects the perspective of Judaism on the depravity of the Gentiles. It seems that Paul's purpose in Rom. 1:18-32 is to demonstrate not only human weakness, but also the perversion of society from the macro-structural perspective, and the impossibility for any human being to do justice under such circumstances. Homosexuality serves as an image of the inversion of values according to the heterosexual view of marriage. Rom. 1:26-27 should not be taken literally, just as also the assertions that *all* Jews or *all* Gentiles are unjust in their actions should not be taken literally. Surely there were good, sincere, and honest people then, as in every society. The problem was that besides human fragility anthropologically speaking, justice that is effective, meaningful, and real in his environment was, in his eyes, impossible to realize without the intervention of God.

35. Tomás Hanks ("El testimonio evangélico a los pobres y oprimidos," *VP* 4 [1984]: 12) recognizes the importance of the forensic meaning for the poor, not only because they also are sinners, but because that meaning testifies to the existence of a supreme Judge who is incorruptible. In the history of Israel itself, the judges were frequently bribed by the rich to the detriment of the poor who sought justice in their courts.

36. Paul continues to speak throughout Romans of an eschatological judgment determined by the practice of human beings. Justification by faith does not annul that. See the classification of Pauline texts concerning judgment in Karl Donfried, "Justification and Last Judgment," *ZNW* 67 (1976): 103.

37. According to Cranfield (*Epistle of the Romans*, p. 167), Paul is referring not to ordinary Jews, but to the teachers—perhaps especially to those who instructed Gentile converts.

38. Segundo, *El hombre de hoy*, p. 370.

39. José Ignacio González Faus, *Proyecto de hermano: Visión creyente del hombre* (Santander: Sal Terrae, 1987), p. 242.

40. Segundo (*El hombre de hoy*, p. 324) emphasizes the anthropological aspect of the reading in Romans. He maintains that Paul changes the political key of the preaching of Jesus to the anthropological one. That is to say, Paul "moves from the accusation of oppression to the most generic or social relations deprived of truth and humanity." It is important to note, however, that there is an intrinsic connection between the two keys.

41. He appears to have made the change deliberately in order to give greater force to the justice of God. In fact, in 3:21-26 Paul will go on to present the good news of the justice of God (*dikaiosynē theou*), will describe God as just (*dikaios*) and justifying (*dikaiounta*), and will speak of God's justifying action (*dikaioō*).

42. Günter Röhser, *Metaphorik und Personifikation der Sünde: Antike Sündenvorstellungen und paulinische Hamartia* (Tübingen: J. C. B. Mohr, 1987), pp. 1-3.

43. Miranda, *Marx and the Bible*, p. 181.

44. His reflection on Christ's liberation of humankind from that fate is also peculiar to Paul. Luise Schottroff, "Die Schreckenherrschaft der Sünde und die Befreiung durch Christus nach dem Römerbrief des Paulus," *EvT* 39 (1979): 497.

45. Bonnard ("La justice," p. 138) believes that Rom. 7:25 summarizes the chapter. In Romans 7, *nous* is a power autonomous from the discernment and consent of the good; but its value here is simply theoretical, with no effect on practice, because it is "sold to sin."

46. Wilckens, *Der Brief an die Römer*, p. 172.

47. One might even say that in those human conditions, the practice of justice itself yields to the vitiated and perverted reality that is turned against the very person who does justice. For that reason one cannot be justified, because it is impossible to be just in an unjust world, where the power of sin reigns. And God cannot simply justify the unjust, forgetting those who suffer because of their injustices. Beyond ceasing to be just, God would be unfaithful to God's own identity and to the poor.

48. Christophe Senft (*Jésus de Nazareth et Paul de Tarse* [Geneva: Labor et Fides, 1985], pp. 71-77) underlines the misunderstanding involved in seeing the forgiveness of sins as the heart of the gospel. See also Krister Stendahl, *Paul Among Jews and Gentiles* (Philadelphia: Fortress Press, 1976), pp. 23-40.

49. The same thing applies to the sentence from Habakkuk that Paul cites. The person who is just, or who has faith, will live. In a given moment, when one's powers are exhausted by the superiority of the enemy hosts, no hope for survival remains for the just person except to count on the sovereign power of God (Leenhardt, *Epistle to the Romans*, pp. 59-60).

50. In Isaiah 59, which Paul knows well and has just cited, God appears, finds no just person, and intervenes to do justice.

51. Käsemann, *Commentary on Romans*, p. 92. This judgment and proclamation are produced within the eschatological framework. In order that the justice of God be truly radical and permanent, it cannot be given in any other way. Therefore Paul speaks various times in the future tense using apocalyptic language. At stake is the opening of a new horizon where the justice of God is presented as a power able to be anticipated in the concrete works of men and women, thanks to the faith of Jesus Christ and of the believers.

52. Simão Voigt ("Estão faltos da glória de Deus (Ro. 3.23): Ambivalência no pensar linguajar de Paulo," *REB* 47 [1987]: 243-69) affirms that in "fall short of the glory of God," one must read both a subjective and an objective genitive—failing to give God glory, and consequently also to receive glory from God. They are thus justified freely, without having received the glory or approval of God, and without necessarily being pleasing to God.

53. Recognize that the announcement of justice for all is situated precisely within the polemic against the Jews who were convinced of their advantage relative to other peoples (3:1-20, 27-37). According to the studies of Luke Timothy Johnson ("Rom. 3:21-26 and the Faith of Jesus," *CBQ* 44 [1982]: 77-90), Sam K. Williams ("Again *Pistis Christou*," *CBQ* 49 [1987]: 431-47), and Leonard Ramaroson ("La justification par la foi du Christ Jésus," *ScEs* 39 [1987]: 81-92), *pistis Christou* is translated as faith of Jesus Christ in the sense of faith lived by Jesus Christ, not faith in Jesus Christ. That translation resolves the redundancy of such important verses as Rom. 3:22, 26; Gal. 2:16; 3:22; Phil. 3:9, and gives internal consistency within Romans to such other passages as Rom. 1:17; 4:1-25; 5:12-21. In addition, that translation makes the faith of the believer dynamic and oriented toward the practice of justice, which has been emphasized in this interpretation.

54. In the parallel with Adam, Paul affirms that by the obedience of Jesus, humanity is made just (Rom. 5:19). For a discussion of the faith of Jesus as obedience, see Ramaroson, "La justification," pp. 89-90.

55. In that sense Jesus is the initiator and consummator of faith in the struggle against sin (Heb. 12:2-4). His faith has a soteriological character and provides the basis for the faith response of others, which by the gift of the Spirit can be like the faith of Jesus (Johnson, "Rom. 3:21-26," p. 89). While analyzing Rom. 3:22, Gal. 2:16, and Phil. 3:9, Ramaroson ("La justification," pp. 90-91) observes two types of faith, one as a beginning point and the other

as an end point. One begins with the faith of Christ in order to arrive at the faith of the Christian. This observation illumines the meaning of the difficult phrase in Rom. 1:17: the justice of God that is revealed from faith to faith—that is, from the faith of Christ to the faith of the believer. The faith of the believer is definitely the faith of Jesus, because the believer lives in Christ. Williams ("Again *Pistis Christou*," pp. 443-44) concludes that the faith of Christ is prior to and distinguishable, at least conceptually, from the faith of the believer in the sense that Christ inaugurates eschatological faith, and that faith is the means by which God's justice is manifest to all persons who make the attitude of Christ their own and thus participate in the consummation of the historical purpose of God.

56. The faith of Christ is the source to which the law and the prophets testify. According to Williams ("Again *Pistis Christou*," pp. 443-44), the phrase *eis pantas tous pisteuontas* means "to those who benefit from the faith of Christ" when they opt for a new style of life before God, inaugurated by Christ.

57. Miranda (*Marx and the Bible*, pp. 182, 189, 191-92) interprets that fact in the following way: God justified Jesus by raising him from the dead. Thus, for Paul justice can come not from the law but from faith: believing that the reign that defines both justice and life has indeed arrived.

58. Peter Stuhlmacher, "Zur neuern Exegese von Rom. 3.24-26," *Versöhnung, Gesetz und Gerechtigkeit* (Göttingen: Vandenhoeck & Ruprecht, 1981), p. 134.

59. Maillot, *L'épître aux Romains*, p. 106.

60. In Judea there was a complaint about the abuse of crucifixions by the Romans as part of the "pacification" of rebel provinces (Martin Hengel, *La crucifixion* [Paris: Cerf, 1981], p. 65).

61. Miranda, *Marx and the Bible*, p. 189.

62. In that sense, "The message of the cross is more than a questioning or a criticism of the law; that message mocks the law" (J. Allaz et al., *Chrétiens en Conflit: L'épître de Paul aux Galates* [Geneva: Labor et Fides, 1987], p. 20).

63. By including both *dōrea* and *charis*, Paul clearly wanted to make it clear that this was a gift. His meaning also needs to be understood in the context of the polemic in which he was engaged with the Judaizers. The author includes this aspect in 3:21-26, in a polemic against those who were under the law as a requirement for justification (3:20, 27), but also against those who were under the reality of the inverted order just described, which makes men and women incapable of doing justice.

64. Käsemann, *Commentary on Romans*, p. 96.

65. Ibid., pp. 101, 172. Note how the terms Paul uses to describe the practice of justice of the person who is justified by faith reflect this relationship of gift and Giver: (1) The love of God has been poured out into our hearts (5:4); (2) those who have received justice exercise dominion in life (5:17); (3) those who live this new life make of their members instruments of justice in the service of God (6:13), and those freed from sin have made themselves slaves of justice; (4) they have been freed from the law to serve with a new spirit, not according to the old letter (7:6). The justice of the law is fulfilled in those who conduct themselves according to the Spirit.

66. Here Paul takes up the language of late apocalyptic Judaism (Käsemann, *Commentary on Romans*, p. 95); Peter Stuhlmacher, *Gottes Gerechtigkeit bei Paulus* (Göttingen: Vandenhoeck & Ruprecht, 1965), p. 187.

67. The gift of justification is part of the eschaton, but not the eschaton itself, and for that reason the creation is still "groaning in labor pains" (8:22). Käsemann (*Commentary on Romans*, pp. 234-35) insists on reading the justice of God and justification from an eschatological perspective.

68. Cranfield, *Epistle of the Romans*, pp. 224-25; Leenhardt, *Epistle to the Romans*, pp. 122-23.

69. Miranda, *Marx and the Bible*, p. 231.

70. The Spanish phrase, *contra toda condena*, is the title of the entire book. In this section the author spells out the ramifications of justification by faith as the gracious cancellation of all condemnation, every punishment, and indeed the entire world view that rewards privilege and merit. Bringing neither pardon nor a declaration of innocence, God's action of justification in the faith of Jesus Christ amounts to a gracious declaration of amnesty for all humankind (translator's note).

71. The justice of the law could not be properly fulfilled (8:3) because it was oriented not by the Spirit, but by the dead letter (2 Cor. 3:6).

72. The law of the Spirit that gives life in Christ liberated humankind (8:1); God condemned sin (8:3); the Spirit of God dwells within humankind (8:9); the Spirit of Christ is life (8:10); the Spirit of the one who raised Jesus will give life (8:11).

73. Paul was not confining his thought to the limited situation of his time. It is that concrete situation that permitted him to conceive in a universal way the perverse character of a logic provoked by the specific injustices of men and women, as well as a certain tendency in human beings to twist things to support their own interests.

74. Miranda, *Marx and the Bible*, p. 191.

75. Bonnard ("La justice," p. 175) underlines the importance of this text, which "constitutes the decisive originality of Pauline thought."

76. This fact must not be forgotten. It would be counterproductive for a believer with economic and political power, who believes himself or herself to be faithful to the truth, to use these words to support his or her power, to the detriment of others. Curiously those are the ones who commonly refuse to recognize themselves as sinners, tending to forget that every human being is a sinner. Some fail to recall their human finitude as sinful beings, while others, who have the clarity to recognize themselves as sinners, need to recall their divinity in Christ.

77. Jorge Pixley, "El evangelio paulino de justificación por la fe: conversación con José Porfirio Miranda," *VP* 6 (1986): 54. Pixley continues, "The life of faith will tend to be a life of someone who knows that he or she is still a sinner, who knows his or her potential for oppressing a neighbor, and who relies on the help of God in the daily struggle against the power of sin that threatens to impose again its dominion over the person who has been freed to live in justice. And whether we speak of persons or of groups, the dynamic is the same." See also Cranfield, *Epistle of the Romans*, p. 319.

78. Rubem A. Alves, *A Theology of Human Hope* (Washington, D.C.: Corpus Books, 1969), pp. 136, 142.

6. FROM A BIBLICAL-HERMENEUTICAL READING TO A THEOLOGICAL REREADING

1. Juan Luis Segundo (*El hombre de hoy ante Jesús de Nazaret: Sinópticos y Pablo*, 3 vols. [Madrid: Cristiandad, 1982], vol. 2, pp. 16-24) notes the need to reread the event of Jesus Christ in light of our reality. That cannot be achieved by repeating what is said in the biblical texts produced in a particular time and place. According to Segundo, it is necessary to "learn to learn," or "to learn as a second step." Paul, then, gives us the criteria for such a reading.

2. J. Severino Croatto develops the concept of the "reservoir" or "surplus" of meaning (*Exodus: A Hermeneutics of Freedom*, trans. Salvator Attanasio [Maryknoll, N.Y.: Orbis Books, 1981], p. 3): "We can speak of a circular dialectic between event and word, and, by the same token, between kerygma and situation, between the biblical word on liberation and our processes of liberation. But a hermeneutic reading of the biblical message occurs only when the reading *supersedes the first contextual meaning* (not only that of the author but also that of his first readers). This happens *through the unfolding of a surplus-of-meaning disclosed by a new question addressed to the text.*"

3. E.g., note the disputes about various types of grace, or about the existence of original sin. See the discussion in Alister E. McGrath, *Iustitia Dei: A History of the Christian Doctrine of Justification* (London: Cambridge University, 1986).

4. The reader "adds" meaning to the reserve of meaning that the text itself possesses. See Croatto, *Exodus*, p. 2; Carlos Mesters, *Por trás das palavras: Um estudo sobre a porta de entrada no mundo da Bíblia* (Petrópolis: Vozes, 1974), p. 131.

5. According to Néstor Míguez ("No como los otros que no tienen esperanza. Ideología y estrategia del cristianismo paulino en la gentilidad. Lectura socio-política de la primera carta

de Pablo a los tesalonicenses," unpublished doctoral thesis [Buenos Aires: ISEDET, 1989], pp. 614-44), the Pauline strategy of powerlessness is based precisely on this objective reality.

7. JUSTIFICATION BY FAITH AND
THE THREATENED LIFE OF THE POOR

1. In this sense we break both with earlier studies of justification and with current treatments of the issue. We begin not with a generic "human," but with specific human beings—men and women who suffer the consequences of the structural sin of our society, whether as victims or as victimizers (José Ignacio González Faus, *Proyecto de hermano: Visión creyente del hombre* [Santander: Sal Terrae, 1987], pp. 237-98). That fact leads us to assume, or at some moments to distance ourselves from, certain approaches of the classical Protestant tradition, which, like the Catholic, does not make such a distinction. The motivation of this theological project is not to discuss whether or not there is anything good in the human being, or to privilege faith over works, or to justify God vis-à-vis the death of the excluded. Since our primary concern is the way people have been condemned to death by structural sin, our purpose is to underline the solidarity of God in justification as a divine act, by appealing to the practice of justice. We are aware that this is not "the meaning" of justification, but one among several that attempt to respond to the present situation. Some of these conclusions on the level of theoretical argument will be the same as those found in the tradition (e.g., justification as the free action of God, as the restoration of the human being, as including both forensic and effective dimensions, and as the forgiveness of sins). However, in addition to rethinking those data, we take into account the background of our concrete history lying behind the discussion. Our principal source will be Latin American theology, but we will take into account also the work of Karl Barth on justification in the *Church Dogmatics* 4/1, 61, trans. Geoffrey W. Bromiley (Edinburgh: T. & T. Clark, 1956), and the Helsinki Document (published as *Justification Today, Lutheran World*, Supplement to No. 1 [1965]), prepared by the Lutheran World Federation (Studies and Reports, Supplement 1, 1965). The work of Barth represents a theological position known and assumed by vast sectors of the Protestant tradition. The Helsinki Document reveals the Lutheran concern to interpret the meaning of justification in today's world. We will note at appropriate points our divergence from those positions.

2. Franz Hinkelammert (*Crítica a la razón utópica* [San José, Costa Rica: DEI, 1979], pp. 240-41) contrasts the satisfaction of necessities with the satisfaction of preferences (such as a choice of products or technology). The latter "must be derived from and subordinated to the former. If there are basic needs to be met, preferences or tastes cannot be the criteria that determine economic ends. The only basic criterion must be precisely that of necessities. . . . *The satisfaction of necessities makes life possible; the satisfaction of preferences makes it pleasant. But in order to be pleasant, first it must be possible.*" On the contrast between criteria of productivity and of the priority of providing basic necessities, see the collection of essays edited by Hugo Assmann (*Tecnología y necesidades básicas* [San José, Costa Rica: DEI, 1970], pp. 13-26) coming out of the meeting in Oaxtepec, Mexico, convened by the World Council of Churches and the Association of Economists of the Third World.

3. We identify ourselves with the following as the primary concern at this time in the history of our continent: the premature death that is imposed today on the people who live in poor nations, and the affirmation of the God of life and Liberator who opts for the poor. This is why we believe that "death and injustice are not the final word of history. Christianity is a message of life, a message based on the gratuitous love of the Father for us" (Gustavo Gutiérrez, *We Drink from Our Own Wells: The Spiritual Journey of a People*, trans. Matthew J. O'Connell [Maryknoll, N.Y.: Orbis Books, 1984], p. 1). See also Franz Hinkelammert, *The Ideological Weapons of Death: A Theological Critique of Capitalism*, trans. Phillip Berryman (Maryknoll, N.Y.: Orbis Books, 1986); Raúl Vidales, "Teología de la vida, Teología de la muerte,"

Cruz y resurrección: Presencia y anuncio de una iglesia nueva (Mexico City: CRT, 1978), p. 349; Jon Sobrino, "The Epiphany of the God of Life in Jesus of Nazareth," in Victorio Araya et al., *The Idols of Death and the God of Life: A Theology*, trans. Barbara E. Campbell and Bonnie Shepherd (Maryknoll, N.Y.: Orbis Books, 1983), pp. 66-102; Leonardo Boff, *Jesucristo y la liberación del hombre* (Madrid: Cristiandad, 1981); Enrique Dussel, *Ética comunitaria* (Buenos Aires: Paulinas, 1986); Dorothee Soelle, *Choosing Life* (Philadelphia: Fortress Press, 1981); Ulrich Duchrow, *Global Economy* (Geneva: WCC, 1987), pp. 139-84.

4. According to Eberhard Jüngel ("Homo Humanus: La signification de la distinction réformatrice entre la personne et ses oeuvres pour la façon dont l'homme moderne se comprend lui-même," *RTP* 119 [1987]: 48-49), to be a "person" does not necessarily imply that one is a "human being." A "person" becomes human when the person is recognized as such by God in the event of justification. To try to achieve that recognition by one's own actions is self-contradictory and can cost one's humanity. For González Faus (*Proyecto de hermano*, p. 487), the Pauline doctrine of justification is "the transformation of the human being from inhuman to 'good,' and even to fully human." The author notes that there is no single word that substitutes univocally and adequately for the word "justification," but on the "modern semantic horizon" one can substitute "human realization," "humanization," "rehabilitation," and others.

5. See the Helsinki Document (*Justification Today*) for a discussion of the secular person in a competitive society (sec. 1, par. 1, pp. 2-3) and the present institutionalized church (sec. 3, par. 9, p. 6; sec. 4, par. 11, p. 6). That affirmation is certainly biblical and we have made it explicit several times. But there are distinct angles that can be explored. Karl Barth (*Church Dogmatics* 4/1, 61, 2, pp. 528-29) assumes the generic, universal angle, considering justification from the perspective of the human being: All equally have sinned, and all equally need justification. The human being is one who is a sinner, unjust, and proud. Other current approaches, influenced by the sin presently visible in the mechanisms of oppression, begin also with the human being as sinner. More specifically, in order to proclaim the grace of God, they begin in the first instance with the one who oppresses and spills innocent blood. From there comes the insistence that such a being recognize his or her guilt, since he or she has sinned against God and against the sister or brother (González Faus, *Proyecto de hermano*, pp. 393-414). According to that same author ("Los pobres como lugar teológico," *El secuestro de la verdad: Los hombres secuestran la verdad con su injusticia (Rom 1, 18)* [Santander: Sal Terrae, 1986], pp. 138-43), it is the poor person who makes another convert to the Lord, because the poor person shows him or her the truth that the human being is a sinner, and at the same time shows the love of God who justifies even sinners. Therefore it is categorically affirmed that the fundamental sin is that of self-affirmation in the sense of wanting to be like God. This is an important aspect of justification. However, for now we want to begin with the spilled blood—that is to say, with Abel and not with Cain. For our question is that of Gutiérrez (*We Drink from Our Own Wells*, p. 7): "How can we thank God for the gift of life when the reality around us is one of premature and unjustly inflicted death? How can we express joy at knowing ourselves to be loved by the Father when we see the suffering of our brothers and sisters?"

6. In the final statement of the Fifth EATWOT (Ecumenical Association of Third World Theologians) Conference, New Delhi, August 17-29, 1983, the theologians spoke about that irruption in the following terms: "Over against this dramatic picture of poverty, oppression, and the threat of total destruction a new consciousness has arisen among the downtrodden. This growing consciousness of the tragic reality of the Third World has caused an irruption of exploited classes, marginalized cultures, and humiliated races. They are bursting from the underside of history into the world long dominated by the West. It is an irruption expressed in revolutionary struggles, political uprisings, and liberation movements. It is an irruption of religious and ethnic groups looking for affirmation of their authentic identity, of women demanding recognition and equality, of youth protesting dominant systems and values. It is an irruption of all those who struggle for full humanity and for their rightful place in history" ("The Irruption of the Third World: Challenge to Theology," in Samuel Rayan et al., *Irruption of the Third World: Challenge to Theology*, ed. Virginia Fabella and Sergio Torres [Maryknoll, N.Y.: Orbis Books, 1983], p. 195).

7. From the perspective of feminist theology, Elizabeth Moltmann-Wendel (*A Land Flowing with Milk and Honey: Perspectives on Feminist Theology*, trans. John Bowden [New York: Crossroad, 1986], pp. 161-65) stresses the importance of justification by faith as radical self-acceptance. To know oneself as good, whole, and beautiful, as opposed to the feelings of guilt and shame promoted by the androcentric society, is part of humanization. Gustavo Gutiérrez (*On Job: God-talk and the Suffering of the Innocent*, trans. Matthew J. O'Connell [Maryknoll, N.Y.: Orbis Books, 1987], pp. 101-3) sees in the poor, women, and indigenous peoples, persons whom society identifies as thoroughly insignificant.

8. Concerning the truth of the idol, the introduction to the collective work *The Idols of Death and the God of Life* affirms: "Much to the contrary of what might be supposed, false gods not only exist today, but are in excellent health! Many are the worshipers who invoke their mercy, their love, and their power, and theologies abound to rationalize a false practice of liberation. The search for the true God in this battle of the gods brings us to an anti-idolatrous discernment of false gods, of those fetishes that kill with their religious weapons of death." According to Pablo Richard, writing in the same book ("Biblical Theology of Confrontation with Idols," p. 3), "In an oppressed world, evangelization must direct its attention mainly to idolatry, not to atheism. The oppressive world of today is a world of fetishes and idols, of clerics and theologians." Hugo Assmann ("Iglesia desde los pobres," in Assmann et al., *Cruz y resurrección: Presencia y anuncio de una iglesia nueva* [Mexico: CRT, 1978], p. 288) affirms that "it is impossible to develop a theology of sin, grace, and the purposes of God toward the poor, without denouncing the idolatrous, structural, and persistent character of the theology of domination—a dismantling that cannot be limited to the purely 'theological' arena." For a discussion of capital as an idol, see Dussel, *Etica comunitaria*, pp. 18, 33, 145-48, 173.

9. Raúl Vidales, "Pagar es morir, queremos vivr," *Pasos* 6 (1987): 43-44.

10. Pablo Richard notes (*La fuerza espiritual de la iglesia de los pobres* [San José, Costa Rica: DEI, 1987], p. 124), "The sinner goes on dying in his or her sin. There is a limit. When one arrives at that limit, the sin kills the sinner. Every criminal is transformed into a beast and the beast ends up killing the criminal."

11. It is here, and only here, that we hear the profound meaning of the early (1919) and opportune affirmation of the *No!* of Karl Barth to everything that signifies self-affirmation, human potential, pride, and insolence before the God who is wholly other, in the reality of progress and abundance that appears to have no limits (*The Epistle to the Romans*, trans. from the sixth ed. by Edwyn C. Hoskyns [London: Oxford University, 1933], p. 38). His well-known *Yes!* to the human being and to the creation would be pronounced later on, when he affirmed the humanity of God in Jesus Christ ("The Humanity of God," in Karl Barth, *The Humanity of God*, trans. John Newton Thomas and Thomas Wieser [Atlanta: John Knox Press, 1960], pp. 37-65). Jorge Pixley ("Un teólogo europeo de la encarnación," *Xilotl* 2 [1988]: 75-84) indicates the importance of maintaining in tension these two affirmations of Barth. Biblically, it would be the equivalent of joining Eccles. 5:2 and Ps. 8:4. Klauspeter Blaser (*Karl Barth 1886-1986: Combats-Idées-Reprises* [Bern: Peter Lang, 1987], p. 127), speaking of Barth, demonstrates that even if the human being were to reclaim his or her autonomous manner of self-possession and to lift himself or herself up, that would still signify liberation.

12. The terminology "long time" and "short time" is taken from Sergio Spoerer, *América Latina: los desafíos del tiempo fecundo* (Mexico City: Siglo XXI, 1980) and from Raúl Vidales, *Utopía y liberación: el amanecer del indio* (San José, Costa Rica: DEI, 1988). We give it a theological connotation: eternity-historicity and universality-particularity.

13. Is it not perhaps in this sense that Karl Barth affirms divine election for the human being in Jesus Christ for all eternity? (*Church Dogmatics* 2/2, trans. Geoffrey W. Bromiley et al. [Edinburgh: T. & T. Clark, 1957], pp. 7-14.)

14. There is a significant connection between justification by faith and resurrection. The Helsinki Document (sec. 5, par. 18) points out the difficulties generated for the Christian life by the understanding of justification that centers on the cross and does not consider the resurrection with the same intensity (*Justification Today*, p. 8). Jürgen Moltmann (*The Way of Jesus Christ: Christology in Messianic Dimensions*, trans. Margaret Kohl [San Francisco: HarperCollins, 1990], p. 214) also urges the reconsideration of the resurrection in justification. Tra-

ditionally justification has stressed the death of Jesus on the cross (Luther, Karl Barth). Recent contributions relating justification to the creation of the human being are emerging from a goal of the framework of Christology to emphasize the manifestation of God the Creator (Käsemann, Stuhlmacher). We intend to grant a privileged place to the relation between justification and resurrection (although the resurrection is always a "child of the cross"). In this way we affirm that the three persons of the Trinity are participants in the event of justification: The Father or Creator-God raises Jesus from the dead. The life of faith of Jesus, his death, and his resurrection are counted as justification for all those who believe in the God who has the power to raise the dead. The Spirit renews, orients, consolidates, and gives testimony to that faith.

15. According to Leonardo Boff (*O destino do homem e do mundo* [Petrópolis: Vozes, 1973], p. 26), "The human being is called to be totally the same in the realization of all of the capacities latent in human nature. He or she is constituted as a knot of relationships upset from all directions—by the world, by the other, and by the Absolute."

16. The project of being brother and sister and the project of being a child of God correspond to each other. The human being is a brother or sister because he or she is a child of God. See González Faus, *Proyecto de hermano*, p. 12.

17. God will always be God and the creature always the creature. See Boff, *O destino*, p. 26.

18. Ibid., pp. 26-27.

19. González Faus (*Proyecto de Hermano*, pp. 94-120) summarizes the various material or formal responses to the content of the image of God. No response exhausts the subject, and all provide access to that content. He is concerned to maintain a healthy tension or distinction between creaturehood and image of God: "The image of God is not only in a pure and facile continuity with human creaturehood. At the same time as continuity, the image results in a rupture, vertigo, and leap to creaturehood." Throughout his book he underlines the importance of establishing "the human distinction between harmony and difficulty, between positive sensation and tragic sensation." Without denying this important point, and accepting as good the responses that theology has given in the definition of the image of God, we want to note in this particular study (situated at the beginning of the decade of the 1990s in the specific continent of Latin America) the importance to relating the image of God to the dignity of the human being as a person and historical subject. Poor people, women, indigenous people, blacks, and those who are denied respect or who are excluded for whatever reason must be recognized as subjects, for that is a divine right authorized in the creation to every human being. The image of God as the dignity of the human person implies "an element of grandness and absolute mystery in the other, that demands total respect, that prevents radical condemnation and prohibits the manipulation of the other. And it implies an element that must not be denied by other people, even though humankind has ignored or destroyed it in themselves, or that coexists within the human being with a large dose of the satanic image" (ibid., p. 100). An affirmation the poor people of the popular Christian communities—and men and women in general—like to repeat constantly is simply that they are sons and daughters created in the image and likeness of God.

20. This is definitely the drama that Gutiérrez posits when he asks how one can speak of the love of God in the midst of such profound contempt for human life. For him, "Job shows us a way with his vigorous protest, his discovery of concrete commitment to the poor and all who suffer unjustly, his facing up to God, and his acknowledgment of the gratuitousness that characterizes God's plan for human history" (*On Job*, p. 102).

21. For Julio de Santa Ana ("Costo social e sacrificio aôs ídolos," *Dívida externa e igrejas: Uma visão ecumênica* [Rio de Janeiro: CEDI, 1989], p. 82), the laws of the "free" market are translated into sacrificial violence. Dussel (*Etica comunitaria*, pp. 145, 173) identifies the idol with capital: "Capital pretends, like a true god, to produce profit, 'out of nothing' *(ex nihilo)*. Its idolatrous character, fetishist, ignores the origin of all the value it contains, that it has accumulated. It believes that it has produced it itself. The person of the laborer is nothing in that process."

22. The revelation of God, God's name, is always linked to a history that leads to the knowledge of God: history of liberation, of death, and of resurrection, of consignment to the world (K. Blaser, *Esquisse de la Dogmatique* [Lausanne: UNIL, 1985], p. 14).

23. The humanity of God as a dimension of that encounter is a subject to which we will need to return. Toward the end of his life (1956), Karl Barth spoke of the humanity of God. Unfortunately, this affirmation by Barth is little known compared with his extensive discussion of the distant God. For the elderly Barth, the divinity of God has a human character insofar as God manifests it not in the emptiness of a being divine in itself, but rather in the fact that God exists, speaks, and acts as a companion of the human being (see "The Humanity of God," pp. 45-46). God's free affirmation of the human being, God's free concern for the human being, and God's free intervention in favor of the human being are what constitute the humanity of God (ibid., p. 51). In Jesus Christ, "The fact is once for all established that God does not exist without man" (ibid., p. 50).

24. "The people shouts and God hears" is the typical movement that one encounters in the memory of God's people in the Hebrew Bible. See Pablo Richard, *Cristianismo, lucha ideológica y racionalidad socialista* (Salamanca: Sígueme, 1975), p. 75.

25. Leonardo Boff, *Passion of Christ, Passion of the World: The Facts, Their Interpretation, and Their Meaning Yesterday and Today*, trans. Robert R. Barr (Maryknoll, N.Y.: Orbis Books, 1987), p. 11. The christological hymn of Phil. 2:5-11 illustrates this journey of solidarity of God.

26. Leonardo Boff writes in a poem in Portuguese, "Jesus is not alone on the cross. His followers are there. They take up his cause, imitate his life, and follow his destiny. There is also the army of the crucified. They are invisible. They are crucified on the other side. The cross always has two sides, that of the Teacher, that of the disciples, and that of all the suffering people of this world. All of them are in the heart of Jesus" (Leonardo Boff and Nelson Porto, *Francisco de Assis: Homen do paraíso* [Petrópolis: Vozes, 1986]). See also Boff, *Passion of Christ*, p. 130.

27. The event of justification is that Jesus was raised from the dead as a proof of his innocence in the face of condemnation (José Porfirio Miranda, *Marx and the Bible: A Critique of the Philosophy of Oppression*, trans. John Eagleson [Maryknoll, N.Y.: Orbis Books, 1974], p. 189), because his condemnation to death on the cross is the consequence of his life of faith (Jon Sobrino, *Christology at the Crossroads: A Latin American Approach*, trans. John Drury [Maryknoll, N.Y.: Orbis Books, 1978], pp. 201-17).

28. The crucified Christ reveals the identity of God as the "power of the weak," who takes the side of the victims of history (Blaser, *Esquisse*, p. 15).

29. Sobrino (*Christology at the Crossroads*, p. 201) demonstrates the scandal of this abandonment by God, and how from the beginning the tradition has tried to give a positive meaning to the reason for the cross, and has focused more on Jesus as the Son of God and on his power. What has been forgotten, he adds, is that God was on the cross of Jesus. The consequence of this forgetting has been not to seek God where God is: "In the Christian view [God's] locus is not only the resurrection, but also the cross of Jesus. In historical terms God is to be found in the crosses of the oppressed rather than in beauty, power, or wisdom."

30. The discussion of the negative consequences of self-affirmation and self-confidence, and the danger of aggrandizing oneself over God, does not belong here. The depersonalized human being needs to recognize himself or herself as a creative subject in order to feel worthy—a free child of God.

31. This phrase of Bonhoeffer has been taken up at a number of points in the christologies of Sobrino (*Christology at the Crossroads*) and Boff (*Jesucristo y la liberación*).

32. As Gutiérrez says, the experience of the freely given love of God—first datum of the Christian faith—is not only situated as if in a historical parenthesis, but rather gives its full significance—from within—to the process of human becoming (*We Drink from Our Own Wells*, p. 112). In this sense, "In the final analysis, to believe in God means to live our life as a gift from God and to look upon everything that happens in it as a manifestation of this gift" (ibid., p. 110). The proper consistency of history is not ignored in this process, but, on the contrary, its deepest meaning is probed.

33. In a theology "from the underside of history" (an expression coined by Gustavo Gutiérrez, *The Power of the Poor in History: Selected Writings*, trans. Robert R. Barr [Maryknoll, N.Y.: Orbis Books, 1983], pp. 169-221), we call solidarity what Barth called reconciliation. Although he kept his gaze fixed on the human being as sinner (through pride, inertia, and lies), we fix our gaze on the one who suffers unjustly from the sins of the powerful. Both have

lost their humanity, and, in Jesus Christ, God returns to both their lost humanity. Solidarity and reconciliation are present in the act of the true God, who comes down in order to dignify and reconcile all human beings. We believe that Jesus Christ is: (1) the true God who comes down in order to be in solidarity with those who are suffering from sin, and in order to reconcile God's creatures (including the suffering); and (2) the true human being lifted up by God and reconciled with God. In these two natures, Jesus is the guarantor of solidarity and reconciliation (Barth, *Church Dogmatics* 4/1, 58, 1-3). Understood in this way, Christ is "God with us" (ibid., 4/1, 57, 1).

34. In Rom. 8:29, Paul affirms that we are destined to "reproduce the image" of God's Son, in order that this one might be the first born of many siblings. To be the first born means "that Jesus is the first in whom the human contradiction has been overcome and creation has been terminated: he is the beginning of the new reality." It also means that "Christ is the goal of all of the creative action of God. He is the image that, in present reality, announces the future" (González Faus, *La humanidad nueva* [Santander: Sal Terrae, 1984], pp. 290-91).

35. Sobrino (*Christology at the Crossroads*, pp. 7-8) makes this affirmation when he criticizes the Christologies that begin with the Christ of the kerygma, even though in the proclaimed Christ no concrete content can be found that would guarantee the authenticity or inauthenticity of existence. For us the proclamation of the kerygma is intimately related to the praxis of the proclaimer, the sincere follower of Jesus. The historical Jesus is present in the kerygma not only because the cross leads us to him, but because the preacher represents—makes present again—the life of Jesus. The testimony of Paul is a concrete example. He himself expressed that idea when he wrote that he was carrying the death of Christ in his flesh, in order that the life of Christ might be manifest to those who hear the kerygma (2 Cor. 4:10-12), and in order that he might bear in his own body the signs of Jesus (Gal. 6:17; see also Col. 1:24).

36. Jesus Christ is the gospel and the justice of God (Rom. 1:16-17). But, as González Faus indicates ("Cristo, justicia de Dios. Dios, justicia nuestra: Reflexiones sobre cristología y lucha por la justicia," *La justicia que brota de la fe* [Santander: Sal Terrae, 1982], p. 143), "Jesus is the justice of God, not by being another type of justice that functions only on the most intimate levels of relationship within the Triune God, removed from relationships between human beings, but by the form in which God realized in him justice between human beings."

37. This phrase was used by Rubem Alves in a dialogue with his community of Campinas, February 26, 1989.

38. González Faus (*Proyecto de hermano*, pp. 487-527) demonstrates the problem in the history of Christian thought of having considered grace a "thing" or a "substance," instead of in terms of personal relationship.

39. Barth discusses the divine witness of God's will for an eternal and original covenant (*Church Dogmatics* 4/1, 57, 2).

40. In the weeping of the child-God pleading for milk from Mary (Rubem Alves, "Fome de Deus—Fome do homem," *Pai nosso: Meditações* [São Paulo: CEDI-Paulinas, 1987], pp. 103-7), in his dignifying friendship with women, in the moments of exhausting work with the marginalized and welcome rest with accused sinners, in his dreams and fears in the company of his disciples, in his moments of agony, that solidarity can be seen. This God, says Duquoc (*Messianisme de Jésus et discrétion de Dieu* [Geneva: Labor et Fides, 1984], p. 198), is a God truly hidden because God is revealed in God's opposite.

41. In Jesus, says Blaser (*Esquisse*, p. 76), all of the abandoned encounter an equal, a brother. The one who was abandoned on the cross reveals a singular love: The abandoned encounter their Father, the impious are justified, and the hostility between God and God's adversaries is overcome.

42. Sobrino (*Christology at the Crossroads*, p. 224) expresses this in the form of a thesis: "On the cross of Jesus God himself is crucified. The Father suffers the death of the Son and takes upon himself all the pain of history. In this ultimate solidarity with humanity he reveals himself as the God of love who opens up a hope and a future through the most negative side of history. Thus Christian existence is nothing else but a process of participating in this same process whereby God loves the world and hence in the very life of God."

43. In the drama represented by Job and his friends, none of them was able to recognize

NOTES TO PAGES 136-40

the presence of God in the rubbish heap, for God was revealed with a face different from that which was expected.

44. Faced with the traditional christological focus on justification, we want to underline the participation of all three persons of the Trinity. In contexts of urgent solidarity, the Trinity is unveiled as a paradigm in itself of perfect communion, and as a communitarian power in the transformation of the human being into the new humanity. See Blaser, *Esquisse*, p. 16.

45. Gutiérrez, *The Power of the Poor in History*, pp. 16-18.

46. If justification were granted because of one's merits, the result would be—in addition to legitimating the law of exclusion, which is contrary to the justice of God—that almost no one would be saved. Under such a merit system, some people perform injustices and others, their victims, are dehumanized. In the process, what is lost is the human vocation of doing justice. On the other hand, we agree with González Faus (*Proyecto de hermano*, p. 519) when he notes that for human existence it is important and liberating to come to the understanding that "the human being has value not for what he or she does, but because God loves him or her. Even just receiving Love enables the human being to act humanly."

47. Ibid., p. 652; see the discussion on pp. 650-52.

48. Xabier Pikaza (*Hermanos de Jesús y servidores de los más pequeños. Mt. 25.31-46* [Salamanca: Sígueme, 1984], p. 308) notes, "What before seemed to be a double movement (on the one hand sharing one's goods with the poor, and on the other following Jesus) turns out to be united: Jesus is discovered in the universal service of help to the needy."

49. Gutiérrez, *We Drink from Our Own Wells*, p. 133.

50. González Faus, *Proyecto de hermano*, p. 652.

51. Leonardo Boff, *Liberating Grace*, trans. John Drury (Maryknoll, N.Y.: Orbis Books, 1979), pp. 4-5, 29-31.

52. Hugo Assmann (Hugo Assmann and Franz Hinkelammert, *A idolatria do mercado. Ensaio sobre economia e teologia* [Petrópolis: Vozes, 1989], pp. 65-66) says that grace should be reflected in the exigency of sociohistorical conditions and not in ritual religious behavior appropriate to automatons.

53. Gutiérrez, *We Drink from Our Own Wells*, pp. 21-25.

54. Gutiérrez (ibid., p. 21) states that what is new in Latin America is not the suffering of the poor, but their awareness of the reason for their poverty and their desire to escape it. That is the propitious time of salvation.

55. According to de Santa Ana (*Pan, vino y amistad* [San José, Costa Rica: DEI, 1985], pp. 104-5), "companion" (Spanish, *compañero*) comes from "company," a term that itself comes from the Latin words *cum* and *panis*. "In the meal is established an intimate companionship with the Spirit of Jesus and among the participants."

56. Ibid., p. 12.

57. Pierre Gisel, "Le Sacrifice," *Foi et Vie* 84 (1984): 66.

58. González Faus, *Proyecto de hermano*, pp. 665-66.

59. It is at this point that Rubem A. Alves (*A Theology of Human Hope* [Washington, D.C.: Corpus Books, 1969], pp. 85-100) contrasts messianic humanism and humanistic messianism. A person holding the latter view falls into anxiety and is dominated by a messianic obsession with the power to make history. Such a person does not live life in gratitude. Messianic humanism preserves both grace and creativity from the perspective of historical experience. The creativity of God ensures the creativity of the human being, both together building the future.

60. Ibid., pp. 98-100; see also the poems of Alves in *Creio na ressurreição do corpo* (São Paulo: CEDI, 1982).

61. Leonardo Boff, *Trinity and Society*, trans. Paul Burns (Maryknoll, N.Y.: Orbis Books, 1988), pp. 118-20. See also his discussion of *perichoreisis* on p. 235.

62. We affirm that justification is the work of the three persons of the Trinity. All of them are involved in human history in order to give life to human beings and to orient them to the way that leads to abundant life without end.

63. Alves compares it to the delight of an "aperitif" ("Aperitivos do futuro," *Pai nosso*, pp. 57-62.

64. According to Barth (*Church Dogmatics* 4/1, 57), justification in Jesus Christ includes a

universal character, since creation and justification are part of the covenant between God and humankind, and that involves nothing less than the totality of human history.

8. JUSTIFICATION AS THE AFFIRMATION OF THE LIFE OF ALL

1. That is the concern of Rubem A. Alves (*A Theology of Human Hope* [Washington, D.C.: Corpus Books, 1969) in his search for a theological language in which men and women might create history. For us, the emphasis on the human being as a subject who creates history is indispensable in situations of exclusion and oppression. We are aware of the theological risk of deifying the human being. Barth and the Protestant tradition are zealous in that respect. However, when one seeks alternatives—new models of life, or the creation of a renewed future—one needs a new theological language. Here the language of Barth and his followers turns out to be limited. It appears·that he does not manage to conceive of the human being as *homo creator*. In his summary of the critique of Barthian language (p. 55), Alves makes the following observations about humanization in the two phases of Barth (the No of judgment and the Yes of election): "Man is not *homo creator*. In the first phase his most creative possibilities are discarded as new forms of rebellion. In the second phase his action is reduced to movement within the given structures." It would seem that Barth believes that history already ended (see the discussion of Barth, pp. 44-55). From the perspective of oppressed women, Dorothee Soelle and Shirley A. Cloyes (*To Work and to Love: A Theology of Creation* [Philadelphia: Fortress Press, 1983], pp. 23-53) note the difficulty in the tradition of identifying the image of God in the human being because of the claim that humankind is also "made of dust," which is superimposed with force on the divine image.

2. We are taking up again the theological concerns of praxis found in the following sources: Alves, *A Theology of Human Hope;* Hugo Assmann, *Opresión-Liberación, desafío a los cristianos* (Montevideo: Tierra Nueva, 1971); and José Míguez Bonino, *La fe en busca de eficacia* (Salamanca: Sígueme, 1977). However, we relate them to the theme of justification, and in particular its relationship to faith, the law, and the sovereignty of God.

3. "Contrary to what a certain romantic notion would hold, the world of the poor is not made up simply of victims, of solidarity and the struggle for human rights. The universe of the poor is inhabited by flesh-and-blood human beings, pervaded with the forces of life and death, of grace and sin. In that world we find indifference to others, individualism, abandoned children, people abusing people, pettiness, hearts closed to the action of the Lord" (Gustavo Gutiérrez, *We Drink from Our Own Wells: The Spiritual Journey of a People*, trans. Matthew J. O'Connell [Maryknoll, N.Y.: Orbis Books, 1984], p. 125). Here Paul's emphasis on the new era inaugurated by Jesus Christ is of paramount importance.

4. Gustavo Gutiérrez, *A Theology of Liberation: History, Politics, and Salvation*, trans. and ed. Caridad Inda and John Eagleson (Maryknoll, N.Y.: Orbis Books, 1973), p. 175.

5. Franz Hinkelammert, *La fe de Abraham y el Edipo occidental* (San José, Costa Rica: DEI, 1989), pp. 28-29.

6. According to Leonardo Boff (*Jesucristo y la liberación del hombre* [Madrid: Cristiandad, 1981], p. 401), the incarnation of God in Jesus of Nazareth took place in order to make divine and humanize the human being, relieving him or her of the burden of inhumanity resulting from historical sin.

7. Regarding the collective, one can see that praxis is not imprisoned in the privatizing model of I/Thou. For Assmann (*Pueblo oprimido, señor de la historia* [Montevideo: Tierra Nueva, 1972], p. 15), "The essence of the biblical message appears to give priority to the relational image I/community or I/brothers and sisters as the basic ethical structure within which to reflect on revolutionary commitment." Referring to the human being as agent of his or her own destiny, Gutiérrez (*Theology of Liberation*, p. 31) discusses the inner liberation to which the human being aspires, in addition to its more public expression. Liberation is understood not as an ideological evasion in the situation of servitude. According to Gutiérrez, the requirements of liberation on a collective and historical plane must include psycho-

logical liberation. "Alienation and exploitation as well as the very struggle for liberation from them have ramifications on the personal and psychological planes which it would be dangerous to overlook in the process of constructing a new society and a new man."

8. Emilio Castro, "Reflection After Melbourne," *Your Kingdom Come: Mission Perspectives,* Report on the World Conference on Mission and Evangelism, Melbourne, Australia, 15-25 May, 1980 (Geneva: World Council of Churches, 1980), p. 229. From a feminist perspective, Letty M. Russell (*Human Liberation in a Feminist Perspective: A Theology* [Philadelphia: Westminster Press, 1974], pp. 64-65) indicates that human beings have the need to be accepted as subjects and not as objects of manipulation. She adds that human beings have the need to participate in the conception of the world in which they live, for they are "creatures of history." For her, the aim is that one build one's own history, both individual and collective.

9. Jon Sobrino, "Pecado personal, perdón y liberación," *RLT* 5 (1988): 23.

10. Alves, *A Theology of Human Hope,* pp. 145-58; Silvio Meincke, "Justificacão par graca e fé: um novo espaço para a vida," *EstT* 23 (1983).

11. This fragment is from Frei Betto's *O dia do Angelo* (São Paulo: Ed. Brasiliense, 1987, pp. 45-46), which presents the life and death of a militant Christian prisoner, his fits of incoherence, and his problems. It tells of the relationship of the character Angelo with God in a way that, from our perspective, allows one to glimpse what justification by faith might mean in those particular situations.

12. In his "third use of the law," Calvin (*Institutes* 2/7, 12) recovered the positive meaning of the law that Luther had dismissed. See *Calvin: Institutes of the Christian Religion,* 2 vols., The Library of Christian Classics, vols. 20 and 21; ed. John T. McNeill, trans. Ford Lewis Battles (Philadelphia: Westminster Press, 1960), vol. 1, pp. 360-61.

13. Klauspeter Blaser, *Esquisse de la Dogmatique* (Lausanne: UNIL, 1985), p. 120.

14. According to Alves (*A Theology of Human Hope,* p. 83), the law by itself, separate from the logic of the spirit of life, destroys the historicity of the human being. "Action becomes imitation. Man does not march toward a new tomorrow, since law and legality, as already given in the past, become the model of his action in the future."

15. Elsa Tamez, *Bible of the Oppressed,* trans. Matthew J. O'Connell (Maryknoll, N.Y.: Orbis Books, 1982), pp. 1-84.

16. And on the contrary, the death of God is the death of the human being (Jon Sobrino, *Jesus in Latin America* [Maryknoll, N.Y.: Orbis Books, 1987], pp. 149-51).

17. Relative to the sovereignty of God, I agree with Blaser (*Esquisse,* p. 18) that "theology does not have the task of establishing the God of Jesus Christ as superior or absolute, or of converting adherents of other faiths to that God or to the religion of Christianity, but rather it has the task of testifying to the victory of God over death in the weakness of the crucified one."

18. Míguez Bonino, *La fe en busca de eficacia,* p. 126.

19. Juan Luis Segundo (*El hombre de hoy ante Jesús de Nazaret* [Madrid: Cristiandad, 1982], pp. 383-408) emphasizes the dimension of a life led with maturity based on faith, which saves the human being from enslavement to the law.

20. "The criterion of discernment is the affirmation of the life of all; that which leads to life is not the law, but the submission of the law to that affirmation" (Hinkelammert, *La fe de Abraham,* p. 30).

21. According to Blaser (*Esquisse,* p. 102), that is precisely what the capitalist society and modern bourgeois mentality have done in making divine the active subject, whose action has no limits. As an eyewitness of such societies, he warns of those dangers and identifies as a myth the notion that human beings forge their own destiny.

22. Martin Luther, "The Freedom of a Christian," in *Martin Luther: Selections From His Writings,* ed. John Dillenberger (Garden City, N.Y.: Doubleday & Co. [Anchor Books], 1961), p. 53.

23. It is a matter of recovering that vocation (Gen. 2:28) from an angle that is both eschatological and fruitful in the present. Faith in God as the Creator "vindicates again, for God, the world as the creation and as the field for human responsibility" (Blaser, *Esquisse,* p. 96).

24. Dorothee Soelle, *Choosing Life* (Philadelphia: Fortress Press, 1986), p. 1.

25. In an article on the intrinsic relation between peace and justice, René Padilla ("Justicia

y Paz," *Misión* 3 [1984]: 141) affirms that when law and order are invoked in order to defend created interests, illegality and disorder are institutionalized. When they are rationalized in order to justify the oppressors, law and order inevitably lose respect for the oppressed and the victims of the system. Thus, ethical values lose their force, and all notion of good and evil is lost as well.

26. The consequence of faith in the resurrection is historical. According to Alves (*A Theology of Human Hope*, pp. 130-31), resurrection describes neither an isolated objective fact nor an isolated subjective fact. It refers to the unity of both with the power of freedom over history, and therefore to the possibility of hope within and for history. "Resurrection, hence, is the language of the ongoing politics of God in history." It is the language of the hope "in which we are saved" (Rom. 8:24), and it announces the triumph of God over the powers that oppress (1 Cor. 15:24-28). The Helsinki Document (sec. 5, par. 24), published in *Justification Today* (*Lutheran World*, Supplement to No. 1 [1965], pp. 9-10), affirms that the resurrection does not confer secular power. We agree only if the framers of the document understand by secular power institutionalized power of the state. For we believe that faith in the one who raises the dead confers power to the excluded in order to struggle in secular society for their own life and that of others, and to defend it. In that sense the life of Paul is exemplary.

27. José Porfirio Miranda, *Marx and the Bible: A Critique of the Philosophy of Oppression*, trans. John Eagleson (Maryknoll, N.Y.: Orbis Books, 1974), p. 231.

28. Soelle and Cloyes (*To Work and to Love*, p. 46) note the importance of believing in this truth.

29. See the analysis of Hinkelammert (*Crítica a la razón utópica* [San José, Costa Rica: DEI, 1984]) concerning the relationship between the impossible and the feasible in the portrayals of utopia in the various categorical frameworks of current economic thought.

30. Alves, *A Theology of Human Hope*, pp. 130-31.

31. Míguez Bonino, *La fe en busca de eficacia*, p. 127.

32. Alves, *A Theology of Human Hope*, p. 67.

33. Sobrino, *Jesus in Latin America*, p. 149.

34. One of the difficulties that Alves notes in the theological paradigm of Barth is that for him eternity is historicized uniquely and exclusively in the time of Jesus of Nazareth, that is to say, in the first years of the first century of the Common Era. This approach closes off the path of the history inaugurated precisely with Jesus (*A Theology of Human Hope*, pp. 51-52). It seems that Paul, on the contrary, insists on historicizing transcendence, the justice of God, by means of faith in the God of life, which occurs in the action of justification. "The revelation of God in Christ does not end history: the future inaugurated in Christ promises the glorification of God in the world, and the end of the humiliation of the human being" (Blaser, *Esquisse*, p. 14).

35. Hinkelammert (*La fe de Abraham*, pp. 15-22) contrasts this antisacrificial history with the tragedy of Oedipus of Sophocles, in which the father commands the son to be killed, and in the end, the son kills the father. According to Hinkelammert, these motifs were introduced into Western Christianity to interpret, with Anselm, God as the Father who kills the Son.

36. These testimonies are collected and systematized by Gutiérrez in *We Drink from Our Own Wells* (pp. 95-135). In them one can see the resurrection as the power of the struggle for life. Note also this feeling of the resurrection from the perspective of Guatemala, and the importance of "knowing oneself resurrected" in that situation, in the poetry of Julia Esquivel: *Threatened with Resurrection: Prayers and Poems from an Exiled Guatemalan*, trans. Maria Elena Acevedo et al. (Elgin, Ill.: Brethren Press, 1982).

37. The disciples were witnesses of the glory of the resurrected one, and as Karl Barth says (*Church Dogmatics* 4/1, 59, 3, trans. Geoffrey W. Bromiley [Edinburgh: T. & T. Clark, 1956], p. 341), "In this seeing and hearing and handling, in this encounter, they were brought to faith and they for their part came to faith."

38. Míguez Bonino, *La fe en busca de eficacia*, pp. 169-70.

39. Ibid., p. 182.

40. Jon Sobrino, *Spirituality of Liberation: Toward Political Holiness*, trans. Robert R. Barr (Maryknoll, N.Y.: Orbis Books, 1988), pp. 51-52. On discipleship, see Sobrino, *Christology at*

the Crossroads: A Latin American Approach, trans. John Drury (Maryknoll, N.Y.: Orbis Books, 1978), pp. 79-145; *Jesus in Latin America,* pp. 131-47; Gutiérrez, *We Drink from Our Own Wells,* pp. 72-135.

41. Sobrino, *Jesus in Latin America,* p. 150.

42. According to Leonardo Boff (*Passion of Christ, Passion of the World: The Facts, Their Interpretation, and Their Meaning Yesterday and Today,* trans. Robert R. Barr [Maryknoll, N.Y.: Orbis Books, 1987], p. 101), "Christ, achieving the goal, strikes to the root of the being of all human beings, whether they are aware of it or not, indeed even if they reject the proclamation of this good news." Faith proclaims Christ "the universal Liberator and Savior." That is because, for Christ, the covenant is a condition of justification, and the covenant is founded on the creation. God "causes the promise and command of the covenant: 'I will be your God and ye shall be my people,' to become historical event in the person of Jesus Christ. . . . God keeps faith in time with Himself and with man, with all men in this one man" (Barth, *Church Dogmatics* 4/1, 57, 3, p. 67).

43. Dietrich Bonhoeffer (*Ethics,* ed. Eberhard Bethge [New York: Macmillan, 1955], pp. 34-35) insists that the good works of the person who has been justified in Jesus carry the mark of simplicity. They are not anything that such a person chooses or judges and takes pride in. Rather he or she does them simply because "the knowledge of Jesus is entirely transformed into action, without any reflection upon a man's self." For the person who is justified, good works are not one possibility among others, but simply doing the will of God.

44. Sobrino, *Spirituality of Liberation,* p. 113. Sobrino theologizes about that which is divine in the struggle for human rights. He concludes that "those who struggle for life encounter God in history, and encounter themselves in history in the sight of God."

45. Míguez Bonino, *La fe en busca de eficacia,* p. 137.

46. Mortimer Arias (*Announcing the Reign of God: Evangelization and the Subversive Memory of Jesus* [Philadelphia: Fortress Press, 1984], pp. 92-99) recalls the list of fifteen hundred names of "priests, nuns, pastors, and lay people [who] had been arrested, searched, interrogated, imprisoned, exiled, tortured, killed, or had 'disappeared'" (p. 93) in the decade from 1968 to 1978, simply because they took seriously the message of the reign of God. The list of martyrs continues beyond those named in Arias's book, to include also the Jesuit priests and humble women assassinated in El Salvador on November 19, 1989.

47. Helsinki Document, sec. 5, par. 23 (*Justification Today,* p. 9).

48. For the believer, the new being is born again in Christ through baptism and the Spirit. According to the Helsinki Document, sec. 3, par. 10 (*Justification Today,* p. 6), the presence of the Spirit, a gift of God, is the divine presence that generates in the human being new possibility and well-being.

49. A concern to keep the two realities of the human being in tension permeates the entire work of José Ignacio González Faus (see esp. *Proyecto de hermano: Visión creyente del hombre* [Santander: Sal Terrae, 1987]).

50. If we have emphasized this sinful reality of the human being, it is because we believe that the present theological need is to underline the dignifying grace of God and the status of the excluded as free sons and daughters of God. However, we know that the dimension of human fragility is also a present need for the leaders and managers of the entire popular movement, who are organizing the struggle aimed at changing structures that exclude.

51. Sobrino, *Spirituality of Liberation,* p. 168. Almost all the writings of Richard Shaull since the decade of the fifties speak about revolution and highlight both the action of God in concrete history and God's purposes directed toward a new and humanized society. Those writings not only allude to the struggle—to the personal and collective call to change—but also, at the same time, observe the eschatological character of God as sovereign and creator, and the importance of the recognition of the person as a pardoned sinner. See, e.g., *De dentro do furacão* (São Paulo: CLAI, CEDI, 1984), pp. 117-222; *The Reformation and Liberation Theology: Insights for the Challenges of Today* (Louisville, Ky.: Westminster/John Knox, 1991), pp. 25-77.

9. OBSERVATIONS ON THE MEANING OF THE SACRIFICE
OF CHRIST, JUDGMENT, AND FORGIVENESS

1. Juan Luis Segundo, *El hombre de hoy ante Jésus de Nazaret* (Madrid: Cristiandad, 1982), p. 442. This author, who analyzes Romans using an anthropological investigative key, indicates that in the study of redemption and expiation, one must consider the cultic-legal key as well. Furthermore, that key can have various interpretations. "Christ died for us" can be read from a broader perspective, without losing the juridical context: "When we understand that even when we were still enemies, Christ consented to go to his death because he loved us, we are radically freed from our moral fears and given a new possibility—that (insofar as we are humanly able) we forget our own destiny to which we are condemned by sin, and that we commit ourselves (insofar as it depends on us) to the building of God's reign or—in Paul's synonym—to the humanization of the human world" (ibid., p. 440).

2. This position is found in Anselm of Canterbury, "Cur Deus homo?" in *Saint Anselm: Basic Writings*, trans. S. N. Deane; 2nd ed. (LaSalle, Ill.: Open Court Publishing Co., 1962), pp. 177-288.

3. Leonardo Boff, *Passion of Christ, Passion of the World: The Facts, Their Interpretation, and Their Meaning Yesterday and Today*, trans. Robert R. Barr (Maryknoll, N.Y.: Orbis Books, 1987), pp. 102-16; Franz Hinkelammert, *La fe de Abraham y el Edipo occidental* (San José, Costa Rica: DEI, 1989), pp. 35-38; Jon Sobrino, *Christology at the Crossroads: A Latin American Approach*, trans. John Drury (Maryknoll, N.Y.: Orbis Books, 1978), pp. 182-201; José Comblin, "O tema da reconciliação e a teologia en America Latina," *REB* 46 (1986): 280-82; José Ignacio González Faus, *La humanidad nueva. Ensayo de cristología* (Santander: Sal Terrae, 1984), pp. 479-520.

4. François Varone, *Ce Dieu censé aimer la souffrance* (Paris: Cerf, 1984).

5. Ibid., p. 45. Varone criticizes the theory that equates the atonement with the satisfaction of a debt owed to God, as reducing the work of salvation to the death of Christ, and consequently reducing salvation itself to a juridical order between God and humanity.

6. For Varone the sentence "Jesus died for our sins" is true but extremely ambiguous. In order not to fall into the religious trap of a God who requires the compensatory death of an innocent person, he proposes that one begin by affirming that Jesus did not in fact die for our sins as a formal demand of God, but because of his prophetic struggle that brought him to the end (ibid., pp. 49, 74). For Pierre Gisel ("Le Sacrifice," *Foi et Vie* 84 [1984]: 42), the important thing is not to affirm that Jesus came to die (for the sake of our sins), but to understand that Jesus came first and foremost as a testimony to God, to a God who gives life.

7. Recall that the pre-Pauline formula in Rom. 3:24-26 arose from Hellenistic circles.

8. A number of interpreters connect the motif of the reign of God found in the Synoptic Gospels and the theme of justification by faith in Paul: Sobrino, *Christology at the Crossroads*, pp. 36-37; Segundo, *El hombre de hoy*, p. 441; Irene Foulkes, "El Reino de Dios en Pablo," *VP* 1 (1983): 9-24.

9. D. Widerkehr (*Fe, redención, liberación* [Madrid: Paulinas, 1979]) notes problems in the current discussion of soteriology, trying not only to make accessible a language alien to modern people, but also to relate the present understanding of salvation and praxis to the fundamental and decisive salvific event of the faith, by emphasizing christological, ecclesiological, and pneumatological points of connection.

10. Varone, *Ce Dieu censé*, pp. 18-19. John Calvin (*Institutes* 2/16, 19) discovers salvation in the Son both before the incarnation and even after the resurrection, in the ascension to the Father (*Calvin: Institutes of the Christian Religion*, 2 vols., *Library of Christian Classics*, vols. 20 and 21; ed. John T. McNeill, trans. Ford Lewis Battles [Philadelphia: Westminster Press, 1960], vol. 1, pp. 527-28). His approach of seeing in Jesus Christ the offices of Prophet, Priest, and King (*Institutes* 2/15, 1-6; vol. 1, pp. 482-90) expands the limited focus on the Christ sacrificed for our sins.

11. Hugo Assmann and Franz Hinkelammert, *A idolatria do mercado. Ensaio sobre economia e teologia* (Petrópolis: Vozes, 1989), pp. 303-23, 341-51.

12. Jorge Pixley ("¿Exige el Dios verdadero sacrificios cruentos?" *RIBLA* 2 [1988]) has already observed that point in the same biblical text.

13. Sobrino, *Christology at the Crossroads*, pp. 201-2.

14. Assmann and Hinkelammert, *A idolatria do mercado*, p. 361.

15. Comblin, "O tema da reconciliaçâo," pp. 281-82.

16. According to Kosuke Koyama ("The Crucified Christ Challenges Human Power," *Your Kingdom Come: Mission Perspectives*, Report on the World Conference on Mission and Evangelism, Melbourne, Australia, 15-25 May, 1980 [Geneva: World Council of Churches, 1980], p. 157), "The crucified Christ exposes the deception of those who 'have healed the wound of the people lightly, saying "peace, peace" where there is no peace' (Jer. 6:14)."

17. Julio de Santa Ana, "Costo social e sacrificio aos ídolos," *Dívida externa e igrejas. Uma visâo ecumenica* (Río de Janeiro: CEDI, 1989), pp. 88-89.

18. This is "costly grace," as Bonhoeffer called it (*The Cost of Discipleship*, rev. ed., trans. Reginald H. Fuller and Irmgard Booth [New York: Macmillan, 1959], p. 47), because it cost God the life of God's own Son.

19. Canaan Banana, "Good News to the Poor," *Your Kingdom Come*, p. 117.

20. Karl Barth, *Church Dogmatics* 4/1, 59, 3, trans. G. W. Bromiley (Edinburgh: T. & T. Clark, 1956).

21. George V. Pixley, "Divine Judgment in History," in Victorio Araya et al., *The Idols of Death and the God of Life: A Theology*, trans. Barbara E. Campbell and Bonnie Shepherd (Maryknoll, N.Y.: Orbis Books, 1983), p. 54.

22. Dietrich Bonhoeffer, *Ethics*, ed. Eberhard Bethge (New York: Macmillan, 1955), p. 79.

23. Jon Sobrino, "Pecado personal, perdón y liberación," *RLT* 5 (1988): 17.

24. Bonhoeffer, *Ethics*, pp. 118-19.

25. Gustavo Gutiérrez, *We Drink from Our Own Wells: The Spiritual Journey of a People*, trans. Matthew J. O'Connell (Maryknoll, N.Y.: Orbis Books, 1984), pp. 99-100.

26. Sobrino, "Pecado personal," pp. 25-26.

27. Irene Foulkes, "Justificación y justicia en parábola: Un sermón sobre Mt. 18.23-24," *VP* 6 (1986): 39-42.

28. Sobrino, "Pecado personal," pp. 26-29.